The Politics of Parody

ᗡᗯᗕ

THE LEWIS WALPOLE SERIES
IN EIGHTEENTH-CENTURY CULTURE AND HISTORY

The Lewis Walpole Series, published by Yale University
Press with the aid of the Annie Burr Lewis Fund, is dedicated
to the culture and history of the long eighteenth century (from
the Glorious Revolution to the accession of Queen Victoria). It
welcomes work in a variety of fields, including literature and
history, the visual arts, political philosophy, music, legal history,
and the history of science. In addition to original scholarly work,
the series publishes new editions and translations of writing from
the period, as well as reprints of major books that are currently
unavailable. Though the majority of books in the series will
probably concentrate on Great Britain and the Continent, the
range of our geographical interests is as wide as
Horace Walpole's.

The Politics of Parody

A Literary History of Caricature,
1760–1830

David Francis Taylor

Yale

UNIVERSITY PRESS

NEW HAVEN AND LONDON

Published with assistance from the Annie Burr Lewis Fund.

Published with assistance from the foundation established in memory of
James Wesley Cooper of the Class of 1865, Yale College.

Yale University Press books may be purchased in quantity for educational, business, or promotional use. For
information, please e-mail sales.press@yale.edu (US office) or sales@yaleup.co.uk (UK office).

Set in Fournier type by IDS Infotech Ltd.
Printed in the United States of America.

Library of Congress Control Number: 2017956284

ISBN 978-0-300-22375-0 (hardcover : alk. paper)

A catalogue record for this book is available from the British Library.

This paper meets the requirements of ANSI/NISO Z39.48-1992 (Permanence of Paper).

10 9 8 7 6 5 4 3 2 1

For Jennifer and Mathilda

Contents

Contents

Preface

This book channels a number of arguments: about parody, about the after-lives of certain texts, about how we use stories to make sense of the political world, and about satire's key role in the broader ideological enterprise of defining (and defending) high literary culture against the encroachments of the "popular." But in many ways its most important argument is its methodology. Attending to the vast archive of satirical prints published in the later eighteenth and early nineteenth centuries—a period sometimes described as "the golden age of caricature"—it registers the frequency and intricacy of graphic satirists' political appropriations of texts by the likes of Shakespeare, Milton, and Swift. Equally, in reading these prints alongside not only literary texts but also newspapers, pamphlets, topical verse satire, criticism, parliamentary speech, fine art, and theatrical performance, it conceives of political caricature as an intermedial form that, in turn, vividly reminds us of the inherent intermediality of Georgian culture itself. In this way, this book offers a challenge to literary history as it is conventionally constructed and insists that we have much to learn by attending to materials and archives usually considered to lie well beyond the discipline's purview. Here, and like a number of others before me, I call for literary criticism and literary history to take better account of literature's shaping of and, more especially, its circulation *as* a visual culture.

As in my previous book on Richard Brinsley Sheridan, I also seek more carefully to map the relations between literary and parliamentary political cultures in the later Georgian period. Of course, *all* literature is political. To represent something, and to encounter the representation of something, is to make decisions both consciously and unconsciously that can never be ideologically neutral. In the Althusserian sense, there is no means of us standing outside ideology; we are always already interpellated by it. But it's precisely the seeming obviousness of this point that, to my mind, too often pushes scholars away from a more serious consideration of the specific roles that literature plays within *parliamentary* politics—within what Terry Eagleton calls the "sordidly historical." Political caricature suggests just how fundamental the stories, characters, and tropes of canonical literary texts were to the workings of parliamentary political culture in that they furnished satirists and other interlocutors with a vocabulary through which otherwise slippery political crises, ideologies, and personalities could be given particular narrative—and moral—structure. I'm concerned with what this process of narrativizing politics might involve, and how this kind of emplotment at once relates the present to the past and gives shape to a sense of history. In parodying a particular literary scene, graphic satirists invoke various forms of the past but they also place the political present within a trajectory that has not only a beginning but a discernable if yet-to-be-arrived-at end. In such instances, the business of satire lies in imagining a political future that both renders the present newly legible and diminishes that present's perils or confusions.

Yet the literariness of graphic satire problematizes the very notion of a public in its more democratic sense. In their sophisticated parodic architecture, the satirical prints considered in this book appeal to the educated eye; they use literary texts to negotiate the boundaries of the public, to make a certain level of cultural capital a prerequisite of political literacy. As this last statement suggests, I'm deeply uncomfortable with any reading that assumes political caricatures—then or now—to be a necessarily radically inclusive or democratic form, and my suggestion that literary parody in these images is largely aimed at, and can be seen as a means of imagining, an elite political public is undoubtedly the most contentious of the arguments I develop here. Thorny though the questions of caricature's readership and parody's reach might be, they are nonetheless central to the way this book undertakes not only to track the political history of literature but also to think in terms of the *literary* history of British politics.

At the same time, my analysis puts pressure upon conceptions of the political in broader terms. I argue that in their delight in parody, prints engage their target texts critically and in ways that are often remarkably alert to questions pertaining to a given work's generic status, strategies of characterization, and formal or thematic ambivalences. To consider these graphic satirical parodies is thus to also engage the politics of form and the politics of the look; it is to think about the politics of the sublime, of history and its trajectory, of parody, and of the literary as a category. It is, ultimately, to find reflected back at us the politics of our own strategies of critical reading. In other words, this book tracks the overlaps between politics in these constellated cultural senses and politics in the more strictly parliamentary sense—a division that becomes increasingly blurred the more it is scrutinized.

The book is divided in two. The two chapters of Part I together offer a long introduction that maps out the issues at stake in considering the literariness of graphic satire. They argue for the value of a literary critical approach to a visual archive that has hitherto been discussed largely by art and social historians; they locate graphic satire within a variety of intersecting cultural matrices; and they set out the key issues of parody, narrative, political containment, and audience that animate this study as a whole. The chapters of Part II then focus on particular texts—respectively, *The Tempest, Macbeth, Paradise Lost, Gulliver's Travels,* and the pantomime—as a means of exploring these matters with greater specificity and of eliciting the fundamental importance of literary character and narrative to the operations of political culture in the later Georgian period. In these chapters I develop two particular lines of argument. The first concerns the critical operations of parody and, in particular, the manner in which parodic caricatures work to excavate the formal and historical contours of literary genre and to apply pressure to the supposed unity of the texts they take up. The second argument has to do with graphic satire's investment in adjudicating between high and low cultures at this time. Here I'm contending not simply that these caricatures circulated within and embodied a reasonably elite literary culture but indeed that they actively fostered and sequestered that culture in important ways. Not for nothing, then, do I turn my attention in the final chapter away from parodies of canonical texts and toward those of pantomime, a form of popular theater at the core of long-standing and pervasive anxieties about the dissolution of British culture. I therefore bring this book to a close by explicitly addressing and historicizing the question that quietly informs my reading of caricatures throughout this book: What exactly is "the literary"?

Over the past few hundred years political caricature has demonstrated a remarkable ability to migrate across different media: from the single sheet in the eighteenth century to the periodical in the nineteenth and then the newspaper by the twentieth. In our own moment the political cartoon is, above all, a digital medium. It is looked at on smart phones, laptops, and tablets, and it crosses fraught cultural boundaries in new and sometimes dangerous ways, as recent chapters in the history of intolerance have shown all too clearly. And though it has undergone considerable change, in terms of its idiom as much as its medium, the political cartoon still delights in cultural allusion and parody: to television, to the cinema, and, yes, to literature. The questions I pose here—about how certain texts equip us with the tools we need to make sense of the world, about how literature functions as a political language, and about who this language embraces and who or what it shuts out—are at least as meaningful in thinking about our present as they are in thinking about the eighteenth century.

Last, a brief word about the devil in the detail. This book engages with the day-to-day intricacies of political scuffles that took place more than two centuries ago. To this end, I've included an appendix that offers short biographies of the major figures who populate the following chapters. Though I introduce each of them on their first appearance, I thereafter leave it to readers to consult the dramatis personae as and when they feel the need.

Note on Citations

Wherever possible I identity the satirical prints discussed in this book by the number they are given in Frederic George Stephens and M. Dorothy George, *Catalogue of Political and Personal Satires Preserved in the Department of Prints and Drawings in the British Museum*, 11 vols. (London: British Museum, 1870–1954), henceforth BMC. All references to Shakespeare's plays are taken from *The Complete Works*, ed. Stanley Wells and Gary Taylor, 2nd ed. (Oxford: Clarendon Press, 2005).

PART ONE

Prints, Parody, and the Political Public

1. The Literariness of Graphic Satire

Reading the Satirical Print

What does it mean to speak of the literariness of graphic satire in the long eighteenth century? Most immediately, perhaps, such a notion troubles that most entrenched conception of graphic satire as a medium that can be adequately comprehended in the space of a moment. In one respect, this misunderstanding inheres in our anachronistic description of images by the likes of James Gillray and George Cruikshank as *cartoons*. First applied to visual satire in the mid-nineteenth century, this term problematically implies a straightforward formal equivalence between the modern editorial cartoon and the political caricature of the Georgian period, which was published and disseminated as a single-sheet etching.[1] But, in fact, the fallacy that such images yield their meaning directly and near instantaneously is an old one. Writing in 1818, and invoking the age-old notion of pictures as the books of the poor and illiterate, one editor of Gillray's works praised graphic satire as "a universal language,—it is a book that is read at a glance."[2] To register caricature's literariness is, at the very least, to refute the assumptions proffered in a statement such as this and instead to insist that the rhetoric of much graphic satire at this time was neither entirely inclusive nor in any way immediate.

Of course, this line of argument will be self-evident to those who have spent time looking at Gillray's works (for they demand time) or who are familiar with the scholarship on eighteenth-century caricature that has burgeoned over the past twenty years. Rather, what interests me about this

statement from 1818 is that even as it asserts graphic satire's absolute difference from the book, from the mechanisms of the verbal, it nonetheless posits
an analogy between the book and the satirical print as commensurate cultural
objects, and, in the paradoxical phrase "read at a glance," introduces the idea
of textual engagement in the very act of claiming caricature's immediacy.
Suddenly, and surprisingly, we are not too far here from Charles Lamb's
assessment of William Hogarth, one that might just as easily be applied to
Gillray or the Cruikshanks: "His graphic representations are indeed books:
they have the teeming, fruitful, suggestive meaning of *words*. Other pictures
we look at,—his prints we read."[3] Later in this book I will consider at greater
length the distinctions between glancing and gazing, looking and reading at
work in adjudications of this kind. For now, I want simply to note that, from
seemingly opposing angles, both Lamb and the early editor of Gillray
conceive of satirical prints in some sense as *texts*. In the first instance, then, to
speak of the literariness of caricature is to recognize and attend to its syntactical and narrative structures: structures that are themselves constituted
through the enmeshing of images and words, the appropriation and parody
of literary scenes and tropes, and often-dense networks of allusions to other
cultural texts, practices, and traditions. In order fully to appreciate the intertextuality, indeed the intermediality, of eighteenth-century graphic satire we
must also position it within the wider cultural matrices of literary quotation
and parody; of the literary marketplace; of print publication, exhibition
culture, and the theater; of the newspaper; and of parliamentary speech. To
trace the literariness of graphic satire is not just to read a given print's elaborate architecture of narrative, characterization, and allusion but also necessarily to acknowledge that a print's meaning and sociopolitical orientation
comes into focus only when seen in relation to the cultural constellation of
which it was a vital and, as we'll see, highly self-conscious constituent.

Graphic satire of the eighteenth and early nineteenth centuries is thus
"literary" in two intertwined senses, first in terms of its formal operations
and appropriations and second in terms of its position within and in relation
to the broader field of literary culture and production. In developing these
ways of understanding the satirical print in this chapter I want to consider in
detail how graphic satire marshals the narratives, characters, and themes of
literary texts as a means of giving shape to the political present and, equally,
why it is that prints from this period have habitual recourse to such sources
and strategies. I will not be offering anything that approximates a

phenomenology of reading graphic satire, but—however skeptical we might be about our capacity to bridge the epistemological gap that separates us from the past—I do hope that close attention both to the narrative procedures of graphic satire and to the kinds of cultural exchange and negotiation those procedures involve will take us a little closer to what Michael Baxandall calls "the period eye," that is, to the way these complex images were viewed, read, and deciphered in their historical moment.[4] And this question of how satirical prints were looked at perforce brings with it that of who was properly equipped socially and culturally to undertake the interpretative labor these prints demand; in this case, the period eye must have been an educated one competent in and comfortable with parsing a variety of cultural codes and playing the game of parody. To speak of the literariness of graphic satire is, finally then, to broach the highly vexed issue of its audience less as a matter of sociology and more as problem of exegesis, for us as much as for a print's first consumers. It is to think primarily in terms of *implied* readers, of the kinds of public caricatures imagine for themselves, and also to map the tight relations between cultural capital and political literacy.

Let me, at this point, offer an example: Isaac Cruikshank's *The Near in Blood, The Nearer Bloody* (fig. 1.1). I take this caricature because it is, in more than one sense, a highly textual print and also because it strives to find coherent meaning in perhaps the most shocking political event in eighteenth-century European history. Published on 26 January 1793, just five days after the execution of Louis XVI in Paris, Cruikshank's satire excoriates the Duke of Orleans for his alleged role in the king's death. Orleans, at this time styled "Citizen Égalité," was Louis's cousin, a Jacobin, and a member of the French National Assembly, and Cruikshank's print baldly regards his support of the Revolution as an underhand scheme aimed at securing the French crown for himself. Orleans is shown wielding the axe over Louis, whose head rests on the chopping block; on the left, Maximilien Robespierre, cast as a grotesque plebeian woman, holds out the basket ready to catch the severed royal head; on the right, Marie Antoinette and the Dauphin plead for the Louis's life.

This is a highly allusive print, and it's worth detailing each of its quotations in full. First, and most obviously, Cruikshank borrows his title from Donalbain's warning to his older brother, Malcolm, in *Macbeth*: "Where we are, / There's daggers in men's smiles—the nea'er in blood, / The nearer bloody."[5] Second, in a large speech bubble Orleans recites a soliloquy slightly adapted from Colley Cibber's 1699 reworking of Shakespeare's *Richard III*,

Fig. 1.1. Isaac Cruikshank, *The Near in Blood, The Nearer Bloody* (S. W. Fores, 26 January 1793). BMC 8292. Library of Congress, Prints & Photographs Division, LC-DIG-ppmsca-05420.

where, as he awaits confirmation of the assassination of the princes in the Tower, the eponymous protagonist speculatively views his murderous actions from the vantage point of posterity:

> Shall future ages, when this tale is told,
> Drop tears in pity of his hapless fate,
> And read with detestation the misdeeds of Orleans,
> The red-nosed tyrant, cruel, barbarous,
> And bloody—will they not say too,
> That to possess the Crown, nor laws divine
> Nor human stopt my way? Why let 'em say it;
> They can't but say I strove to obtain the Crown;
> I was not fool as well as villain.
> Now for the deed Cousin farewel,
> To me there's music in your passing bell.

Meanwhile, Marie Antoinette's entreaty repeats almost verbatim Lady Anne's hissing dismissal of Richard as he approaches her before the corpse of her father-in-law, Henry VI, lines again taken from Cibber's adaptation and which are part Cibber, part Shakespeare: "How canst thou do this deed? Could not the laws of man, of nature, nor of heaven dissuade thee? No beast so fierce, but knows some touch of pity." Finally, at the foot of the print we are given the following text, in which Cruikshank alters only the proper name (originally "Richard") in the final, damning line:

> Thrice is he arm'd that has his quarrel just,
> And he but naked, though lock'd up in steel,
> Whose conscience with injustice is corrupted,
> The very weight of Orleans guilt shall crush him.[6]

This rally cry is spoken by Richmond (soon to be Henry VII) as he prepares to meet Richard's troops at Bosworth Field in the final act of Cibber's play, but with the exception of the final line—which is Cibber's invention—these words are lifted from Shakespeare's *2 Henry VI*, where they are spoken by the king. Cruikshank's print thus cites two plays on one reading and three on another. In taking up Cibber's tragedy it reworks a text that is already a tissue of sources and voices, an appropriative move that, combined with its additional citation of *Macbeth*, gives this caricature an especially palimpsestic texture.

Yet before we have chance to perform the work of reading and piecing together this intertextual assemblage of quotations, what most immediately strike us is the sheer abundance of text that Cruikshank's print includes (almost two hundred words in all). *The Near in Blood, The Nearer Bloody* reminds us just how verbal a form is eighteenth-century graphic satire. Dorothy George calls on us to think of satirical etchings as "graphic pamphlets," while Peter Wagner, striving for a term adequate to the task of describing the complex composite verbal-visual structure of these prints, arrives at the neologism "iconotext." As Eirwin Nicholson observes, understanding of these caricatures has been impeded by the persistence of a logophobic analytical paradigm that regards their verbal components as distracting and tautologous, and which implicitly insists on the fundamental opposition of word and image.[7] When we assess the intricate negotiations between the visual and the verbal in caricatures, then, we need to be alert both to the different registers of text they offer (titles, subtitles, epigrams, publication lines, labels, keys, speech ribbons) and also to how these portions of texts are differently and complicatedly embedded within and oriented in relation to a given print's iconography. Some words are integral to the central image in that they give voice to the figures shown therein, or are materially present within the (distorted) world being depicted, say in books, papers, and the ephemera of the street; other words occupy the frame, where they establish context or offer commentary.

How are we to understand the operations of these various kinds of text within the verbal-visual matrix of a caricature? Roland Barthes, for instance, contends that an image's linguistic message serves the function either of anchorage, whereby words direct and organize the reader's perception, or of relay, whereby words provide supplemental information essential to a total understanding of the image. But the copious textuality of a print such as *The Near in Blood* exposes both the problematic dualism of this framework and also its implicit privileging of the image as something anterior to text; for Barthes, the text always comes *after* the image, the polysemous possibilities of which it works to counteract and circumscribe.[8] By contrast, as we'll see over the course of this book, the framing words of satirical prints commonly sit in productively tensile, even contrapuntal, relationship with the image they orbit, while the impact of the words *within* that image are often, as David Bindman notes, "visual facts in themselves." Equally, a number of prints from this period play with a reified language and imagine orators eating or spewing verbiage as physical matter in satires that call into question the very ontology of political speech in an age of newspapers and printed parliamentary records.[9]

At the same time, *The Near in Blood* suggests how, quite apart from the presence of words, eighteenth-century satirical prints are textual at the level of what we might call their rhetorical form. In essence, the experience of looking at a print such as Cruikshank's is discursive.[10] To some extent this is a distinctive feature of eighteenth-century visual culture in general; as art historians have noted, in a period that clung to the classical ideal of *ut pictura poesis,* "English paintings . . . often aspired to the condition of a readable text."[11] As is implied by Lamb's praise, Hogarth's engravings generically align themselves with contemporary verse satire, most especially the mock-epics of Alexander Pope and Jonathan Swift.[12] Isaac Cruikshank and Gillray thus inherit from Hogarth's works, which generally include far less text than their own, a syntactical structure that requires readers carefully to parse the relations between a profusion of discrete compositional details in order fully to engage with what amounts to an argument, a commentary, an attempt to narrate the moment. As Gary Dyer and Vincent Carretta have suggested, these later eighteenth-century prints also need to be read alongside and perhaps understood as contiguous with contemporary satirical writing.[13] Gillray's surviving ink-and-wash sketches, drawn with feverish lines and covered in writing, disclose just how textual his works are in their conception and architecture. For instance, the thickly annotated margins of the preliminary drawing for his 1806 caricature *News from Calabria!—Capture of Buenos Ayres!* (fig. 1.2)—which imagines an irate Napoleon chasing from his presence a messenger who brings news of French defeat—show Gillray experimenting with the phrasing of his title and subtitle, recording details taken from daily newspapers ("London Gazette . . . ᴛᴏᴏᴏᴏ 9000 French destroyed by 4000 English"), and noting a line from *Richard III* ("Out on you, owls! nothing but songs of death?") to be spoken by Napoleon in a speech balloon in the final etching.[14] Taking us toward an archaeology of graphic satire, the sketch shows the extent to which caricatures—especially Gillray's elaborate exercises in the form—coalesce around and through a scaffolding of wordplay and multiple textual sources, only some of which remains visible within a final design.

As this drawing vividly testifies, the discursive character of the satirical print is in part the result of the way in which, almost as a formal imperative,

Fig. 1.2. James Gillray, preparatory sketch for *News from Calabria!—Capture of Buenos Ayres!* (1806). © The Trustees of the British Museum.

it traffics in allusions to and appropriations of a remarkable range of materials, and undertakes these exchanges in a highly self-reflexive manner.
Graphic satire of the eighteenth century is, through and through, an intermedial cultural form, and it was so well before the period I address in this book,
the so-called golden age of caricature.[15] Mark Hallett has traced at length how
prints of the first half of the century are defined by their insistent hybridity,
their intermixing of "high" and "low" cultural modes, and, ultimately, the
degree to which they foreground their own "strategies of pictorial fracture,
assemblage and instability." Such habits were pushed to their extreme, as
Hallett observes, in the staged discordances of the medley prints especially
popular in the 1720s, which offer still lives of overlaid print ephemera—
newspaper cuttings, ballads, playing cards, mezzotint portraits, and sheet
music, among other things—and which delight in generating meaning
through ostensibly random juxtapositions and correspondences.[16] This intermediality in fact goes back further still, for already in the seventeenth century
graphic satire was, as Helen Pierce contends, "a form of interdisciplinary
media" shaped by its interaction with "related forms of polemical ephemera."[17]

What is discernably different and new about prints of the later eighteenth and early nineteenth centuries is that this compulsive cross-cultural
borrowing tends to take on a markedly more coherent and sustained parodic
form. Satirical prints routinely focus on a single, noteworthy moment from a
text and elaborately restage it within the political present, carefully and
suggestively matching statesmen and other key figures to particular characters. *The Near in Blood* is somewhat unusual in this regard, for, perhaps
awkwardly, it condenses the action of an entire play rather than lighting
upon a moment of choice, but it nonetheless makes apparent this analogic
approach: Orleans becomes Richard; Marie Antoinette, Lady Anne; and
Louis XVI, by extension, Edward IV. Such parody sometimes serves to
register and even augment the gravity of an occasion, as is the case with
Cruikshank's caricature, but the effect is just as often one of deliberate
disjunction and even mock-heroism, as the banalities of everyday politics are
inscribed within an incongruously mythic structure.

Political Parody and the Work of Narrative

The first to recognize the caricatures of Gillray and others as sustained
exercises in political parody was William Hone, the radical satirist of late

Georgian London and in many ways parody's first true historian. At his trials for blasphemous libel in December 1817, Hone defended his publication of three liturgical parodies (*The Late John Wilkes's Catechism, The Political Litany,* and *The Sinecurist's Creed*) by invoking and reciting examples of comparable parodies that had in the past gone unprosecuted. Foremost among Hone's legion of examples were what he referred to as "graphic parodies," including George Cruikshank's *Boney's Meditations on the Island of St. Helena* (August 1815; BMC 12593), a parody of Satan's address to the sun in book 4 of *Paradise Lost,* and Gillray's *Disciples Catching the Mantle* (25 June 1808; BMC 10992), which casts former prime minister William Pitt the Younger as the prophet Elijah.[18] What for our purposes is significant about Hone's discourse is not only that he regarded these graphic satirists as parodists in their own right and set their prints within a longer tradition of literary parody that assuredly encompassed both verbal and visual publications, but also that he considered them to represent one of two distinct varieties of parody. Hone insisted that while some parodies aimed "to ridicule the thing" in question, ironically inhabiting a text that is also the satirical object, he, along with the likes of Gillray and George Cruikshank, practiced a different kind of parody, "one in which a man might convey ludicrous or ridiculous ideas relative to some other subject." Parody of this type, Hone assured the court, was "a ready engine to produce a certain impression on the mind, without at all ridiculing the sentiments contained in the original work."[19]

On the one hand, we are familiar with parody in this sense. Samuel Johnson's definition of the form—"A kind of writing, in which the words of an author or his thoughts are taken, and by a slight change adapted to some new purpose"—gives its operation as that of re-functioning rather than satirically mimicking an extant text, and other writers of the eighteenth century, including Pope, conceived of parody's work in similar terms.[20] On the other hand, however, and with the important exception of Augustan mock-epic, we often overlook parody along these lines in our overwhelmingly focus on parodies in which, as Swift succinctly puts it, "the Author personates the Style and Manner of other Writers, whom he has a mind to expose."[21] In doing so, we ignore a vast archive of political parodies from this period, topical pieces that were published in newspapers and pamphlets and parallel texts, and, concomitantly, we fail to register graphic satire's embeddedness within this dynamic culture of parody. I will say more about this culture later in the chapter. For now I want to press home just how much we as literary critics have to gain by reading graphic satire in the manner suggested by Hone, for it directs our attention toward the mechanisms by which satirical prints recycle the structures, plots, personae, and tropes of literary texts as a means not only of generating satires of something else but also of *narrativizing* politics.

In this way, in *The Near in Blood*, Shakespearean (or pseudo-Shakespearean) drama furnishes Isaac Cruikshank with a syntax of regicide and Machiavellian politicking through which a seemingly incomprehensible event might be understood. By drawing on *Richard III*, the print both makes legible—encounterable—the execution of an anointed king and offers a political diagnosis of Orleans's character. And in its inclusion of Richmond's lines about the self-destructive nature of the guilt-ridden conscience and the indomitability of virtue, it also prophesies the future restitution of benevolent and righteous authority, the overthrow of a tyrant by a "just" sovereign. In general terms, such recourse to narrative reveals its indispensability to all human cognition, what Mark Turner refers to as "the literary mind." For Turner we cannot think without narrative; it remains essential to the rational processes by which we negotiate the everyday world around us and understand relations between past, present, and future.[22] More specifically, though, Cruikshank's fashioning into a tragedy of an event that eroded long-established categories of political and ontological thought bespeaks the narrative shape of history. Like the historian, the caricaturist—who is as much a chronicler as a satirist—uses plot to bring coherent order to the white noise of unfolding reality, where there is no immanent hierarchy of agencies and no immanent chronology of cause and effect. As Hayden White observes, the narrativity of historical representation is driven by a moralizing imperative.[23] *Richard III* brings to Cruikshank's depiction of regicide not only a literary structure but also an ethical one; or rather, at least for Enlightenment readers who invariably approached cultural experiences in terms of the Horatian ideal of *utile et dulce* (instruction and pleasure), literary narrative is always already an ethical structure. *The Near in Blood* uses Shakespeare bluntly to establish a rhetoric of blame. Orleans, the print insists, is solely responsible for the king's death, and a bloody event that modern historians regard as the culmination of dynamic and long-evolving social, economic, and political factors is presented to the viewer as a consequence of familial intrigue and personal ambition, rather than of underlying ideological crisis. The print perhaps offers something approaching tragic catharsis, with the threat of communal violence reassuring displaced onto a convenient scapegoat, whose future death, we're told, will certainly bring about the rehabilitation of the legitimate state.[24]

Unlike the discourse of history, however, which for White seeks to repress the very narrative mechanisms it both needs and is embarrassed by, satirical prints plot politics in highly self-reflexive ways.[25] As Margaret Rose argues, parody often "forces our attention on to both the problem of representation in the fictional work, and its interpretation by the reader," and one of the most striking features of graphic satirical parody is the manner in which it cultivates the viewer's awareness of its own appropriative and narrative impulses.[26] In *The Near in Blood* it is significant that the soliloquy spoken by Orleans is one in which Richard quite consciously curates his own ruthlessness from the perspective of "future ages," expressly imagining himself within the present of history's reader or spectator. Cruikshank both recycles Shakespearean history and entreats his audience to register the way in which he is framing current affairs from the comfortingly safe vantage point of a stable future. In the strange, exposed temporality of this print, the political present is given to the reader as if it were the political past.

We can observe a similar concern with the shape of narrative in Gillray's *Slough of Despond* (fig. 1.3), a print published just a few weeks before Cruikshank's *Near in Blood*. In December 1792 the majority of the opposition Whig party, troubled by events across the Channel and the efflorescence of radicalism on their own shores, opted to support the government in a move that isolated their sometime leader Charles James Fox, who was seen to be sympathetic to some revolutionary ideals and who was unwilling to countenance allying himself with the prime minister, Pitt the Younger. Gillray responds to Fox's political alienation in a parody of the scene early in John Bunyan's *Pilgrim's Progress* in which the protagonist, Christian, finds himself mired in the slough of despond. In Gillray's *Patriots Progress*—the print's subtitle—Fox is shown floundering in the bog, the mud almost up to his neck. Just as Bunyan's Christian carries the burden of his sins on his back, so Fox is fatally weighed down by his treasonous Francophile politics, with the bundle on his back inscribed: "Contents French Gold, French Loyalty, French Daggers, And Crimes, more num'rous than the sands, upon the Ocean's shore." He has lost his Whig Club (an easy visual pun), his tricolor cockade, and his book—not the Bible that Christian carries with him but

Fig. 1.3. James Gillray, *The Slough of Despond;—Vide—The Patriots Progress* (Hannah Humphrey, 2 January 1793). BMC 8286. Courtesy of The Lewis Walpole Library, Yale University.

rather a "Gospel of Liberty"—and he calls out for aid, declaring that his "Former Friends" have forsaken him.

This is a richly detailed print that, once again, includes a significant amount of text. It contrapuntally plays the militant secularism of the French Revolution against Bunyan's uncompromising evangelism, and it also likely provided a source of inspiration for William Blake.[27] But what is more germane to my present discussion is Gillray's use of *Pilgrim's Progress* to satirize the very notion of diachronic movement, narratological and political. In the distance we see Fox's wished-for destination, the fortified entry to "Patriot's Paradise" beyond which lies a ladder that rises toward but stops well short of a crescent moon. Gillray folds into a single image a depiction both of Fox's present crisis and also of the empty idealism of the egalitarian future that radicals were then imagining for themselves, what Fox here calls "the Promis'd Land." Even if this revolutionary traveler escapes the slough, he will get nowhere. But Fox, in Gillray's scathing assessment, would just as soon go backward as forward: "My feet are stuck so fast in the Mire, that I can not get back, 'tho I try," he cries desperately. Fox, it emerges, is less a parodic version of Christian—the pilgrim determined to achieve salvation at all cost—and more a political reimagining of Pliable, the all-too impressionable character who briefly accompanies Christian only to turn back upon encountering the slough. Much like Hogarth's modern moral subjects, this print relentlessly ironizes the concept of progress; it exposes advance and retreat to be entirely interchangeable, and thus equally meaningless, goals. Politics is given a narrative in this satire only for it to be taken away again.

In their harnessing of literary narratives by the likes of Shakespeare and Bunyan, Cruikshank's *Near in Blood* and Gillray's *Slough of Despond* suggest the extent to which graphic satire is preoccupied with projecting discernable if yet-to-be-arrived-at ends. If these prints respond to and are in intimate dialogue with crises of the immediate moment, then their broader concern is to plot the trajectory of a political future, whether as an exercise in irony, in reassurance, or both. Cruikshank and Gillray implicitly understand—and make clear their understanding—that the dynamics of a story are predicated on the eschatological assumption that, as Frank Kermode noted, "an end will bestow upon the whole duration and meaning."[28] This, then, is the real value of literary narrative to the caricature parodist, for it makes sense of the now, whatever that might be, by expressly placing it in relation both to a particular past (such as the Wars of the Roses) and, more crucially, to an imagined future. So, as we'll see in Chapter 4, *Macbeth* appeals to graphic satirists as a text about prophecies and omens, a text that therefore enables those satirists at once to posit unequivocal and often bloody conclusions to ongoing affairs of state and also to thematize the fundamentally conjectural nature of their own form.

To broach graphic satire in terms of its literariness is thus also to recognize the critical operations that underlie its parodic play. We are not dealing here with the vocationless "blank parody" that Fredric Jameson sees in pastiche.[29] In its appropriation of a particular text, a print will often open up to scrutiny not only its own strategies of political emplotment but also the narrative procedures of its target text. Gillray's *Slough of Despond*, for instance, problematizes the theological efficacy of Bunyan's central conceit by questioning the neat teleology that inheres in the notion of a journey. It casts into doubt not only Fox's progress but also, more broadly, the very ideological coherence of "progress" as an idea and ideal. Equally, though, in relocating the allegory from the spiritual to the parliamentary-political world, Gillray elicits the often-overlooked satirical valency of Bunyan's personifications and symbolic topography of swamps and entryways. Though *The Near in Blood* seems less engaged with its source text, it too reminds us that parody is, in Linda Hutcheon's much-quoted formula, "extended repetition with critical difference," for the caricature's double citation—of *Richard III* and *Macbeth*—discloses anxiety about the political tensions and instability of the first of these plays.[30] As we've just established, the pivotal quotation here is the one given at the foot of the print ("Thrice is he arm'd that has his quarrel just . . ."), and as long as these words guide us to Cibber's drama, and to the redemptive persona of Richmond, the political logic of Cruikshank's satire holds. If, however, these lines instead direct us to Shakespeare's *Henry VI, Part II,* then they rather conjure a weak monarch besieged by both a fractious court and, resonantly, Jack Cade's popular rebellion. The danger is that Cibber's audience, and now Cruikshank's audience, hear the king whom Richard kills rather than the king who kills Richard. Certainly, we might read this print as struggling to find the most secure way of positioning its message of hope. The words of Cibber's Richmond, of Shakespeare's Henry VI, are bodiless here, and the trope of the "just" man adequately "arm'd" with virtue seems incongruous beside the hopelessly prostate figure of the about-to-be-beheaded Louis. Yet in its allusion to *Macbeth,* which overlays *Richard III* with a second tale of a bloody tyrant whose inevitably gruesome fall is written in the very path of his success, the print seems alert to the contradictions it inherits from Cibber's text; double citation functions as an ideological buttress, reinforcing the efficacy of the poetic, and political, justice in which the viewers are asked to place their faith. Once again, political parody is by default a mode of political exegesis. In repurposing their target texts, and in putting them to work in manifestly presentist ways, both Gillray and Isaac Cruikshank show themselves to be highly attentive to the nuances and ambivalences of those texts. In looking at their prints we are invited to read them reading a text we already know, or thought we already knew. As literary critics, we find in these images a dark glass that reflects our own interpretative procedures back at us.[31]

But not all texts were of equal appeal to graphic satirists of this period. In fact, satirical prints mined a fairly narrow range of literary works. Shakespeare's plays were by far the most common source of material, as Jonathan Bate has shown; or rather, *some* of Shakespeare's plays provided a seemingly inexhaustible repertoire of motifs and situations for political caricature.[32] *Macbeth* was especially popular, and was quoted or travestied in more than sixty of what Dorothy George terms "political" prints—in contradistinction to "social" prints—between the 1750s and the 1830s; *Hamlet* (at least forty-nine prints) was also repeatedly drawn upon, as were the two parts of *Henry IV* (twenty-two), *Richard III* (nineteen), *The Tempest* (thirteen), and *Othello* (eleven). Beyond the Shakespearean canon, John Milton's *Paradise Lost* was the most routinely cited text and features in at least fifty-five prints, while references to *Don Quixote* (forty-one), *Gulliver's Travels* (thirty-six), *Hudibras* (seventeen), *The Pilgrim's Progress* (thirteen), and the epics of Homer and Virgil (together, nineteen) were also common across the period.[33] In many ways this list is unsurprising in that it comprises many of what were regarded as the key works of the emergent vernacular canon. Certainly, and in the cases of Shakespearean and Miltonic allusion especially, graphic satirists consciously wield the cultural authority of the texts they appropriate. Caricature aspired to, and often achieved, considerable cultural prestige, and in its delight in literary parody it can be seen to contribute to the ongoing project of canon building by continually reinforcing the cultural currency of certain texts and ensuring their ready circulation within the print culture of the metropolitan political classes.

Yet if canonicity is a precondition of a literary text's availability for political appropriation, it cannot alone explain why some works were repeatedly parodied by graphic satirists while others were ignored. George's distinction between "social" and "political" satirical prints has been much maligned for imposing an arbitrary binary upon a complex archive, but it nonetheless provides a useful heuristic in addressing the question of what's distinctive about those texts that entered the grammar of graphic satire.[34] What George terms "social" satires commonly include epigraphs from a wide range of British poets, from Shakespeare to John Dryden to Pope, but such prints rarely engage in the elaborate literary parody I've been describing. Populated not by individuals but rather by recognizable stereotypes—the cleric, the lawyer, the cuckold, the quack, the fop—they have little need to import a moral structure because this cast of stock characters already, and inherently, offers one. On the other hand, political prints—and by "political" George more precisely means "parliamentary"—are concerned with the particular actions and affectations of identifiable members of Parliament (MPs) and ministers of state, and such satires therefore have need of the moral typology of narrative, with its heroes, villains, and martyrs. In other words, in their attempt to give legible satirical and ethical contours to political events and personalities, graphic satirists look to well-known fictional scenarios and characters as a means of reading individuals *as* or *through* types. As Richard III, Orleans becomes the tyrant; as an ironic version of Bunyan's Christian, Fox is the misguided pilgrim.

The literary texts that were most ripe for political parody were therefore those especially conducive to typological reading, those that readily operated as allegories. What I'm tracing in this book is, in simple terms, the elevation of certain works to the status of myth, an elevation enacted in recurrent habits of appropriation that mark a narrative as a communally shared and ostensibly timeless repository of tropes. This use of literature goes well beyond the material and time frame considered here, of course. During the First World War, as Paul Fussell has shown, British soldiers reflexively turned to Bunyan's *Pilgrim's Progress,* then a staple school text, as a quest narrative that lent meaning to their experiences at the front line and, in the slough of despond, provided a scenario that gave uncanny descriptive legibility to the unremitting mud and blood of the trenches.[35] Myths, as this example suggests, resonate with and serve to codify the realities of life precisely because their stories and characters are not recognizably lifelike, and in this respect it's to be expected that the texts most parodied by eighteenth-century graphic satirists are fantastical, offering a repertoire of characters that caricaturists could easily recast in their allegories of the moment: ghosts, witches, monsters, magicians, angels, demons, giants, dwarves, shapeshifters. And in their titles, which mimic the syntactical formula adopted by the period's plays ("short title; or, longer subtitle"), prints also repeatedly and consciously align themselves with the theater; as Hogarth understood, the medium of graphic satire is performative in that it is always the outsides—physiognomies, expressions, gestures, voices, groupings—that count. "My picture is my stage," he wrote, "and my men and women my actors, who were by means of certain actions and expressions to exhibit a dumb show."[36] There is no real attempt at interiority in satirical prints; morality's only vocabulary is that of the body; all has to be made visible through surface effects and the play of types. What they offer is often something close to a political morality play.

This, then, is why there are so many graphic-satirical parodies of *Macbeth, Paradise Lost,* and *Gulliver's Travels*—texts that are fundamentally otherworldly and spectacular—and none at all of novels such as Samuel Richardson's *Pamela* or even Daniel Defoe's *Robinson Crusoe,* which attempt to represent interiority and contemporaneity by recalibrating the intimate modes of epistolary writing or spiritual autobiography. This is not a matter of "flat" versus "round" characters. After all, who would claim that Macbeth or Richard III are the former? Rather, it is a question, to cite Deidre Lynch, of how dominant practices of reading understood and constituted fictional characters. Resisting Ian Watt's rise of the novel narrative, Lynch charts the move away from the "typographical culture" of the early and mid-eighteenth century, in which "character," in the then complementary senses of printed letter and personality, functioned in terms of "generalizability" and "replicability," and toward a culture in which readers and critics increasingly sought to locate depth and complexity in fictional characters old and new as a means of tying individuality to subjectivity.[37] In its literary parody, and evident preference for texts that lent themselves to typological reading, graphic satire shows that this older symbolic economy was far from moribund at the end of the eighteenth century. In political prints, character remains first and foremost a technology of legibility.

This argument troubles much received wisdom on the development of graphic satirical practices across the period, most especially the supposed shift in the form's prevailing visual idiom, from one of emblem in the earlier part of the century to one of caricature, in the sense of physiognomic exaggeration, from the 1770s and 1780s onward. For Amelia Rauser, "earlier, emblematic prints feature, above all, things—symbols, allegories, and layers of objects and texts—while later caricatural prints feature, above all, selves."[38] Yet the problem with this all-too teleological narrative is that it reads the rhetoric of an image through iconography alone and thus fails to register the insistency with which the "selves" of caricature are typologically defined, coming into focus as much through a constellation of intermedial and parodic references as through satiric portraiture. In their marshaling of literary texts, that is, caricatures retain the very emblematic structure they ostensibly reject; as Bunyan's pilgrim or Milton's Satan, Fox steadfastly remains a symbol, a motif, an allegorical figure, even as his particular likeness is meticulously captured and distorted. Indeed, as Diana Donald rightly observes, it was only in the 1780s that the strategies of sustained parody and the mock-heroic become commonplace in political prints, and it's no coincidence that this is also the decade in which those prints show a decisive predilection for physiognomic representation and hyperbole.[39] To be sure, there are a few examples of such parody as early as the 1750s, but without question the bulk of those I've found date from the 1780s onward, and this historical concentration suggests that in their turn to the idiom of caricature graphic satirists necessarily sought out new strategies for emblematizing politics.[40] It is less the political print in general, then, and more precisely political *caricature* that has need of the typologies offered by literary narratives by virtue of its special commitment to portraying specific public individuals.

Of course, my attempt here to map the ways in which graphic satire narrativizes politics has described these procedures as far more secure, hermeneutically and ideologically, than they ever could be. In their parodies of works by Shakespeare, Milton, and Swift, caricaturists are engaging with polysemous texts that ultimately frustrate the imperatives of reduction and simplification. If such texts furnish satirists with typologies of political character, then they also bring with them fluid networks of association and connotation that are not to be controlled or suppressed. Graphic satire's consumers were, to use Michel de Certeau's wonderful phrase, "poets of their own acts."[41] Unwarranted or unintended readings will always be possible, especially in a form such as parody, which asks its readers to track mobile ironies and to work across different and sometimes discordant cultural codes. As I detail in Chapter 5, caricatures of the 1780s tread a dangerously fine line between ridicule and its opposite in their analogic use of Milton's Satan. In part, this reaffirms Lynch's understanding of the changing patterns of reading character. Under the pressure of new readerly impulses to locate subjectivities and imagine inner lives, the types that populate late-century graphic-satirical parodies might easily give way to more complex, morally equivocal characters. But this is also an issue of the way in which what Jameson terms the "political unconscious" of a text makes itself felt within these parodies. In its harnessing of literary structures, graphic satire takes on narratives that already seek imaginatively and formally to resolve deep-lying social contradictions, and that generate new tensions in this dialectical process. In this sense, narrative is both a necessary and a singularly unfit tool for the political satirist, for it is an array of frictions as much as (or because it is) a structure that attempts coherence.[42] For the literary critic, then, the most interesting and telling features in the satirical prints at which we will be looking are those—such as the double citation of *The Near in Blood*—that disclose a parodist's struggle to close down the routes to alternative and countervailing inference; or conversely, those features which show a parodist actively welcoming the ambivalences and ambiguities that inhere in a source text. The latter is true of Gillray's prints especially, which repeatedly marshal polyvalence and paradox as themselves signifiers of political crisis and instability.

All of this returns us once more to the question of graphic satire's intermediality, for such inevitable play of meaning reminds us that the literary texts taken up by satirical prints are always already mediated by and through other modes of cultural production. So, in its preference for Cibber's play, *The Near in Blood* draws upon the version of *Richard III* that appeared on the contemporary stage, a version that offered audiences a more bluntly villainous and obsessively soliloquizing protagonist than is to be found in Shakespeare's drama.[43] Or, to take another example that looks to the same play, *Charles the Third, King of all the Orkneys* (fig. 1.4), a print of June 1784, arrives at Shakespearean history through still more strata of mediation and re-mediation that include not only theatrical adaptation and practice but also painting and celebrity culture. In a parody of Hogarth's famous portrayal of David Garrick as Richard as he wakes from a dream crowded with the spirits of his victims (fig. 1.5), Fox gesturally replicates the iconic Garrick "start" as he registers the full horror of his corrupt and dissipated actions, the paraphernalia of which lies strewn around his couch: a sword of "Injustice," a "Helmet of Unrighteousness," a list of purchased votes, and a portrait of his supporter and alleged lover, the Duchess of Devonshire. Fox is here the man who would be king, a charge routinely applied to him in the months surrounding the 1784 general election, as we'll see. This complex parody exposes Fox's turpitude and also casts him as a political anachronism; dressed as a Tudor monarch and grasping at arbitrary power, Fox seems woefully out of his time. But he is not so much one Richard as four—Shakespeare's, Cibber's (from which the print quotes), Garrick's, and Hogarth's—and their accretion significantly complicates the direction of the caricature's satire. If Fox is the Richard of Shakespeare or Cibber, we might interpret this image as a political prophecy, an assertion that no man can evade his crimes or conscience indefinitely. But if Fox is Garrick, the actor performing Richard or posing as this character for a picture, then this caricature instead offers a dissection of Fox's audacious insincerity: he is the celebrity statesman, the consummate performer for whom politics is a matter of ego over principle. These two readings are not mutually exclusive. Rather, the print's layered parody holds them in a state of permanent, and productive, tension.

Fig. 1.4. *Charles the Third, King of all the Orkneys, and would be Monarch of the East. Or the Effects of a Bad Conscience* (S. W. Fores, 16 June 1784). BMC 6622. Courtesy of The Lewis Walpole Library, Yale University.

Fig. 1.5. William Hogarth, *Mr Garrick in the Character of Richard the 3d* (1746). By permission of the Folger Shakespeare Library.

Charles the Third testifies to the foundational importance of Hogarth to the literariness of later graphic satire. Hogarth—certainly a skilled parodist—did not himself engage in sustained literary parody, but in the absence of a native tradition of art, his work sought almost programmatically to establish a British artistic culture that derived its materials, aspirations, and institutional validity from the enshrined literary canon. *The Painter and His Pug* (1745), in which the oval canvas of his self-portrait rests on casually stacked volumes of Shakespeare, Milton, and Swift, is Hogarth's manifesto for English painting as, in Ronald Paulson's words, "a branch of literature rather than art." Following Hogarth's example, the high art that flourished within the new exhibition culture of the later eighteenth and early nineteenth centuries was self-consciously literary, as is evidenced by the many paintings of scenes from literature shown at the Royal Academy and, more obviously still, by projects such as John Boydell's Shakespeare Gallery, Henry Fuseli's Milton Gallery, and Thomas Macklin's Poets' Gallery.[44] If the marked increase in elaborate literary parody in the graphic satire of the 1780s is in part symptomatic of the move toward an aesthetic of caricature, then it also bespeaks the extent to which canonical literary texts permeated and animated visual culture of this period. By the final twenty years of the century, the likes of Shakespeare and Milton were circulating within a visual economy as much as a print one.

Yet, as *Charles the Third* evinces, what distinguishes graphic satire's engagement with literature from that of Academy art is its unrelenting attention both to the mediatedness of culture and to its own position, as at once mediated and mediating, within this proliferating matrix. Once again, it is the self-reflexivity of graphic satire's parodic practices—where satirical prints often seem to tell us what they are doing and all that they are negotiating in the very process of that doing and negotiating—that's so striking. In its parody of Hogarth's picture, *Charles the Third* summons its viewers to think not just about Fox's politics but also about Garrick's curation of Shakespeare, which is also a curation of his own acting expertise; about Hogarth's staging of these acts of curation; and, finally, about how, as a satirical print, it is inserting itself within this cascade of appropriations. If we follow Clifford Siskin and William Warner in understanding the Enlightenment as "an event in the history of mediation," an event in which print played a starring role, then the single-sheet satirical print might well be regarded as an Enlightenment cultural form par excellence.[45]

Literature and the Limits of Political Literacy

Who, though, possessed the interpretative dexterity and cultural expertise to decipher satires such as *Charles the Third* and Gillray's *Slough of Despond?* To some extent this is a question that I have been posing—and perhaps answering—all along in my elaboration of the complex parodic and analogic play in which these prints engage. In their literariness, these caricatures could have appealed to and have been fully understood by a limited audience only. Graphic satire is not a "universal language," and it invites not the glance but the educated gaze. This argument is by no means new. For all that the issue of graphic satire's audience remains a vexed topic, there is a broad level of consensus among most historians about who likely looked at and purchased satirical prints in the Georgian period. Bindman, for instance, notes that political caricatures of the later eighteenth century "carried with them the aura of a gentlemanly hobby," not least because it was Grand Tourists who had first brought the Italian practice of *caricatura* to England's shores in the early part of the century. The likes of Gillray, the Cruikshanks, and Thomas Rowlandson were, Bindman goes on, "sophisticated purveyors of luxury goods aimed at the wealthy and politically powerful who might open their volumes of satires underneath their portraits by Thomas Gainsborough or Joshua Reynolds." Other historians—among them Roy Porter and Timothy Clayton—agree that satirical prints were part of an "elite" culture and spoke to a political class that at most included propertied professionals.[46]

It needs to be emphasized that these scholars are describing not graphic satirical culture in general, which was quite heterogeneous, but more precisely its "high end" amid the significant cluster of printshops that by the final quarter of the century came to be concentrated in London's fashionable and expensive West End. Gillray's large and ornate images, printed on high-quality paper and sold by Hannah Humphrey from her shop in St. James's Street, are far removed from the cheap, sometimes pirated, usually less polit-ical designs published by Thomas Tegg from his Cheapside premises.[47] With the exception of a few small engravings that appeared in periodicals such as the *Westminster Magazine,* it is to this more rarified marketplace of satirical prints that the parodies which form the focus of this book belong. Such etch-ings cost between one and six shillings, depending on their size and coloring, with the average price above three shillings and the highest as much as thir-teen shillings, sixpence. As Vic Gatrell points out, at five shillings a large print would have cost the same as an everyday coat.[48] Available information, which admittedly is scarce, suggests that print runs for single-sheet satires might have been around the five-hundred mark in the first instance, with this number rising in cases of especially successful prints. The numbers in which caricatures circulated do not stand comparison with those of newspapers and periodicals; by the end of the century, for instance, the print runs of the *Monthly Magazine* and the *Morning Post* were respectively 5,000 and 4,500.[49] What statistical data we have thus supports the conclusion that only those of considerable means would have been able and willing to purchase commodities—and caricatures were commodities—that cost so much and were printed in such small quantities. Certainly, this was the hard truth that confronted Gillray when he initially marketed the prints of his propagandistic sequence *Consequences of a Successful French Invasion* (1798) at just sixpence. As he informed Sir John Dalrymple, who commissioned the ill-fated engravings to accompany his own text, "there has hardly been one sold but to people who would have paid Half a Crown as willingly as sixpence." In an effort to recoup production costs, the prints were quickly repriced at two shillings, a change, the *Morning Post* noted, that ensured the horrors imagined by Gillray would be "confined to the view of the rich."[50] It's hardly surprising, in this context, that satirical prints were subject to neither stamp duty nor censorship.

Yet against the weight of this evidence, the conception persists of graphic satire as a "popular" medium, what one scholar describes as "a national pastime."[51] In particular, those who maintain this position invariably cite printshops' customary practice of exhibiting caricatures in their windows, thereby making them available to pedestrians from all social classes and extending their potential audience almost indefinitely. This is a highly problematic but tenacious argument that oversimplifies what was a complex site of visuality and cultural exchange, and I engage with its premises and sources at length in the next chapter. For now, let me simply note that, like all ideas, this notion of the inclusivity of graphic satire has its own genealogy; it was, as we've seen, articulated by Gillray's editor in 1818, and as early as 1765 one newspaper was suggesting—or, more accurately, worrying—that prints were "a universal Language, understood by Persons of all Nations and degrees."[52] In other words, we inherit the conception of graphic satire as a democratized and democratizing medium from the period itself, and before we rehearse it once again we need to understand how and why it emerged. It is this task of historicization that I take up in the following chapter.

What more directly concerns me here is that the two books which arguably come closest to my own in their attendance to the literary character of graphic satire—Jonathan Bate's *Shakespearean Constitutions* and Ian Haywood's *Romanticism and Caricature*—are both unabashed advocates of this populist thesis. Published almost thirty years ago, Bate's pioneering study of the use of Shakespeare's plays by late Georgian political caricaturists broke new ground in its embrace of satirical prints as a form of literary historical evidence and its rigorous focus on questions of political appropriation, while Ian Haywood's more recent monograph parses the textual and iconographic intricacies of a selection of prints by Gillray and Rowlandson in a sequence of extended close readings that are informed as much by Derridean deconstruction as new historicism. Both, however, fall back on the entrenched notion of caricature as "popular." Writing before the wave of scholarship on graphic satire that began in the 1990s and continues today, Bate equates caricature's cultural presence and function with that of television; Haywood is circumspect in his use of the term *popular*, which he rightly recognizes as working across and encompassing all classes, but he nonetheless insists that this aptly describes the wide cultural reach of satirical prints. The result is an irresolvable disconnect between methodology and argument: between, on the one hand, the sophisticated critical procedures Bate and Haywood use to excavate the intended meanings of these images and, on the other hand, their repeated avowals that these images could be and were comprehended by something approaching a mass public.[33]

In contrast, I'm interested in elaborating the ways in which these satirical prints thoroughly entwine cultural and political literacies by making political understanding conditional on a deep and ready knowledge of the English classics. I have repeatedly drawn upon the term *legibility* to describe the operations of literary appropriation in graphic satire, and it's important to keep in mind that to render something legible—a political crisis, a political personality—is not simply to make it known and knowable but necessarily to do so for those specific constituencies that possess the requisite expertise to read the vocabulary being used. What is in question here is an implied readership more than the actual one, for if a caricature targets and imagines for itself a particular kind of consumer in its pricing, then it does so too in its predilection for literary parody. If satirical prints circulated primarily among an elite political class, then this limited audience was constituted in rhetorical as much as commercial terms.

Parody, as Simon Dentith observes, usually works to "draw a circle around initiated readers to exclude ignorant ones," and the readers and writers of the eighteenth century were entirely cognizant of this in-joke imperative, as is clear from Henry Fielding's blithe comment that the mock-heroic passages of his novel *Joseph Andrews* were "chiefly calculated" for the "Classical Reader," and therefore needn't be pointed out.[54] "The pleasure we take in parody," wrote Maria Edgeworth in 1816, "arises from the self-approbation we feel from our own quickness in discovering the resemblances and recollecting the passages alluded to"; should we, Edgeworth continues, "not immediately remember them, or if the resemblance must be pointed out, or the allusion explained, our pleasure must be diminished" and we feel "pain" and "mortification."[55] This nascent phenomenology of parody suggests the manner in which it entices the educated reader by offering a reaffirmation of her or his self-image as one of the discerning few and thus, in turn, reinforces the boundaries between that (imagined) community of the culturally enfranchised and everyone else; and it also reminds us how far difficulty was cherished and fostered within eighteenth-century culture's models of textual enjoyment. Writing of the "love of pursuit" that is innate to human nature in his *Analysis of Beauty* (1753), Hogarth noted that "it is a pleasing labor of the mind to solve the most difficult problems; allegories and riddles, trifling as they are, afford the mind amusement."[56] Like the rebus prints that proliferated in this period, which invited readers to decode a language of hieroglyphic signs (see fig. 4.1), parody was then thought of as a puzzle. For example, *The Near in Blood* requires its viewer to register multiple character analogies, to detect the subtle but important changes that Cruikshank makes to the speeches of Richard and Lady Anne, to recognize the title's quotation, and then, constellating these various components, to grasp the way in which Shakespearean drama is being grafted onto and used to frame contemporary crisis. All of this presumes a complex horizon of expectations on this viewer's part, who must come to the print with some knowledge of the event in question (likely from the daily press) and an extensive familiarity with Cibber's *Richard III* and *Macbeth* (through performances and/or published texts), and who also has to be able to identify the figures shown and distinguish their relations to one another. The payoff for those able to perform this work of overcoming parodic difficulty are the "pleasures," to use Edgeworth's word, of political understanding, of satirical engagement, and, woven with these, of a renewed sense of one's own cultural capital. Admittedly, not all satirical prints of the period make such significant demands on their readers, but the frequency with which graphic satirists have recourse to literary appropriation, making things difficult even as they make things legible, nonetheless reveals the base level of cultural know-how that their consumers were expected to possess.

Certainly, the public for satirical prints significantly overlapped with the readerships of newspapers, periodicals, and pamphlets, and with the spectatorships of the major theaters, and it needs to be remembered that caricatures were part of a wider political culture of literary parody and quotation. For instance, the late 1770s witnessed a flurry of antiwar parodies of Richard Brinsley Sheridan's plays that cast the Tory ministers then overseeing the military campaign against the rebelling American colonies as the misguided profligates and compulsive fraudsters of contemporary comedy.[57] Elaborate parody of this kind pervaded the period's newspapers and periodicals, too. In 1771, the Wilkesite *Middlesex Journal* reimagined the speech in which Joseph Addison's Cato ruminates upon the immortality of the soul as a monologue in which a vacillating George III ponders how best to deal with the radical John Wilkes; at the end of 1793, across two months and seventeen numbers, the *World* serialized a parody of *The Beggar's Opera* that took aim at the Whig club; from 1792 to 1805 the *Gentleman's Magazine* included a regular section entitled "Parodies of Shakspeare," in which famous soliloquies were often adapted to speak to the parliamentary moment ("To stand, or not to stand . . .," or "Is this a mitre that I see before me . . ."); and, most obviously, William Gifford's *Anti-Jacobin* (1797–98), which featured etchings by Gillray, deployed parody as a primary strategy of conservative political critique.[58] Even beyond these examples of sustained parody, and there are many more, one can register the reflexively appropriative and analogic nature of political discourse at this time in the brief literary references that routinely punctuate articles in the daily and periodical press. So, just two days after the publication of *The Near in Blood*, and seemingly unaware of Cruikshank's caricature, a paragraph in the *Public Advertiser* noted "the resemblance of the Royal Tragedy acted in France to that of Shakespeare's Richard III."[59] Far from dwindling in the second half of the century, as Robert L. Mack has contended, overtly political parody flourished right across the reign of George III.[60]

Throughout this book, then, I place caricatures alongside those travesties and appropriations that were appearing in adjacent venues and forms within eighteenth-century print culture. Yet in tracking these cross-media relays I don't want to lose sight of what it is that makes the satirical prints of Gillray, the Cruikshanks, and others distinctive, formally and culturally. Exclusively textual parodies often incorporate clues, notes, and patterns of insinuation that catalyze understanding, or even offer readers parallel texts that enable them to shuttle between an original and its distorted imitation at will, as is the case with the *Middlesex Journal*'s reworking of *Cato*. But, even accounting for its pronounced verbality, the satirical print rarely aids its readers to this degree; it is a work of considered economy that has the space of just a single sheet, and this necessitates a peculiar kind of unpacking and close reading. The reviews of Gillray's prints published in the Weimar-based journal *London und Paris* between 1798 and 1806 vividly suggest, in their alertness to nuance and parodic sophistication, the intricate paths that such reading might take; its article on *End of the Irish Farce of Catholic Emancipation* (see fig. 5.15), for instance, extends to thirty-eight pages.[61] And these essays also reveal the particular prestige associated both with Gillray's caricatures as a cultural form and with the kinds of cultural competence they exercised in their readers. Though there is a frustrating absence of equivalent commentary in Britain, it is telling that by 1806 the *Monthly Magazine* took to including brief summaries of some satirical prints, Gillray's especially, in its "Monthly Retrospect of the Fine-Arts."[62] In graphic satire, then, we encounter political parody that works and circulates in a specific way, one that firmly locates us within what Peter de Bolla, in his discussion of the culture of visuality that emerged in Britain in the 1760s, terms "the regime of the picture." For de Bolla, this was a mode of looking that privileged and enacted identification and prolonged engagement, and which—in contradistinction to the experience of immediate recognition offered in "the regime of the eye"—embedded its viewer within "a particular sociocultural space of knowingness and expertise."[63]

Within this culture of the educated gaze the objects of graphic satire's caustic ridicule were also among its most faithful consumers. Sheridan, a Foxite Whig politician as well as a playwright, is said to have purchased six copies of Gillray's *Uncorking Old Sherry* (10 March 1805; BMC 10375), a merciless response to a spluttering speech he'd delivered in the House of Commons.[64] Equally, driven partly by his delight in satire and partly by his unflagging vanity and insecurity, the Prince of Wales, later George IV, bought many hundreds of caricatures (sometimes purchasing entire runs, the plate included, to suppress images that cut too close to the bone), and this royal collection now makes up the bulk of the nine thousand prints held by the Library of Congress. But nowhere are the intimacies between graphic satirical and parliamentary cultures more visible than in the aspirations of the precocious young Tory MP George Canning. Educated at Eton and Oxford before entering the Commons, where he would later rise to the ranks of foreign secretary and prime minister, Canning sought to persuade Gillray to caricature him by lobbying their mutual friend, the Reverend John Sneyd. Canning recognized that a "*debut*"—the word is Sneyd's—in Hannah Humphrey's window would unequivocally signal his arrival on the political stage, and having achieved this aspiration by 1796, he would go on regularly to supply Gillray with ideas and to showcase his own parodic talents in Gifford's *Anti-Jacobin*.[65]

On this account, caricature represents a thoroughly institutionalized mode of political satire, and its use of literary allusion and parody bespeaks its proximity to, almost its imbrication with, the rhetorical culture of Parliament mapped by Christopher Reid. Satirical prints offer some of the most colorful records we have of oratorical performance; they frequently reproduce verbatim the phrases and passages of members' speeches, and the likes of Gillray were often to be found in the Commons's Strangers' Gallery. But graphic satire did more than just document the words spoken on the floor of the House; more profoundly, it shared with parliamentary speech certain rhetorical protocols. Like caricaturists, orators quoted from literary sources—most notably Virgil, Horace, Cicero, Shakespeare, Milton, and Pope—with uncommon frequency and deliberateness, and in doing so, as Reid argues, they mobilized "a literary tradition, asking [their] audience to recognize it as a shared inheritance, to recognize themselves in that inheritance, and to find there an identity in common." The literariness of graphic satire is thus, more broadly but also more specifically, the literariness of Westminster culture. As we will see across this book, politicians, in their speeches, and satirists, in their etchings, cited and played with the same works of literature, often doing so in similar ways; and in drawing upon these texts as a common repository of ideas and tropes, they were generating and renewing the "quotation community" that Reid regards as central to parliamentary political culture in the eighteenth century. Graphic satirists and MPs were speaking the same language to the same limited public of culturally literate citizens; for both, literary quotation served as "a means of summoning gentlemen to meet on common ground." In this context, and to use Pierre Bourdieu's term for the acquired skills and dispositions shared across and constituting a social class, literary appropriation and parody were part of the habitus of an educated elite who regarded their own cultural capital as guaranteeing and self-authorizing their hold on political power.[66]

Such a claim perforce needs to be qualified. For one, texts by Shakespeare, Milton, and Swift were certainly well known within the *functionally* literate population of late eighteenth-century Britain. The size and development of this reading public are hard to plot with precision, but it would have been considerably smaller than the 60 percent of men and 40 percent of women able, by the 1790s, to sign their names in a marriage register.[67] William St. Clair contends that the print marketplace was flooded with more affordable editions of older works after 1774, when in the *Donaldson v. Becket* case the House of Lords determined that copyright was not perpetual. For St. Clair, this decision represents "the most decisive event in the history of reading in England since the arrival of printing," for the marketplace of cheap books to which it gave rise in turn fostered a new level of public familiarity with and sense of ownership of literary texts that was foundational in establishing a national canon. Indeed, for Trevor Ross, the Lords' adjudication effectively instantiated the idea of "literature in its modern sense."[68] Yet J. E. Elliott has challenged the evidence on which this admittedly compelling narrative is grounded. Pointing especially to auction sale catalogs, he argues that book prices in fact did not fall after 1774 and that the Lords' verdict encouraged publishers not to release cheaper editions but rather to "splinter" authors' works into many more volumes. Noting that "a second-hand edition of Shakespeare's plays . . . would have been equivalent to a day's labor among the relatively well-to-do and more than a week's among the clerical and mercantilist classes," Elliott ultimately corroborates Richard Altick's claim that if "the prices of new books were high before 1780, they were prohibitive afterward to all but the rich."[69]

In light of such arguments, we cannot regard the explosion of literary parody in graphic satire of the 1780s as implying a sudden dilation of the reading public. The increasing literary saturation of exhibition culture and the discernable shift toward a caricatural idiom remain, as I've suggested, the key enabling matrices in the satirical print's embrace of sustained parody. Put differently, parody requires its readers to possess a special degree of familiarity with a target text; it is not enough simply to have read, say,

Paradise Lost, when a print calls upon its viewers to undertake the dexterous negotiation of thinking across a political event and a particular phase of Milton's poem, a negotiation that requires not only a deep knowledge of both the text and event in question but also, crucially, the cultural confidence needed to read that event *as* a text, and vice versa. For this reason, my concern is with literary parody and not allusion per se. Allusion is local and can be usually missed, in a poem as much as a print, without entirely inhibiting a reader's comprehension of the whole; parody, by contrast, is oriented in total toward something outside of itself, and the reader who lacks proper knowledge of that something is necessarily excluded from the space of understanding. Parody is, in this way, resistant to index learning. The lines from *2 Henry VI* quoted at the foot of *The Near in Blood* were repeatedly included in anthologies and miscellanies under headings such as "Conscience" and "Innocence," and would likely have been known to many through such collections, but Cruikshank's satire would have been illegible to such readers unless they also possessed a sound knowledge of Cibber's play in its entirety.[70] This is not to ignore the extent to which these complex prints yield their meaning across a scale of intersecting interpretative levels, but it is to insist, like Edgeworth, that at the certain point the distinction between understanding and not understanding will always be binary.

Moreover, we know that the size and development of graphic satire's audience was neither stable nor linear and that it appealed to and likely reached larger or smaller constituencies at different moments in the eighteenth and nineteenth centuries; not least, the often crudely designed prints published during the Wilkesite agitation of the early 1760s almost certainly proliferated in greater numbers than the caricatures of the 1790s.[71] In broaching prints in terms of the kinds of cultural competence they expect of their prospective consumers, I hope further to illuminate this uneven history. After all, different texts circulated in different ways, and a parody of *Gulliver's Travels,* which in part makes its jest through juxtapositions of size and which was readily available in fairly inexpensive abridgments, may have found a wider audience than Gillray's elaborate, mock-epic play with Milton. In its deployment of literary parody, graphic satire can be seen to be continuously negotiating and renegotiating the limits of political engagement.

As should become clear later in this book, the pressures of the Napoleonic Wars had a discernable impact on patterns of literary appropriation as the urgency with which satirical prints were required to perform as propaganda compelled them to extend their legibility. At the very same time that images of an inclusive public looking into printshop windows began to appear—an emergence I trace in the next chapter—Napoleon was being cast in the roles of Gulliver and Harlequin in parodies of texts (in the broader sense of this word) that had some presence within popular culture. But the exigencies and anxieties of a given political moment could just as easily induce satirists to address a markedly contracted public. During the "Days of May" in 1832, a period of civil unrest precipitated by the House of Lords' vetoing of the third Reform Bill, Tory satirist John Doyle retreated to the safety of Homeric reference in his print *The Great ~~Wooden~~ Stalking Horse* (fig. 1.6), a parody of *The Iliad* that depicts Lord Grey and his associates hauling the Trojan horse of "Reform" within the walls of the British state. Here, only the title and label on the horse's headband are given in the vernacular; all other text, including two speech ribbons, an inscription, and an epigraph, appear in Latin. Facing up to and working against the imminent possibility of an enlarged franchise, the caricaturist speaks only to those who are classically educated.

Fig. 1.6. John Doyle, *The Great ~~Wooden~~ Stalking Horse, A Modern Antique* (Thomas McLean, 10 May 1832). BMC 17028. © National Portrait Gallery, London.

In this way, what is most important to an understanding of graphic satire at this time is less the actual boundaries of the reading public than the intensity with which that public's constitution was being imagined and contested. According to Paul Keen, the 1790s witnessed a "crisis of literature" brought about by competing prescriptions of how the republic of letters ought to function within and as a public sphere. Where reformists such as William Godwin projected literature as an ideal vehicle for the wider diffusion of knowledge necessary to the creation of a better and more equal society, conservative commentators conjured nightmarish visions of a democratized reading public in which cherished texts and ideas where freely open to abuse and misuse. Both sides of this debate, Keen argues, drawing on the work of Isaac Kramnick, were confronting and striving to reconcile the tension between a still prevailing ideology of classical republicanism, which envisaged the citizen as someone who actively contributed to and acted in the interests of public life, and a social reality of rampant commercialism that was structured around the tenets of bourgeois liberalism, which recognized only the labor of individuals competing against one another for their own private ends.[72]

As commodities that were trafficked within a luxury consumer market and that ironically mimicked the rhetoric of high art in their dizzying depictions of public degradations and animosities, satirical prints could be seen to erode confidence in the ideals of such classical republicanism, and this was a view articulated by the painter James Barry in 1798 when he wrote disdainfully of "the profligate caricatura furniture of print-shops."[73] Such print-shops were for some commentators, as we'll see shortly, worrying sites of cultural accessibility and immorality. Yet graphic satire shares far more with those who feared the democratization of culture than with those who sought and heralded it, as Doyle's caricature readily reveals in the stridency with which it responds to the threat of an enlarged political public by directing itself toward an exclusive and self-selecting cohort of readers. The implied reader of much graphic satire is what in 1784 the *European Magazine* described as the "man of the genteel world" who was equipped to "pass through life with decency" because he possessed considerable knowledge of "history and politics, moral and natural philosophy, and polite literature."[74] We're accustomed to recognizing the scorn that certain discourses of romanticism poured upon a supposedly squalid culture of commercialized entertainment and popular tastes (think of William Wordsworth's preface to *Lyrical Ballads* or

Charles Lamb's essay "On the Tragedies of Shakespeare"). But satire's part in this broader cultural program to fortify literature and art against what Wordsworth nervously called the "many-headed mass" of spectators has gone largely unnoticed. It's this story that I want to tell here.[75]

Ultimately, for all that it habitually conscripts other cultural discourses and media, I do not regard graphic satire as addressing or augmenting a bourgeois public sphere along the lines posited by Jürgen Habermas. For Habermas, and his many interlocutors within the discipline of eighteenth-century studies, such a public sphere emerged as a space in which those newly endowed with economic power but still on the margins of or excluded from the traditional structures of political authority could wield increasing influence through the venues and discourses of public opinion.[76] Satirical prints, by contrast, addressed first and foremost a patrician constituency that was already enfranchised (in the multiple senses of this term) and that had long occupied the centers of social and political privilege. Distributed in small numbers at considerable cost, prints both mocked and catered to an audience of high-status men—and of high-status women, too, as we're reminded by the caricature collection of the antiquarian Sarah Sophia Banks, daughter of a Lincolnshire MP. This is not to suggest that only those within these circles purchased, understood, and enjoyed caricatures. The profiles of the satirists themselves give the lie to such a notion. Gillray, the son of a Chelsea pensioner, owed his education to his Moravian upbringing, while Isaac Cruikshank, the son of a Jacobite customs inspector, spent his childhood surrounded by the publishers of Edinburgh, whose conversations were animated by matters of art, music, and literature; both satirists were intelligent, highly culturally literate artisans. But in their personal histories and more significantly in their art, Gillray and Cruikshank nonetheless affirm how necessary it was for anyone who hoped to enter or engage the field of politics to be conversant in a language of art and literature that "the aristocracy of culture," to use another of Bourdieu's terms, considered their right and natural inheritance.[77]

It was exactly for this reason that William Hone's parodic practice so troubled the political establishment. As Olivia Smith, Marcus Wood, and Kyle Grimes have shown, Hone's parodies took up texts—the Bible, the liturgy, the nursery rhyme—that circulated widely in both print and oral cultures; reproduced rapidly and inexpensively (selling for as little as twopence), they were read or heard by laborers as well as gentleman and therefore struck not only at the political elite's corruption but also at its claims to ownership of certain cultural discourses and modes.[78] Published in the year of the Peterloo Massacre, *The Political House that Jack Built* (1819), a pamphlet collaboration between Hone and George Cruikshank that took the form of a children's book, sold in excess of one hundred thousand copies in just a few years. As the attorney general acknowledged during Hone's trials, his primary misdemeanor was not to have engaged in liturgical parody per se but rather to have done so in a cheap format that could be—and was— easily disseminated among the lower classes: "There may be many writings which sensible men may read in their closets," declared Sir Samuel Shepherd, but Hone's parodies willfully courted an audience "among the ignorant and uninformed," where they were "calculated to have a gross effect."[79] Parody, according to the Crown's representative, was a gentlemanly form that properly belonged in the study or library—within the private spaces of the educated and affluent—and that became dangerous when it was wantonly removed from the self-selecting communities who possessed the cultural competency to understand its subtleties and instead offered within a public forum to the "uninformed" masses, who were liable to misread complex cultural codes never intended for their consumption.

Haywood insists not only that the prints of Gillray and Rowlandson were popular but also that in their penchant for the scatological and carnivalesque they exhibit a "deep-seated resistance to authority," an assumption which in part reflects his exclusive focus on historical junctures (the 1790s and the years around 1819) that represent high-water marks of a radical counterculture in Britain.[80] But such a contention fails to register precisely what was different, and manifestly subversive, about Hone's work, a difference Hone himself drew attention to by highlighting the institutional embeddedness of parody. The roll call of earlier parodists he mustered to his defense—including Martin Luther, Robert Harley, Edmund Burke, and George Canning—were all either of high religious or parliamentary standing or in the employ of those who were, and Gillray was an especially important figure for Hone's legal case not only because he regularly mined scripture for material but also because he was in the pay of the Pitt government and "had a pension for his parodies" (as Gillray did from 1797 to 1801).[81] So, while Hone's own publications might support Mikhail Bakhtin's reading of parody as that which speaks irreverently and recalcitrantly outside of and back to official culture, Hone's understanding of the history and cultural politics of parody is much closer to that articulated by Robert L. Mack, who regards its emergence as a major literary mode as symptomatic of efforts by the cultural authorities of late seventeenth-century Britain to protect the "privileged status" of the printed word during an "aggressively appropriative" era of literary history.[82]

In line with this essentially prophylactic conception of parody's cultural and ideological functions, we can discern a surprisingly consistent politics to the way graphic satire conscripts literary character during this period. If legibility is one imperative that drives such appropriation, then a second is containment. The picture that emerges across the case studies that form the second half of this book is one in which parodists repeatedly harness arche-typal rebels who, in their identities and narrative arcs, simultaneously embody threats to the established constitution and reassuringly reveal such political peril to be either illusory or self-neutralizing. Cruikshank's equation of Orleans and Richard III aims at exactly this effect by representing a regicide who fatally overreaches himself in his very ascent to power. Admittedly, an unquestionable sense of menace continues to pervade the print despite the implications of impending self-defeat carried in the Shakespearean analogy. But this is far from typical. As we'll see in the use of such diverse characters as Caliban, the weird sisters, Satan, and Harlequin, caricaturists often work hard to find modes of political response that at once vividly imagine and thoroughly defuse the possibility of subversion. Insurgency is and must inherently be comedic in these prints; challenges to the political status quo, by which I mean the sovereignty of the king-in-parliament, are exorcised in the very act of naming them.

This is not a question of prints endorsing a particular partisan agenda; rather, it is to note the deep conservatism that informs a medium often mistak-enly assumed to be "radical" simply on the basis of its carnivalesque play and Juvenalian satirical tenor. (In fact, as Gary Dyer notes, in this period Juvenalian satire was "generally allied with the ruling Pittite ministry.")[83] When we look at graphic satire we see governments criticized and leading statesmen excoriated, but, in a form that obsessively reads the political present through a projected political future, potential revolution has always already failed. The parodies of Gillray and others might appear to us to operate as countercultural inversions of art and literature, but they ultimately reveal themselves to be decisively hegemonic in operation; they take up literary narratives not only to speak to a limited political class but also to

propagate fantasies in which all threats to the power of this class are comfortingly blunt.

As this statement suggests, the eighteenth-century Britain on view in
this book is largely one of oligarchy and exclusion. While I would not go so
far as to characterize this as an ancien régime, as does J. C. D. Clark, I agree
with Roy Porter that the immanent paradox of this period is that it was simultaneously a time of rapid, even radical socioeconomic change and of a stable,
intractably traditional society in which the system of governance ensured
that "the many were ruled by the few both in theory and in fact."[84] By
attending to satirical prints as texts, as documents in literary history, I offer in
this book a uses of literature narrative that adumbrates the manner in which
canonical texts were being marshaled as a means of buttressing and, to some
extent, constituting this carefully circumscribed political public; I unfold a
countervailing picture to the common account that emphasizes the democratizing role "literature" played during the period. I would not quibble with the
notion that some contemporary writers and cultural figures understood literature as exactly such a vector, but I do want to resist the political teleology
that often informs literary history and to demonstrate the continuing purchase
of an older paradigm of literary culture even as new ones were beginning to
emerge.

For Trevor Ross, the course of the eighteenth century involved a
fundamental epistemological shift away from an aristocratic "rhetorical
culture" that sought "solidarity through the power of words" and regarded
aesthetic value as something "conferred by a real or fictive community of
verbally adept 'learned readers,' " and toward an ascendant bourgeois
"objectivist" culture in which aesthetic value was rather seen to inhere within
texts themselves. As we'll see, in its quiet effort to insulate the likes of Shakespeare from certain kinds of topicality, graphic satire does bear witness to,
and even facilitates, the emergence of a modern understanding of "literature" predicated on aesthetic autonomy. But caricature also allows us to push
back against the neat linearity of Ross's cultural narrative, for in its elaborate
parodic architecture we can trace exactly the aristocratic conception of literature—one that emphasizes its social instrumentality and reads it in presentist terms—that Ross sees as having been almost entirely supplanted by the
end of the century.[85] Here, and to follow John Guillory in recognizing that
the ideology of literature is a matter of how it is presented and used institu-
tionally, the literary canon is above all the form of cultural capital that

constituted the basis of and the right to political literacy. If graphic satire is an Enlightenment form, as I suggested earlier, then it is so not only in the self-consciousness with which it stages its own procedures of mediation, or in its insistence that the powerful be subject to mockery, but also in the kinds of exclusion it inscribes and masks. The Enlightenment's embrace of "everyone," the literariness of graphic satire reminds us, rarely embraces everyone.[86]

2. Looking, Literacy, and the Printshop Window

Sociability, Social Anxiety, and the Satirical Print

For all that the preceding chapter sometimes thought in terms of the individual viewer, in truth the single-sheet satirical print was fundamentally a social form; it was designed to be seen, enjoyed, and lingered over by the group far more than the solitary reader. As the sites of display and modes of engagement that structured the culture of caricature make abundantly clear, prints not only invited but were in many ways predicated on practices of communal reading and consumption. Most obviously, the exhibition of engravings, satirical and otherwise, in the shopwindows of London's print sellers—a ubiquitous custom by the midcentury—ensured that prints were part of the texture of everyday pedestrian experience in Georgian London. Contemporary commentators and tourists regularly commented upon (and often grumbled about) the large, impromptu throngs that would gather to look at such displays. One Frenchman, visiting the city in 1802, observed that the only way to catch a glimpse of the latest Gillray caricatures posted in the window of Hannah Humphrey's shop was "to make your way through the crowd with your fists," while in 1823 a popular periodical counseled pedestrians: "In passing through a street well frequented with carriages, but narrow in the footpath, you come to that barrier called a print shop."[1] And once customers entered the shop they would find themselves within a retail environment that further cultivated a sense of mutuality, though now one of a more regulated and self-selecting nature. At his premises in Oxford Street in 1788, William Holland began charging an admission fee of a shilling—the same as the Royal Academy—to his "Exhibition Rooms," which he claimed to hold "the largest collection of Caricatures in Europe," and Samuel Fores followed suit a year later at his own shop on Piccadilly.[2] The publication line at the top of *The Near in Bloody, The Nearer Bloody* (see fig. 1.1) thus proudly announces that Fores "has again opened his Caricature Room to which he has added many hundred Old & New Subjects admittance 1 shilling." But sometimes a name said as much as an entry fee. From 1798, Rudolph Ackermann styled his printshop in the Strand "The Repository for the Arts," while even Thomas Tegg, in some ways an outlier in Cheapside, dubbed his shop the "Apollo Library." If such commercial strategies point to the anxious determination with which print sellers sought to gentrify themselves and their wares, then they also remind us that the printshop fashioned itself as a site of polite cultural exchange and social interaction, a gallery space that catered for and brought into being a distinct viewing public.

Equally, within the home, especially the houses of the gentry and aristocracy, graphic satire was principally to be found in the communal space and rituals of the drawing room. In this domestic context, as families or parties gathered to look at prints pasted into albums or portfolios, the viewing of caricature became a media event that served the imperatives of leisure and social lubrication.[3] Writing in the mid-nineteenth century Grantley Berkeley remembered "the book of caricatures" as providing an "unfailing resource for the entertainment of guests in large country houses. . . . Those unfortunates who cannot be got to talk, or are nervously reserved, are usually set by the hostess to find entertainment, and become social over a portfolio of ludicrous scenes in which celebrated personages have acted with more or less success."[4] In some cases, the practice of pasting satirical prints onto walls or items of furniture, such as screens, transformed particular spaces into what might be understood as dynamic, walk-in albums; Ackermann even sold colorful paper borders expressly for the framing of prints displayed in this manner.[5] The turn-of-the-century caricature room at Calke Abbey, Derbyshire (fig. 2.1)—the walls of which are densely covered with hundreds of prints by the likes of Rowlandson, Gillray, and the Cruikshanks—vividly suggests graphic satire's overlapping, indeed mutually constitutive, functions as decorous commodity, cultural-political text, and social prop. By the

Fig. 2.1. The caricature room at Calke Abbey, Derbyshire. Author's photograph.

1790s, the appeal of print consumption as a form of shared domestic amusement was great enough that print sellers such as Fores began lending folios of
caricatures for the evening, thereby enabling the aspiring middle classes to
embrace a cultural habit that had until then been prohibitively expensive.[6]

The gratifying difficulty of much graphic satire is inextricably bound
up with its social orientation. In considering the images discussed in this
book, it's vital to keep in mind that the deciphering of a print, the process of
identifying its key figures and negotiating its allusive architecture, took place
within shared spaces and occasions and through acts of collective looking
and conversation. Reading of this kind leaves little archival trace, but *The
Scandalizade,* a satirical poem of 1750, includes a scene that offers at least a
glimpse of such activity. Here the narrator stands among a crowd gathered
before the window of a "Printseller's Shop" and vocally criticizes what he
believes to be an engraving of "Father *Tobit* . . . with his Dog," only to be
informed by a fellow spectator that the image in fact shows "*Hogarth* himself
and his Friend honest *Towser*" (the self-portrait with pug of 1745).[7] The jest
is at Hogarth's expense, with the narrator soon going on to propose that man
and animal look much alike, but the poem nonetheless provides an ironic
record of the culture of communal interpretation that developed around
eighteenth-century prints.

At the same time, the spontaneity and raucousness of the printshop crowd described in *The Scandalizade*—the "elbowing" and "Argumentation"—gesture toward the unease that attended graphic satire's presence within the street. The shop and drawing room were sites of controlled engagement with caricature, places that were stridently coded in terms of behavior and class. Within the unregulated, open-access space of the metropolitan thoroughfare, by contrast, the sociability of the satirical print took on a more threatening and potentially disruptive character. In particular, as Brian Maidment has explored at length, the areas in front of the city's printshops were perennially associated with criminality; in the press of multiple distracted bodies, pickpockets thrived.[8] "Never stop in a crowd, or to look at the windows of a print-shop or shew-glass, if you would not have your pocket picked," cautioned the *London Adviser and Guide* of 1786.[9] Reports of such criminal activity only reinforced fears that the public spectacle of the printshop window openly incited vice and delinquency. As early as 1752, Henry Fielding's *Covent-Garden Journal* brought print sellers before its "*Court of* Censorial Enquiry," where they stood charged with "exposing in the windows of their shops, several lewd and indecent Prints."[10] In 1789, one Londoner, alarmed at the "amazing increase of Print-Shops within a few years," complained in a letter to a newspaper that "obscene prints publicly exposed in almost every shop, must have a poisonous effect upon the minds of young persons in particular," while John Corry's 1804 *Satirical View of London* similarly opined that "caricature and print shops, which are so gratifying to the fancy of the idle and licentious, must necessarily have a powerful influence on the morals and industry of the people."[11]

These commentaries play upon entrenched fears of the power of images. Of course, I've spent much time elaborating caricature's textuality, but I do not wish this emphasis to obscure the satirical print's value, function, and frisson as an image; as Barbara Maria Stafford and W. J. T. Mitchell rightly warn us, something vitally important gets lost when we read pictures as nothing more or other than language.[12] In contending that the sensuality and supposed simplicity of prints rendered them especially dangerous to adolescents or the uneducated, critics such as Corry were reanimating the tropes of the Reformation iconoclasts, who had insistently employed a vocabulary of seduction and fornication to decry the troubling efficacy of images.[13] In *Letters on the English Nation* (1755), John Shebbeare makes clear this rhetorical debt in his complaint that "every printshop has its windows stuck full with indecent prints, to inflame desire thro' the eye." Yet, writing in the satirical guise of an Italian Jesuit, he also inverts the traditional coupling of Catholicism and idolatry by claiming that the proliferation of coarse visual satires was in fact a direct consequence of governance by "protestant legislators," for whom "liberty is the word."[14] For Shebbeare, the political freedoms of the post-1688 Protestant state only encouraged a new age of iconophilia to take root.

In the final twenty years of the eighteenth century, these anxieties about printshop windows took an increasingly political inflection. The Gordon Riots of 1780—six days of civil disorder that witnessed unprecedented property damage and the breaking open of Newgate Prison—transformed elite attitudes toward the lower classes, replacing in the cultural imaginary the legitimate popular politics of the multitude with the alarming and potentially radical violence of the mob.[15] A decade later, the French Revolution presented the menace of mob power to the British establishment in still more lurid terms, with reactionary polemic haunted by images of the crowd, only the most infamous of which is Edmund Burke's "swinish multitude."[16] In response to these changed political sensitivities a new and more urgently articulated criticism of the satirical print emerged, one first expressed by Vicesimus Knox in his 1788 essay "On the Effect of Caricaturas exhibited at the Windows of Print-Sellers." Warning the governing class that they would do well to remember the actions of "kennel-rakers, shoeblackers, chimney-sweepers, and beggars" during "the memorable month of June 1780," Knox contended that the display "of the first magistrate, and of great statesmen, in caricatura, must contribute to diminish or destroy that reverence, which is always due to legal authority, and established rank."[17] Earlier worries that the printshop window threatens the populace's moral well-being are here displaced by deeper fears that it erodes the foundations of power and privilege. In 1792, the Earl of Abingdon protested to the House of Lords that "the libellous prints that are daily exhibited in every print-shop of this city" served "to draw down contempt where reverence and respect are deservedly due . . . and to level all things with that dust and dirt, out of which these monstrous designs were formed,"[18] while in December 1795, the month in which the Pitt government passed the Gagging Acts to suppress radical activism, one conservative newspaper went so far as to brand printshops "complete warehouses for Sedition."[19]

Of course, these statements reflect the tense and polarized political climate of the late eighteenth century. They tell us more about the febrile imagination and rhetorical excesses of British Toryism at this time than they do about either the social realities of the printshop window or the political efficacy of caricature. As I noted in Chapter 1, satirical prints were never subject to censorship; there is little evidence to suggest that the authorities deemed them a threat to the establishment and an abundance of material that demonstrates the extent to which the social elites of Georgian Britain embraced graphic satirical culture. Beside the anxieties of an Abingdon we need to set the unabated use and consumption of prints within the aristocratic home; the purchase of caricatures by the very statesmen they lampooned; and the desperation with which George Canning sought to cajole James Gillray into caricaturing him. Even Knox emphasized that the "contempt thrown on the higher orders . . . by ludicrous representation on the copper-plate" originated within and radiated out from elite society and "must have been diffused through the higher and middle ranks, before it descended" to the laboring classes.[20]

Far removed from the unrest and paranoia of the revolutionary decade, late Georgian and early Victorian recollections of the printshop crowd unfold a rather more benign picture. One reviewer of 1825, discussing the printshop as a "memorial of times past," laughed at the unthreatening sight of "staring cockneys and bumpkins" looking at a window displaying "the identical engravings which it did some forty or fifty years ago,"[21] while in 1840 William Makepeace Thackeray wistfully remembered how the " 'gratis' exhibition" of George Cruikshank's works in the window of John Fairburn's shop in Ludgate Hill would bring "a crowd . . . of grinning, good-natured mechanics, who spelt out the songs, and spoke them for the benefit of the company."[22] Thackeray reminds us again that prints were viewed and understood collectively, but his nostalgia is shot through with a bourgeois condescension that finds working-class engagement with graphic satire not just innocuous but even, damningly, heartwarming.

The difference between these earlier and later accounts of the politics of printshop spectatorship takes me to the heart of the concerns that I want to address in the rest of this chapter. Through detailed readings of a selection of the many *visual* depictions of pedestrians gazing at the window displays of London's printshops I want to consider the degree to which these images are shaped by the ideological tensions of their historical moment, and, concomitantly, the manner in which they stage and perhaps seek to resolve the vexed relationship between class, political engagement, and satirical-print literacy in the later Georgian period. Quite obviously these issues are central to any study of eighteenth-century graphic satire, which must always grapple with debates about the size and composition of its audience, but they are especially important to this book because attention to the self-conscious literariness of the political print necessarily raises questions of access and understanding—of implied readership. Both the parodic content of a particular print and the representation of a printshop crowd work in different but equally complex ways to imagine and prescribe graphic satire's audience.

Certainly, the printshop window remains as much a site of contestation for today's social and cultural historian as it did for the likes of Vicesimus Knox over two centuries ago. Without wishing to restate the historiograph-ical disagreements I've already outlined, it should suffice here to point out that those scholars who claim caricature to be a genuinely "popular" form point to the printshop window display as a means of circumventing the problem of the prohibitive cost of the satirical print. "People too poor to buy a single print," John Wardroper boldly claims, "could still stand laughing (and extending their political education) . . . in front of a printshop window's crowded panes."[23] Accordingly, the images that depict this practice are granted special heuristic value. We need only glance at the cover of Diana Donald's landmark study *The Age of Caricature* (1996), which is adorned with Gillray's *Very Slippy-Weather* (see fig. 2.9), a print I turn to at the close of this chapter, to appreciate that the image of the printshop window often serves as a synecdoche of Georgian graphic satirical culture as a whole—one which stamps that culture as inclusive and democratic.

Too often this illustrative prominence is attended by a marked absence of critical interrogation, as if the import of these prints was somehow trans-parent or obvious. Almost thirty years ago, in a critique that remains all too pertinent to our current practices of scholarship, Roy Porter warned against naive assumptions that prints "register events, rather like the Bayeux Tapestry," and can therefore be "quarr[ied] . . . to archaeologize the material culture of the past."[24] As we'll see, prints of printshops are not documentary snapshots but rather elaborate, carefully constructed representations—on occasion, fantasies—of their own exhibition and cultural function. They are images about the act of looking at images, caricatures about the display and consumption of caricature; they are what W. J. T. Mitchell terms "metapi-ctures": "pictures that show themselves in order to know themselves."[25] We must therefore attend to their self-reflexivity with care.

Thankfully, two discussions of the print of the printshop window have taken up Porter's challenge that we refuse to take the "explicit subject" of a caricature at "face value." Mike Goode rightly posits that these images "encourage reflection on the activity of caricature viewing itself," while Brian Maidment observes that their "depictions of the street are constructed by ideas concerning social order."[26] Building on these insights, I want to register the difference between one print of printshop spectatorship and the next. The virtue of a cluster of images such as this, images that represent the same practice again and again over many years, is precisely that it allows us to attend closely to the repeated deployment and modification of a distinct set of visual conventions *in* history and so to achieve a better sense of the changing cultural and ideological work those conventions perform across the period.

It's also important to recognize that these prints are generically complex. First and foremost, they are advertisements published by the very printshops they depict.[27] But in their representation of social interactions, emphasis on leisure, fashion, and commodity, and investment in imagining a "public," prints of printshop spectatorship are also, as C. Suzanne Matheson notes, variations on the traditional conversation piece.[28] More exactly, they relate to—and arguably parody—the subgenre of conversation paintings that depict galleries populated with patrons, such as Johann Zoffany's *Tribuna of the Uffizi* (1772–77) and J. H. Ramberg's *Exhibition of the Royal Academy* (1787). In turn, recognition of this correspondence reminds us that prints of printshops belong to an Enlightenment culture that was, to borrow Martin Jay's term, ocularcentric.[29] These images reflect and comment upon a society that was obsessed with, animated by, and anxious about new practices and technologies of looking. Like so many artistic, literary, scientific, and episte-mological texts of the period, they are manifestly concerned with ways of seeing.

Or rather, they are concerned with the problems, limitations, and cultural politics of sight. These prints remain satirical, and like any satire, they are engaged critically with issues of representation and perception; the distortions of a caricature work to elicit the biases and elisions that inhere in the way others, especially those in power, represent the world or represent themselves to the world. The iconography of eighteenth-century graphic satire is replete with optical devices (telescopes, quizzing glasses, camera obscuras) and gazing figures (think of Rowlandson's repeated mockery of the connoisseur), and if the present discussion establishes this book's interest in the constitutions of caricature's audience, then it also foregrounds my recurrent attention to graphic satire's metaphorics of sight. As we'll see throughout the book, prints marshal the look as a political trope with remarkable verve and frequency.

In what follows I show that these images of printshops and their pedestrian viewers are far more prescriptive than descriptive: they make judgments—judgments that are far from ideologically neutral—about the kinds of looking and the types of looker they depict, and they compel us, the actual viewers, to orient ourselves in a particular way in relation to the fictional spectators they stage. The nature of that relationship, I suggest, is symptomatic of the given pressures of a cultural moment. In its emergence in the early 1770s, the print of printshop spectatorship is stridently satirical; its depiction of a failure to see, to read properly, works proprietorially to disavow the cultural credentials and graphic-satirical literacy of new classes of print consumer. Only during the Napoleonic Wars, when it became politically desirable and expedient to imagine a nation of democracy and inclusivity, do these images valorize the printshop crowd as a socially diverse public. Here, as with my discussions of literary parody in Part II, I'm concerned with the means by which a satirical print works rhetorically to imply or construct an ideal of its own public.

Imagining the Printshop Public

The earliest depictions of printshops and their crowds are closely bound up with the macaroni craze of the early 1770s, a phenomenon that was driven as much by print media as by fashion and consumerism. Macaronis were young, well-traveled aristocratic men who theatrically embodied their Continental manners through flamboyant dress, elaborate wigs, and affected behavior. Such performances of foreignness and effeminacy disturbed the accepted taxonomies of class, nation, and, most especially, gender in the mid-eighteenth century.[30] "*Macaronies* are a sex / Which do philosophers perplex," chimed one critic; "if the present Macaroni Taste should prevail . . . the *Women* will become the best *Men*," wrote another. Recognizing the rich satirical and commercial potential of this "amphibious creature," the print sellers Matthew and Mary Darly began publishing macaroni prints in 1771.[31] As Shearer West has shown, these images not only fueled but significantly extended and recoded the very cultural discourse they seized upon by casting a range of social and professional types—clerics, lawyers, butchers, bricklayers—as macaronis.[32] Equally, as Amelia Rauser argues, the proliferation of these prints, by the Darlys and their imitators, served as a key catalyst in propelling caricature (as in the art of physiognomic exaggeration) into the prominent position within metropolitan culture that it was to occupy by the 1780s.[33]

The Macaroni Print Shop (fig. 2.2), published in July 1772, celebrates the cultural impact of the Darlys' macaroni prints by depicting their shopfront on the Strand as a site of interest and animation and also by prompting its viewers to laugh once again at macaroni affectation. Each of the figures stood gaping at the prints posted in the Darlys' windows is stridently caricatured, and the comedy of this image pivots on the manifest incongruity between grotesque bodies—large noses, pointed chins, emaciated or

THE MACARONI PRINT SHOP.

Fig. 2.2. Edward Topham, *The Macaroni Print Shop* (Matthew and Mary Darly, 14 July 1772). BMC 4701. Metropolitan Museum of Art, New York, www.metmuseum.org.

misshapen frames—and extravagant fashions: one man sports a sword and a colossal wig; another wears a bow twice the size of his head; a third is dressed in a large lace jabot. Like the caricatured personae on display, and as was the visual convention in the Darlys' prints, these pedestrians are shown in full profile. The flattened composition of the etching collapses the distinction between the figures in and before the window; the street and the shop front rather appear as consecutive and complementary layers, a foreground and background, of macaroni portraits. And one further detail stands out. In front of the shop door is a tradesman so taken in by the scene before him that a cup tilts in his grasp, spilling its contents onto the pavement. The body of this working-class character is no less awkward or flat than those around him; it is his dress, particularly the bedraggled cloth apron around his waist and the frayed elbows of his jacket, that marks his difference—and this is precisely the point. These spectators, the print suggests, are plebeians ineffectively playing at being patricians.

That the image of the printshop window first emerged in the early 1770s not as a celebration of the open sociability of caricature but rather as a satiric strike at certain classes of consumer is even more evident in John Raphael Smith's *Miss Macaroni and her Gallant at a Print-Shop* (fig. 2.3). Published in April 1773 by John Bowles, this mezzotint shows two pairs of spectators standing before Bowles's premises at 13 Cornhill in the heart of the City, in the windows of which social satires, mostly featuring macaronis, jostle for attention with portraits of religious personalities. In the first, eponymous pairing, a foppish gentleman draws the notice of his lady, "Miss Macaroni," to a caricature that can be identified as *P'sha You Flatter Me* (fig. 2.4). He laughs at the affected posturing of the extravagantly dressed, high-haired woman depicted in the print but patently fails to register that his companion closely emulates this caricatured figure: "While Macaroni and his Mistress here, / At other Characters, in Picture, sneer," read the verses at the foot of the print, "To the vain Couple is but little known, / How much deserving Ridicule their own." Smith delineates a look that constitutes a failure to see. Vanity and ignorance prevent the macaroni from recognizing his or her own reflection.

At first glance, the second pair in Smith's print serves as a visual counterpoint to this couple: the two men are soberly dressed and earnestly discussing a mezzotint of the Methodist preacher George Whitefield (fig. 2.5). Yet here too one figure points to a specific print that the other appears to mimic, for the man with his back to us replicates Whitefield's pose: hands raised, palms open. The relationship between image and spectator remains one of facsimile. In this instance, the duplication implies this man's "enthusiasm," a word that carried distinct and pejorative charge in the eighteenth century, meaning, as Johnson's *Dictionary* tells us, " "hot imagination" or "violent passions" and also "one who has a vain confidence of intercourse with God."[34] As this second definition suggests, "enthusiasm" was a keyword of anti-Methodist discourse, at once denoting and censuring a spiritual experience so excessive as to transgress the bounds of rational thought and moral restraint.[35] We cannot see the face of the man looking at the print of Whitefield, but whether he is surprised, enraptured, or enraged it is certain that he is *affected* by the image of the preacher in such a way that his reasoning self is carried away, for he is oblivious to the fact that the spaniel belonging to the macaroni couple urinates on his shoe. The dog, like the epigraph, glosses an inattentiveness that is ironically folded into the very structure of looking. The macaroni is a figure of myopia, the other man of distraction. Both spectators embody a comic disconnect between the image in the window and the reality of the street.

No look is directly met, returned, or shared in Smith's print. In *Miss Macaroni and her Gallant* only the spaniel successfully makes eye contact. It gazes up and out of the pictorial plane to establish a connection with us, the real spectators of Smith's satire, at the very moment it excretes upon one of those within the print: derision of the failed viewers before the printshop window and acknowledgment of the presence of the viewers *not* represented (but rather looking at this representation) are part of single gesture. I'm not simply suggesting that the four figures of Smith's print are the objects of our gaze as well as the gazing subjects. Rather, I'm contending that this image strives to construct a particular audience for itself by depicting this audience in negative; it prescribes a spectatorship by *not* showing it. This print invites and enfranchises its real consumer at the expense of the inept consumers it depicts. An imagined ideal of the "public" is articulated, made present, through its exact absence.

In answering the question of who this public might be, it's first important to recognize that *caricatura* was very much an aristocratic form in the mid eighteenth century. First brought to Britain in the 1730s by the Grand Tourists, who had seen the works of caricaturists such as Pier Leone Ghezzi in Rome, caricature quickly became "a popular parlor game" among the

Miſs MACARONI and her GALLANT at a Print-Shop.

While Macaroni and his Mistress here,   So the vain Couple is but little known,
At other Characters, in Picture, sneer,   }   How much deserving Ridicule their own.

Printed for Jenn Bowles, at No 13 in Cornhill.

Fig. 2.3. John Raphael Smith, *Miss Macaroni and her Gallant at a Print-Shop* (John Bowles, 2 April 1773). BMC 5220. Courtesy of The Lewis Walpole Library, Yale University.

Fig. 2.4. *P'sha You Flatter Me* (Carington Bowles, 1773). BMC 4528. © The Trustees of the British Museum.

P'SHA YOU FLATTER ME.

The Reverend M.r George Whitefield, A.M.
Chaplain to the COUNTESS *of Huntingdon.*

Fig. 2.5. John Greenwood, after Nathaniel Hone, *The Revd. Mr. George Whitefield* (Robert Sayer, c. 1768). © National Portrait Gallery, London.

social elite.[36] Indeed, the Darlys' business model actively took advantage of this aristocratic vogue by encouraging *"Ladies and Gentlemen"* to submit designs for professional engraving, and in the 1750s they published the pioneering political caricatures of the MP George Townshend, later Marquess Townshend.[37] As we've seen, caricature remained a vital part of the political culture and leisure practices of the nation's aristocracy well into the nineteenth century, but, according to Rauser, caricature also began to find an audience among the affluent bourgeoisie in the 1770s. Again, it needs to be stressed that the macaroni phenomenon was marked as much by the emergence of new forms of print culture as by new codes of fashion and behavior. The macaroni print's play with social types and, more especially, its appeal to prosperous consumers in general paradoxically muddied the very class distinctions that it seemingly set out to reinforce.[38]

Here, then, lies the deeper and more complex intersection between the macaroni craze and the sudden need to create images of the printshop window. *The Macaroni Print Shop* and *Miss Macaroni and her Gallant* are satirical commentaries less on the figure of the macaroni per se than on the specific social and cultural ripple effects of the macaroni print (works produced by the very purveyors of such satires). These prints place before the printshop window figures that imperiled the constellation of elite values in eighteenth-century Britain—the religious enthusiast, the macaroni, the parvenu who apes the macaroni—precisely as a means of ridiculing the pretensions of these people to the cultural domain of print consumption. The earliest images of printshops respond to the broadening social appeal of caricature by proprietorially striving to reaffirm the cultural power of its traditional high-class consumers. Satire, as Frederic Bogel states, "begins in a relation of threatening proximity and then works to establish difference."[39] Indeed, it's noteworthy that *The Macaroni Print Shop* is the effort of a gentleman amateur, the Eton- and Cambridge-educated Edward Topham. Drawn by a young and ambitious member of the gentry, it mocks his social inferiors for both their ersatz civility and their misplaced aspirations as an audience of caricature.

Peter de Bolla contends that the increasing variety of spectacles on offer in mid-eighteenth-century Britain—the theater, the pleasure garden, the first public exhibitions—were constitutive of "a culture of visuality in which seeing and being seen were crucial indices to one's social standing, to one's self-definition." Early images of the printshop window, another key site of metropolitan spectacle, testify to just how much was at stake, socially and politically, in representing and credentialing the practices of seeing. Like the painterly depictions of looking examined by de Bolla (tellingly, conversation pieces), *The Macaroni Print Shop* and *Miss Macaroni and her Gallant* "pictorially argue for a particular attitude to visual culture."[40] Their comedies of failed seeing are concerned with demarcating the limits and status of graphic-satirical literacy. In Bourdieuian terms, they seek to distinguish those who possess the taste, the cultural capital, to look at and understand graphic satire, from those who do not, those whom the prints therefore subject to satire.[41] Quite simply, there are no elite spectators before Topham's and Smith's print-shop windows because, within what John Barrell calls "the republic of taste," *their* status as consumers of caricature was not in question.[42]

To find an image that portrays a genuinely diverse audience for graphic satire we need to jump ahead some thirty years to Piercy Roberts's *Caricature Shop* of 1801 (fig. 2.6). The group of pedestrians now gathered in the street before the printshop window—that of Roberts's new premises at 28 Middle

Fig. 2.6. Piercy Roberts, *Caricature Shop* (Piercy Roberts, 1801). Courtesy of The Lewis Walpole Library, Yale University.

Row, Holborn—is of a radically different character to those shown in Smith's and Topham's earlier prints. Roberts depicts not a small, loose cohort of strangers but rather a large crowd that encompasses figures spanning the social, generational, and racial spectra of metropolitan society. In stark contrast to the derogation of the macaroni, of the other, in comparable images of the 1770s, Roberts's *Caricature Shop* openly embraces a disabled man and a black man as members of the public it describes and defines. This is urban pastoral. Roberts offers an almost mythic projection of social cohesion, unthreatening heterogeneity, and enraptured pleasure—of an innocent and intuitive delight distilled in the child who, at the very center of the etching, reaches toward the window.

This image is still satire. Its mode remains that of caricature (not least, tellingly, in the facial features of the black man), but the hyperbole is of a softer kind; bodies are not, as in Topham's print, pushed toward the grotesque. Equally, Roberts punctuates his idyll with ironic details that qualify its fiction. An older bespectacled gentleman in the foreground pruriently scrutinizes an image of a female nude, while a man further back surreptitiously glances not at the window display but rather at the young lady beside him, who is unaware of being watched. Though these figures of voyeurism complicate the grammar of looking here, they do not compromise its idealized construction of community. Rather, these erotically charged gazes introduce into the design a strain of social commentary and irreverence that validates Roberts's idealization precisely by asserting that it remains subject to the imperative of satire.

Barrell has argued that the period's landscape paintings included carefully sanitized representations of the hardships of agricultural labor in order to legitimize their pastoral illusion precisely by tempering it. Quiet, moderated details of rural poverty enabled viewers to embrace the sociopolitical fantasy of a pictured landscape as a version of truth. In a similar fashion, if in a radically different pictorial mode, Roberts's acknowledgment of the sexual desire of the spectator in *Caricature Shop* allows him to pass off, in Barrell's words, "mythic unity . . . as an image of actual unity."[43] The presence of the voyeurs supports the fiction of inclusive rapture here by admitting that such inclusion must always incorporate less innocent gestures and bodies of longing, and that such rapture necessarily spans a variety of desires. Many print sellers dealt in both satirical and erotic prints, and as I've argued elsewhere, the generic boundaries between Georgian pornography and caricature were porous at best.[44] Yet where the likes of Fielding and John Corry voiced their alarm at the display of lewd prints, Piercy Roberts unashamedly draws the same "licentious" engravings into his celebration of caricature's public appeal. In *Caricature Shop* arousal is only the most extreme variant of the ecstatic enthrallment experienced by the printshop crowd. Graphic satire, in all its vulgarity, engenders community.

Crucially, Roberts depicts himself standing directly beneath his own name in the shop doorway, an etching needle balanced in the fingers of his half-raised hand. Maidment suggests that his presence serves to mark the spatial divide between the unregulated assembly of the street and the consumer-connoisseurs of the shop interior.[45] But Roberts's demeanor is not nervously proprietorial; he seems rather to look at the animated group that has gathered before his window with a sense of professional pride. This gaze, this act of acknowledgment, legitimizes the crowd. Remember that in *Miss Macaroni and her Gallant* the outward glance of the urinating dog distinguished between the real spectators (those who see) and the represented spectators (those who fail to see). In Roberts's etching there is no such gaze (and the dog, who claws at the shop front, is as excited by the spectacle as the rest of the group). No distinction is drawn between the spectators of this caricature and the spectators within it. By looking at this print we are necessarily engaged in the same activity as those it portrays. *Caricature Shop* summons us, its actual consumers, not at the expense of the consumers it depicts but rather by compelling our identification with them: we too can be, indeed already must be, members of this public. Roberts's print at once emphasizes and enacts inclusivity.

But this image is just as profoundly shaped by the anxieties of its cultural matrix as those earlier depictions of the printshop window. I've already suggested that the discourse surrounding printshops and their pedestrian spectators underwent a significant shift of emphasis in response to the Gordon Riots and French Revolution, and in graphic satire the iconography of the crowd was subject to the same political pressures. Diana Donald has noted a discernable decline toward the close of the eighteenth century in prints depicting large metropolitan crowds as motifs of legitimate public opinion or consensus, commenting that the "myth of the freeborn, ebullient English crowd which had formed such a notable feature of eighteenth-century print imagery could not withstand the political *reality* of popular clamour for constitutional change in the post-revolutionary era."[46] In the

1780s and 1790s images of printshop spectatorship—prints that foreground the formation of spontaneous gatherings in the city street—reflect this symbolic shift by their conspicuous absence.

I have found four prints from the early to mid-1770s that show pedestrians engaging with displays in printshop windows.[47] Over the next quarter century, however, only two further prints of printshops were published— Robert Dighton's *Real Scene in St. Pauls Church Yard, on a Windy Day* (c. 1782–84; BMC 6352) and an anonymous recasting of this mezzotint entitled *A High Wind in St. Paul's Churchyard* (1793)—and in neither of these works is anyone actually looking at the printshop window, which functions as no more than a vivid and commercially convenient backdrop for meteorological comedy. In these satires the city's gales work to churn up and fragment the public, precluding the possibility of a crowd emerging from the hubbub of pedestrian life that is shown. Only in two unpublished drawings—*not* reproductive prints—are communal acts of looking at graphic satire represented at this time. A watercolor by J. Elwood (c. 1790) shows a street corner with people gathering before and passing by Carington Bowles's shop, while a sketch by Richard Newton (c. 1794) takes us inside William Holland's exhibition of caricatures, the entry for which, you'll recall, was one shilling. At a moment of increasing governmental concerns about the threat of radicalism, Newton depicts an interior site of viewing that is safely removed from the unruly semiotics of the street and accessible only to elite consumers. In the 1790s, when a crowd was always a potential mob (institutional logic formally acknowledged by the Seditious Meetings Act of 1795), visual representations of graphic satire's pedestrian spectators became something of a political impossibility.

Caricature Shop was, then, the first new print of a group looking at a printshop window to be published for some twenty-five years. By 1801 radical activity had subsided in Britain, and with the threat of Napoleon now undeniable, there was finally popular and parliamentary consensus for a war against revolutionary France that had proved so politically divisive in the years immediately after 1793. Piercy Roberts made a name for himself in the 1790s with prints that depicted the British naval heroes of this conflict. The bellicose patriotism of an expensive stipple engraving like *British Admirals: Britannia Viewing the Conquerors of the Seas* (fig. 2.7) is typical of his loyalist output. His move into graphic satire in 1801 represented a change in direction iconographically but not politically. In caricatures such as *Iohn Bull Drowning the Enemy*

Fig. 2.7. Piercy Roberts, *British Admirals: Britannia Viewing the Conquerors of the Seas* (William Holland, 1800). © The Trustees of the British Museum.

(c. 1803) and *National Contrasts or Bulky and Boney* (fig. 2.8), Roberts juxtaposes an inept and emaciated Napoleon with a robust, irreverent, and well-fed Britain in the shape of John Bull. His satires construct the reassuring image of a confident, ebullient nation that is amused and not alarmed by Napoleon. *Caricature Shop* is no different in this regard. As in *British Admirals,* where the figure of Britannia proudly gazes at thirteen carefully arranged cameo portraits of celebrated naval officers, Roberts depicts the act of looking as an expression of patriotism, with the added implications that this gratified gaze is both communal and directed at graphic satire. This latter point is significant because, by the beginning of the nineteenth century, the ability to look and laugh at caricature was considered to be a notable marker of British exceptionalism.[48] So, toward the end of the Napoleonic Wars, J. P. Malcolm noted that his *Historical Sketch of the Art of Caricaturing* (the first such history to be published) would ultimately "narrow into that of English Caricatures; for the

NATIONAL *Contrasts or* BULKY *and* BONEY

Fig. 2.8. Piercy Roberts, *National Contrasts or Bulky and Boney* (Piercy Roberts, c. 1803–7). Courtesy of The Lewis Walpole Library, Yale University.

obvious reason, that in no other country has the art met with equal encouragement, because no other portion of the globe enjoys equal freedom."[49] In his print of a printshop window, Roberts depicts an inclusive community in the act of exercising the liberty that is their particular birthright as British subjects. At a time of war (a conflict perhaps made visible in *Caricature Shop* by a disabled man who may be a veteran) Robert's printshop crowd imagines a public that is united, content, and emphatically free.

The differences, rhetorical and ideological, between the images of Topham and Smith in the early 1770s and that of Roberts at the turn of the century help us to register the extent to which graphic satire's representations of its own consumption responded to the specific and changing anxieties of the cultural hegemony, and that such representations were readily conscripted in the service of this regime. Before the end of the Napoleonic Wars in 1815 a further three images of diverse printshop crowds were published: Thomas Rowlandson's *Genii of Caricature bringing in Fresh Supplies* (c. 1808), which portrays a large group gathered before Thomas Tegg's printshop in Cheapside; George Cruikshank's *Grievances of London* (c. 1812; BMC 11985), in which a generic printshop and its audience feature as part of a crowded, Hogarthian street scene; and Gillray's *Very Slippy-Weather*, a complex rendering of Hannah Humphrey's shopfront, to which I turn now. In picturing the diversity of the gazing crowd, these prints document less the democratic appeal of graphic satire than the urgency with which wartime Britain heralded graphic satirical culture as evidence of its own political freedom and social cohesion. Such fantasies of inclusivity, of universal print literacy in which everyone can enjoy the joke, suddenly appear in the early 1800s because it had become politically expedient to create images of the metropolitan public that could metonymically stand for a nation of tolerance and democracy. Donald is right to note that prints of printshop windows often "consciously evoke the social diversity of the gazing crowd," but such a statement alone does not address the vital question of *why* they do so.[50] In fact, such diversity is only imagined and celebrated at a precise moment in graphic satire's history, when such conceptions of the agency and constitution of the public were needed to undergird an image of the political nation that was in some way imperiled.

Gillray, Literature, and the Fiction of Inclusion

And so, finally, to Gillray's *Very Slippy-Weather* (fig. 2.9), the best known and perhaps also the most evocative of its genre. I've deferred discussion of this print until now, first, because it offers by some distance the most complex representation of the printshop window and its audience, a representation that negotiates between the rhetorical imperatives of differentiation and identification, exclusivity and mutuality, that are advanced in Topham's *Macaroni Print Shop* and Roberts's *Caricature Shop*, respectively; and second, because Gillray's satire achieves this balance in part by marshaling literature, or more accurately literariness, quietly to distinguish between one kind of consumer and another, between the educated gaze and its opposite. *Very Slippy-Weather* is an image about reading as much as looking, one that fore-grounds the relationship between the allusive literary structure of much graphic satire and the issues of how and by whom such prints could be read. As a caricature that is centrally concerned with the constitutive interplay between literature, political language, and the public—a caricature, more-over, that showcases in miniature two of the parodic prints I consider in later chapters—it thus points the way for the material and questions I address in the second part of this book.

As we'll see in Chapter 6, some of Gillray's most inventive and enduring work emerged through collaboration with amateur caricaturists of the gentry and aristocracy. Such is the case with *Very Slippy-Weather*, which

Fig. 2.9. James Gillray, after John Sneyd, *Very Slippy-Weather* (Hannah Humphrey, 10 February 1808). BMC 11000. Courtesy of The Lewis Walpole Library, Yale University.

was etched according to an original design by the Reverend John Sneyd, the Oxford-educated rector of Elford in Staffordshire, a friend of Gillray's and George Canning's, and the man responsible for recruiting the caricaturist to the *Anti-Jacobin* in 1797.[51] As in the images of the windy city streets of the 1780s and 1790s, the printshop window here provides a backdrop to meteorological comedy, with the foreground of the caricature taken up by the figure of an older gentleman who tumbles to the icy pavement of St. James's Street, losing his hat, wig, and the contents of his pockets in the process but managing to keep grasp of a thermometer (showing the freezing temperature), which stays miraculously upright. As in Jonathan Swift's 1710 poem "A Description of a City Shower," the weather in this print itself is a satirical force that works to strip London's inhabitants of their pretensions to civility and politeness.

Unlike the earlier images of the wind-beaten street, however, the shop-window of *Very Slippy-Weather* does have an audience. Gillray depicts five people looking at his own caricatures, the central three shown entirely from behind. Clothing tells us all we need to know about the professional and class identities of these spectators: a coachman, garbed in plain brown and wielding his whip, stands beside a well-dressed gentleman in a white wig and tricorn hat, who in turn stands next to a guardsman decked out in full military regalia. Sneyd and Gillray offer, on the one hand, a comedy of juxtaposed body shapes and social types and, on the other, a compelling scene of interclass encounter and assembly, one that is reaffirmed by the profile figure of a working-class boy—a "street urchin" as one historian describes him—who stands beside the other gazers.[52] As in Roberts's *Caricature Shop*, this image of diversity projects the alluring fiction of a nation unified in its opposition to Napoleonic France, for prominently placed at the center of Hannah Humphrey's window display are two of Gillray's anti-Bonaparte satires: *Tiddy-Doll, the Great French-Gingerbread-Baker, drawing out a new Batch of Kings* (23 January 1806; BMC 10518) and the more famous *The King of Brobdingnag, and Gulliver* of 1803 (fig. 6.1). (It is worth noting here that the exhibited caricatures are in reality of varying sizes: the neatness and symmetry of the display is itself a fantasy of orderliness).[53] The inclusion of *The King of Brobdingnag*, in particular, deepens the complexity of this depiction of the printshop window. A parody of book 2 of *Gulliver's Travels*, the caricature shows George III, cast as the wise and benevolent monarch of Swift's land of giants, using a spyglass to scrutinize a tiny Napoleon, in the role of the Gulliver, who stands on his open right palm. I offer a detailed reading of this print in Chapter 6, so for now let me just note that Gillray reworks the specific moment at which Gulliver's bravado is summarily punctured by the king's incisive criticism and that the caricaturist also riffs on the theme of sight that is central to Swift's satire in both the scene in question and the text as a whole.

The King of Brobdingnag pictures an encounter not just between the big and the small but between the perceptive and the blind; it gives to George III a look that is direct and powerful and that sees through the self-aggrandizing fictions of the pretender. Napoleon is belittled by the Englishman's gaze.

This depiction of the printshop window is thus an image of gazing that contains another image of gazing. By nesting *The King of Brobdingnag* within *Very Slippy-Weather,* Sneyd and Gillray align the looking of the king with the looking of the spectators before Humphrey's shop. This correspondence is made especially clear in a detail at the far left of the street scene, where a man holds a quizzing glass to his eye as he examines the window, gesturally repeating the interrogative pose of the earlier print's George III. More explicitly than in Roberts's *Caricature Shop, Very Slippy-Weather* works to establish the act of gazing at graphic satire as a constitutive act of Britishness and British supremacy. In both the print and the print-within-the-print the satirical look—of the public as much as the king—defeats Napoleon. As an early editor of Gillray's works recalled in 1818, *The King of Brobdingnag* "had a wondrous effect upon the opinions of the common people of England. . . . John Bull laughed at his pigmy effigy strutting in the hand of the good King George. When this well-conceived satire upon the braggadocio invader first appeared, the heads of the gazers before the shop-window of Mrs Humphrey were thrust over one another, and wedged so close, side by side, that they might be likened to the wood-cut of the children in the cave in the story of the Ogre."[54] Note here that the writer celebrates an inclusive, patriotic nation brought into being through graphic satire and, in the same breath, reaffirms the language of social difference by comparing the "common people" to children. As in Thackeray's nostalgic evocation of the "grinning, good-natured mechanics" outside Fairburn's shop, the commentator defines the curiosity of the lower-class viewers of *The King of Brobdingnag* as innocent and simple-minded. It's not just that the printshop crowd reminds him of a group of children but that it calls to mind a specific woodcut illustration to the popular fairy tale of "Little Thumb," one that was included in the first edition of Charles Perrault's *Histoires ou contes du temps passé* (1697), where the story of "Le petit Poucet" originally appeared, and subsequently reproduced in cheap English translations of that book across the eighteenth century (fig. 2.10). Showing the young captives huddled in the cave while Little Thumb steals the ogre's magic boots, it is a striking but crude image— and this, surely, is why the commentator invokes it. His analogy characterizes

Fig. 2.10. Woodcut illustration from *Histories or Tales of Past Times, told by Mother Goose. With Morals. Written in French by M. Perrault, and Englished by G. M. gent*, 10th ed. (Salisbury: B. C. Collins, 1791). Reproduced by kind permission of the Syndics of Cambridge University Library.

the printshop crowd as infantile or primitive three times over: they are like children; they are like the children of a children's story; they are like the children naively depicted in a woodcut in a children's story. Taking its cue from *The King of Brobdingnag*, which makes use of *Gulliver's Travels* to literalize Napoleon's insignificance, the writer's reference to another popular tale of big and small works to suggest that the "common" spectators of that caricature are themselves no more than "pigmies."

Likewise in *Very Slippy-Weather*, Sneyd and Gillray represent the plebeian presence before the printshop window, and its famous anti-Bonaparte caricature, in such a way as to suggest that though all spectators are equal, some are self-evidently less equal than others. The working-class boy keeps his physical distance from the rest of the viewing group. Other readings of this image have assumed that he gazes up at the prints in the window but his position suggests that he could just as easily be looking at the other pedestrian spectators.[55] Either way, the boy's engagement with the window display is set in distinct contrast to that of the man on the far left, whose quizzing glass implies a gaze that is educated and connoisseurial. It is a well-dressed gentleman, not the scruffy boy, whose manner of looking replays that of George III in *King of Brobdingnag*. The quality of the look is indexical of the social status of the spectator.

This visual opposition is reinforced by Gillray's treatment of physiognomy. Of the five figures before Humphrey's shop, we see only the faces of the man with the quizzing glass and the boy. While the man is barely caricatured, the boy is given the simian features—a flat, skeletal nose, bug eyes, and oversized lips and mouth—that Gillray employs exclusively when portraying the working classes, as is made disturbingly clear in his 1798 satire *London Corresponding Society, Alarm'd* (fig. 2.11). In that print and in the boy of *Very Slippy-Weather* Gillray works in a language of the grotesque that dehumanizes the laboring class no less powerfully than does the reactionary polemic of Burke. Sneyd's and Gillray's image of printshop spectatorship thus reaffirms the social and political disenfranchisement of the working-class body in its very inclusion of that body within the assembly of viewers. The boy's presence underlines the print's projection of a diverse public without threatening the established categories of social and cultural prestige. As a consequence, the caricature's positioning of its real spectators is especially complex, for it allows, even compels, identification and distinction in the same moment. The elite consumers of *Very Slippy-Weather* can feel themselves as part of this community without losing their cherished sense of difference from, or indifference to, the plebeian population in the city street.

Fig. 2.11. Detail of James Gillray, *London Corresponding Society, Alarm'd* (Hannah Humphrey, 20 April 1798). BMC 9202. Courtesy of The Lewis Walpole Library, Yale University.

This folding of exclusion into the fiction of inclusivity is extended by means of a further antithesis between the boy and the two customers, both parsons, who closely inspect a print within Humphrey's shop. Proximity and, in particular, touch distinguish these consumers from the working-class figure just a few feet away. The clergyman is not exempt from Gillray's satire—his blotchy red face and rotundity suggests a life more sybaritic than spiritual—but his grasp of the print and, most especially, his smile suggest at once his approval and understanding of the caricature in question. On the other hand, the boy is prevented even from touching the window by the iron railings in front of the shop, which also impede his view. The customers, like the man with the quizzing-glass, conduct the detailed examination of satirical prints necessary to decipher them. Whether or nor the boy is literate, he can neither hope for an advantageous viewing position in the street nor aspire to enter the printshop as a prospective customer.

In the first instance, this juxtaposition is one of space. As John Brewer has written, the distinction between inside and outside was politically coded in graphic satire of the period: " 'Out of doors' was open, 'democratic,' space; indoors, the world of aristocracy and oligarchy prevailed. And if the caricaturist wished to contrast 'high' and 'low' politics, he often portrayed the former in an enclosed space and the latter in the open air."[56] In distinguishing the spectators within the shop from those before it, *Very Slippy-Weather* establishes a similar binary and qualifies the street's ungovernable variety of gazes and gazers by firmly reinforcing the sociospatial boundaries that regulated spectatorship and consumption in Georgian London. And in respect of these overlapping metropolitan geographies of class, politics, and viewership, it's also important to recognize that in moving from Piercy Roberts's to Hannah Humphrey's shop we have left Holborn—that part of the capital populated by "middling sort" professionals—for St. James's Street, at the heart of the city's fashionable West End. As the correspondent for *London und Paris* wrote in 1805: "Caricature shops are always besieged by the public, but it is only in Mrs Humphrey's shop, where Gillray's works are sold, that you will find people of high rank, good taste and intelligence."[57]

At the same time, Gillray and Sneyd map this politics of space, of inside versus outside, on to differences of cultural proficiency. Maidment rightly notes that the marked distinction between exterior and interior in *Very Slippy-Weather* divides the "gaper" in the street from the "knowing connoisseur who has brought the print for his own purposes."[58] The caricature at which the customers inside Humphrey's shop are looking is Gillray's *End of the Irish Farce of Catholic Emancipation* (see fig. 5.15). As we'll see in Chapter 5, this satirical response to the opposition's failed attempt to petition for Catholic Emancipation in Parliament in 1805 elaborately travesties Milton's description of the Paradise of Fools in *Paradise Lost*. It is an iconographically dense, text-heavy, highly allusive print that assumes and requires a significant level of cultural expertise on the part of its imagined viewer. As is implied in the knowing smile of the parson in *Very Slippy-Weather*, Gillray's Miltonic parody appeals to the educated eye. Literature is thus a crucial means by which this image of print consumption parses street and shop, pedestrian spectators and culturally enfranchised patrons. On one side of the door is *The King of Brobdingnag*, a caricature that, as we'll see, plays with a text that had been successfully repackaged and cheaply printed as a children's story since the 1770s; a satire that, finally, does not depend on knowledge of Swift's book to appreciate its anti-Bonaparte jest, and which, at least according to the Gillray's 1818 commentator, found a ready audience among the "common people." On the other side of the door, Gillray and Sneyd place an intertextual print that demands both considerable graphic-satirical literacy and a deep familiarity with *Paradise Lost*, not a poem that was read only by the social elite, to be sure, but certainly a work of unquestionable cultural prestige and also one that circulated less widely and more expensively within early nineteenth-century print culture than *Gulliver's Travels*. In its imagining of a public for caricature—its imagining, by extension, of the political nation—*Very Slippy-Weather* attends to the literariness of the satirical print as a means of marking the boundary between elite and popular cultures, between those who see and those who just gawp.

PART TWO

Plotting Politics

3. *The Tempest;* or,
The Disenchanted Island

In this chapter I want to model a literary history that is constructed, first and foremost, from the archive of satirical prints. To do so is both to suggest the ways in which the parodic reflexes of graphic satire illuminate—and catalyze—the evolving political histories of specific texts and also to trace the reciprocity of caricature's relations to the matrices of print and perform-ance. This second point is especially important because what I'm undertaking here and in subsequent chapters is a kind of cultural triangulation, which maps the proximity and continual interaction between graphic satire and other forms of literary production. I do this, it should be said, on the under-standing that a text's movement within a culture and across time must always be an intermedial process. In this case, the text in question is Shakespeare's *Tempest,* a play I've chosen for the very reason that it was *not* a particular favorite with eighteenth-century graphic satirists. In the seventy or so years between the close of the Seven Years' War (1762–63) to the beginning of the reform era (c. 1830), a period in which thousands of political prints were published, I have located just nine caricatural parodies of the play. A number of Shakespeare's others works, including, as we'll see, *Macbeth,* were far more regularly cited and travestied, and so circulated more prominently within the period's political culture of literary appropriation. This compara-tively small, historically dispersed group of *Tempest* parodies makes possible an approach that looks at all extant prints both in detail and across time—an approach not attempted elsewhere in this section of the book but which here, in its plotting of a broad chronology, will I hope render especially clear the value of graphic satire as a form of literary historical evidence. Equally, the relative infrequency of these *Tempest* prints makes what we will see to be their discernable ideological coherence all the more remarkable, and elicits the consistency with which this text was invoked to negotiate and to give legible form to a distinct set of political concerns.

Thanks to Jonathan Bate we are readily alert to the ubiquity of allusions to Shakespeare's works in political caricatures of the later Georgian period. For Bate, this habitual practice of appropriation both tells once again, and in new colors, the rise of bardolatry in the period and suggests the ideological plurality of his plays, the degree to which they were used to articulate a broad spectrum of political positions.[1] Yet for all that Bate rightly points to a significant cultural phenomenon, his synoptic frame necessarily privileges the cultural work performed by invocations of "the author" and gives far less attention to the differentiated political syntax of the individual plays. At the close of the next chapter I also want to think about what kind of "Shakespeare" emerges from graphic satirical culture, but it is first important to attend at much greater length than does Bate to how a single play functions as a self-contained political typology, an exercise that will also allow us to register graphic satire's responsiveness to contemporary dramatic practice.

What I offer here, then, is a history of *The Tempest* as political theater. Though the persistence and modulation of this political reading through to the early decades of the nineteenth century have yet to be fully studied, we are certainly familiar with its beginnings.[2] In their 1667 adaptation *The Tempest; or, The Enchanted Island,* John Dryden and William Davenant took up Shakespeare's drama as a performative laboratory for their post-interregnum exploration of patriarchal power, casting Prospero as a father-king—of the kind subsequently prescribed by Robert Filmer's *Patriarcha; or, The Natural Power of Kings* (1680)—and Caliban and company as parodic, stridently plebeian figurations of the 1640s parliamentarians.[3] This Restoration reworking reminds us that the play's political valency rests on a deceptively simple act of surrogation. As Bate notes, "The enclosed 'Enchanted Island' potentially a Utopia but harbouring a rebellious faction consisting of a monster and two upstart drunkards, becomes a favourite image of England or of the realm of high politics."[4] Yet if the political appeal of *The Tempest* resides largely in its dramatic elaboration of "islandness," this concept was far from straightforward at a time when the topography of Britain was regarded by its inhabitants as constitutive of its distinct, and distinctly superior, cultural and political identity. As Kathleen Wilson argues, "At the precise moment when England was *less* an island than ever before . . . English people were most eager to stress the ways in which their nation was unique, culturally as well as topographically. The trope of the island, in other words, although long powerful in imaginary literature and material policies, began to serve not only as metaphor but also as explanation for English dominance and superiority in arts and arms. And as islands became important devices in the examination of self, society and species, they also served as the engines for new ways of thinking about nation, race and gender."[5]

In pointing to the ideological commitments and anxieties that underwrite the eighteenth century's troping of islandness, Wilson helps us to understand why *The Tempest* was such an important—and, on the stage, popular—play during the period.[6] The second half of the eighteenth century witnessed Britain's ultimately unsuccessful struggle to retain control of its American colonies, the East India Company's consolidation of British hegemony in India, recurrent conflict with France, and, at home, the ongoing party-political contest to define the character and extent of royal power—a debate intensified and transformed by the creation of republics in America and then France. The islands imagined in graphic satirical parodies of *The Tempest* are, in this way, not only proxies for Britain; more precisely, they serve as complex satirical articulations of the precariousness of prevailing conceptions of the territorial, constitutional, and cultural exceptionalism of the nation as it was challenged by forces and events within and outside its coastal borders. Unsurprisingly, then, graphic satirists press the play into service at times when—as a consequence of the threat of invasion or the redrawing of the boundaries of Britain's empire—the nation is acutely conscious of its own borders, or, equally, when events work to push into the political foreground the tensile boundary between king and parliament that lay at the center of party-political debate and division from the Revolution Settlement of 1688–89 onward. In satirical prints, Prospero's isle is nearly always a space in which royal sovereignty is both asserted and contested. The "enchanted island" offers, ironically, a space of anxiety and disenchantment.

At the same time, and beyond these significant continuities, to read caricatures reading *The Tempest* is to track shifts in the play's political coding across this period. In this chapter I identify two such shifts. The first, which is localized to the 1780s and 1790s, sees the play closely and publicly associated with the group of opposition Whig MPs led by Charles James Fox, who in the final decades of the century ran a concerted campaign against the influence of the Crown. The second shift is, by contrast, diachronic. Taking place at first almost imperceptibly, and finding lucid expression only in the 1820s, this recoding involves the increasing obsolescence and final inversion of the once secure interpretation of *The Tempest* as a typology of British monarchical paternalism. For all that the rest of this book determinedly shies away from such neat teleological narratives, the sequence of images with which I'm concerned here does tell an overarching story—one in which Prospero the father-king is shadowed and finally usurped by Prospero the despot.

Island States

The precise historical moment at which *The Tempest* makes its first appearance in graphic satire is revealing. Published anonymously in the autumn of 1762, as the Seven Years' War reached its conclusion, *The Tempest or Enchanted Island* (fig. 3.1) responds to two specific events, which together placed particular pressure on the ministry of Lord Bute and, indeed, on the geographical and ideological foundations of British exceptionalism. The first of these circumstances was the French capture, in June 1762, of Newfoundland, where they had destroyed the vessels and English fisheries based there. It represented a bad start for the new government—Lord Bute having replaced the popular wartime leader William Pitt the Elder in March—and an embarrassing loss in the face of a war that had already been won (though Britain would recapture Newfoundland in September). The second event was the ratification of preliminary articles of peace, the details of which were greeted with widespread dismay when reported in the London press from late August. Though the proposed treaty consolidated British hegemony in North America, India, and the West Indies, it granted France retention of the islands of Guadeloupe and Martinique, as well as its trading posts in India, and it recognized Spain's possession of Manila and Havana. Bute was anxious for appeasement, but his opponents vociferously denounced the preliminary articles for failing to bring the defeated Bourbon powers to their knees. "All ranks and degrees of people," wrote a correspondent for the *London Evening Post*, were "alarmed, and highly discontented at the infamous preliminaries of peace which are handed about," concluding that they offered "a peace so very dishonourable and detrimental to their King and Country."[7] Together the loss of Newfoundland and the acceptance of a "soft" peace exposed the Bute government to sustained public criticism for jeopardizing the imperial nationhood that the war, and Pitt the Elder's premiership in particular, had aggressively fostered.

The Tempest was a play already woven into the history of cultural responses to the Seven Years' War. In February 1756, and with the papers saturated with reports of the looming conflict with France, David Garrick had mounted his own operatic adaptation of the play at Drury Lane.[8] The performance was prefaced with a dialogue between "Heartly, an Actor" and "Wormwood, the Critic." Wormwood complains that Garrick's adaption "will make an eunuch" of Shakespeare by transforming The Tempest into an opera, which the archetypally xenophobic critic regards as a foreign and effeminate form. Heartly, however, asserts that the present opera makes use only of English music and that popular songs such as "Britons Strike Home" and "God Save the King" will rouse the patriotism of Englishmen and inspire them to "drive every monsieur into the sea."[9] Garrick thus deployed his

Fig. 3.1. *The Tempest or Enchanted Island* (September 1762). BMC 3958. Courtesy of The Lewis Walpole Library, Yale University.

Tempest to draw the cultural and political battle lines and to reinvigorate the analogy between Prospero's island and a bellicose, war-ready Britain.

It is fitting, then, that the anonymous print of 1762 mines this same correspondence at the close of the war and that it does so in order to dramatize events which have called into question the meaning of the victory that Garrick's *Tempest* prophesied. The caricature's complex, chaotic design shows the detonation of two landmines that cause Bute and the Dowager Princess of Wales (George III's mother) to be tossed into the air and Henry Fox, then leader of the House of Commons, to be thrown to the ground. These fougasses are ignited by the allegorical figure of the City of London at the instigation of Pitt the Elder, who stands on the far right. In the foreground, meanwhile, the novelist Tobias Smollett and the playwright Arthur Murphy, who contributed, respectively, to the pro-Bute journals the *Briton* and the *Auditor,* are mauled by a lion—either that of the City specifically or that of Britain in general. In stark contrast to this imagined demise of government penmen, the print stridently emphasizes the power of opposition discourse. While one of the fougasses is charged with the documents that have brought shame upon the prime minister (a map of Newfoundland, the articles of peace, and the "Additional Duties" the government intends to impose on English trade), the other is loaded with anti-Bute publications: a poetic satire entitled *Gisbal* and two opposition journals, the *North Briton* and the *Monitor.*[10] These periodicals serve to introduce a further actor into the print's drama: the radical journalist, MP, and libertine John Wilkes, whose opposition in the 1760s and 1770s to constitutional encroachments upon the political rights of the ordinary British subject earned him popularity and notoriety in equal measure as "the champion of liberty." Wilkes, who supported Pitt the Elder, was a regular contributor to the *Monitor* and had established the weekly *North Briton* in June 1762 as a vehicle for attacking the Bute administration—an antigovernment campaign that culminated in the infamous No. 45 (23 April 1763), which led to Wilkes's imprisonment for libel.[11] In *The Tempest or Enchanted Island,* then, Wilkes is present not in body but, appropriately, in print. And the printed word is accorded a very real agency in this caricature, for Wilkes's publications are here quite literally incendiary. Promoting and reifying the impact of Wilkesite polemic, this image is a satire that asserts the political efficacy of satire.

The title of the print, which replicates that of the Dryden-Davenant adaptation, is a more significant choice than it may at first appear, for by 1762 this Restoration version of the play had not been staged in London for twelve years.[12] Most obviously, the borrowing serves immediately to emphasize the image's concern with space, with the contested territory of two islands: Newfoundland, which has been all too easily captured by the French; and Britain, whose colonial borders, extended by the military victories of the Seven Years' War, are now threatened by Bute's overzealous pursuit of peace. But this print is as much about polity as territory, and its Shakespearean framework also functions to differentiate two opposing modes of political power. Opponents, and polemicists such as Wilkes in particular, repeatedly alleged that Bute owed his rapid rise to power to the clandestine and unconstitutional influence he wielded over George III, who had acceded to the throne two years earlier at the age of just twenty-two. Not only was Bute a royal favorite and the king's former tutor; he was also, it was suggested, the sexual partner of the Dowager Princess, a figure herself seen as possessing too much control over the young and all-too-pliant monarch.[13] The print thus implies the promiscuity of the princess; she is not only thrown into the air by the explosion but also positioned in such a way that Henry Fox peers directly up her dress. And crucially, her question to Bute and Fox, "O when shall we three meet again" (*Macbeth*, 1.1.1), marshals the political typography of a second Shakespeare play. The princess, the graphic satirist implies, is the malign witch who instructs her Macbeth—that is, Bute, who is shown in tartan and calls to "Belphegor, Ashtaroth, & Belial" for aid—to siphon power from the Crown. As in *The Near in Blood, The Nearer Bloody,* we are confronted with a double citation, but the allusion to *Macbeth* here, which mobilizes the Scotophobia that was a perennial feature of Wilkesite attacks on Bute, functions contrapuntally. Where *The Tempest* charts the restoration of the true patriarch and the rehabilitation of the political elite that had cast him out, *Macbeth* dramatizes regicide, political cataclysm, and civil war.

The satirical meaning of the print thus hinges on the juxtaposition of Macbeth-Bute, who employs underhand means to appropriate royal power without popular consent, and Pitt, who deposes the pretender and reasserts both his own authority and, therefore, the will of the people. In this way, we might understand Pitt to be the Prospero of this political *Tempest,* with the figure of the City occupying the role of Ariel (and note too that there is a beast, the lion, who could be seen to parallel Caliban). I don't wish to push this reading too far, however, for the caricature ultimately frustrates the very allegory it invites. Pointing to the fougasses, Pitt tells the City, "Touch on that Point & Heaven direct thy aim." It is a mandate that perhaps resonates with Prospero's commands to Ariel—"Hast thou, spirit, / Perform'd to point the tempest that I bade thee?' (1.2.194–95)—and which also draws on the City of London's motto, "Domine Dirige Nos," or "Lord direct us." Pitt the Elder owed his popularity and power in large part to the sustained backing he received from the City and its various corporate bodies. Yet, as Marie Peters has shown, this support was far from unconditional.[14] So in the print the City's reply to Pitt, "Tis done my Son & Justice shall take Place," suggests that she is by no means his subordinate. Unsurprisingly, given its Wilkesite agenda, this is a drama in which the personification of public opinion wields considerable power.

Yet if *The Tempest or Enchanted Island* does not present us with its own Prospero, it nonetheless appropriates the narrative arc of Shakespeare's play. The print depicts a scene in which Pitt, as commander in chief, retakes possession of the island from the corrupt, militarily inept Lord Bute in a maneuver notably witnessed and applauded at the left of the design by the Dukes of Cumberland and York (the king's uncle and brother, respectively), both of whom had served in the Seven Years' War. Like *The Tempest*, it offers a fantasy of political recuperation. Territorial borders are reaffirmed, the displaced and beloved leader is returned to power, and the constitutionally ratified regime is rehabilitated. As the verses at the foot of the print make clear, this island has been made secure against incursions both territorial and constitutional: "Hence boundless Ambition this Maxim may gain, / That Liberty's Sons all Encroachments disdain."

I have extrapolated the Shakespearean framework of this print at length because it discloses the specific political grammar—the sovereign status of the island state, the limits of (royal) authority—that *The Tempest* comes to embody in the eighteenth century. Thus, when the play reappears in graphic satire twenty-two years later, and at the end of another protracted global conflict, the American War of Independence, it articulates much the same political preoccupations. Published in the middle of the general election of 1784, William Dent's *Reynard's Hope, A Scene in the Tempest between Trinculo, Stephano and Caliban*, of 15 April (fig. 3.2), satirizes the power hunger of Whig leader Charles James Fox. Just as his father, Henry Fox, was frequently portrayed with vulpine features in prints of the 1750s–60s, as is the case in *The Tempest or Enchanted Island*, so "Reynard" became a common satirical moniker for Fox junior, the charismatic man-about-town who emerged as a key Whig politician in the 1770s. Unlike that earlier caricature, however, Dent's print closely parodies a particular moment in the play: act 3, scene 2. Fox becomes Stephano; the Prince of Wales, Trinculo; while Lord North, the recently deposed prime minister and Fox's adversary-turned-ally, is cast as Caliban. Dent numbers the speech ribbons of these figures to confirm the chronology of their dialogue:

> FOX: Taffy—when the Island's ours—my brave Boy—I—I'll
> be King—and you shall be Viceroy.
> PRINCE: Give me dear woman—and give me good wine—and
> you may govern all things else as thine.
> NORTH: My Jove, I'll lick your shoes & obey your nod,
>   And his, for sure he's Bacchus, the bloated God.

North and Fox closely adapt lines spoken by their respective characters: Caliban's "I will kiss thy foot. I prithee, be my god" and Stephano's "I will be king [. . .] Trinculo and thyself shall be viceroys" (2.2.148 and 3.2.107–8).

Fig. 3.2. William Dent, *Reynard's Hope, A Scene in the Tempest between Trinculo, Stephano and Caliban* (J. Brown, 15 April 1784). BMC 6535. Courtesy of The Lewis Walpole Library, Yale University.

The prince, in what is likely a jab at his dissoluteness, singularly fails to follow any script.

Dent carefully matches his political players to their parts. Throughout the American war, Fox and his opposition Whig colleagues had excoriated the Tory ministry of Lord North (1770–82) for its pursuit and mismanagement of the conflict. The short-lived coalition between North and Fox, which governed from April to December 1783, was therefore viewed as a marriage of gross political expediency, and graphic satirists routinely deployed the trope of transvestism, dressing North as a lady, as a means of figuring the former premier's apostasy and political emasculation.[15] Caliban, "half a fish and half a monster" (3.2.29), likewise offers an image of strange hybridity, while in his naive idolatry of Trinculo he also operates as a motif of mistaken subordination—symbolism here reinforced by North's dialogue and supplicatory posture. Dent is similarly incisive in his casting of the Prince of Wales as Trinculo. The prince's public association with the notoriously fast-living group of Whigs surrounding Fox served further to alienate him from his father (no fan of Fox for reasons made clear below) and amplified concerns that his dissolute behavior undermined the monarchy. In this way, Dent shows us an heir-turned-jester, his fool's cap and bells incongruously adorned with the prince's heraldic ostrich feathers and motto, "Ich Dien" (I serve).

Fox's assumption of the role of the drunken steward is a reference to his own, infamous profligacy, and the dice box inscribed "Compass" that he clutches in the print plays on his reputation for heavy drinking and gambling. More significantly, Dent's casting of Fox as Stephano indexes his political position. From their beginnings as a party in the 1670s, the Whigs cohered around a determination to limit the power of the Crown and assert the authority of Parliament, but the distinct Whig faction that emerged under Fox at the close of the American war were animated by a renewed and especially vocal campaign for the restriction of the royal prerogative.[16] George III's use of the arteries of state patronage to engineer the downfall of the Fox-North coalition in December 1783—an event I consider at length in Chapter 5—only strengthened Fox's already firm conviction that the king exercised his prerogative unconstitutionally, deliberately striking at the powers of Parliament enshrined by the Bill of Rights of 1689. The "influence of the Crown" was, Fox had exclaimed to the House of Commons in 1781, the "one grand domestic evil, from which all our other evils, foreign and domestic, had sprung."[17] For his supporters, such rhetoric made Fox the "man of the people" (though, like most of his Whig associates, he was an aristocrat); for his detractors, it suggested Fox's hubristic determination to appropriate the powers of the Crown for Parliament and himself.[18] As Stephano in Dent's print, Fox thus is the alcohol-soaked commoner who claims the island as his own, an act of self-coronation that is rendered yet more absurd in this caricature's parody by his appointment of the prince as a mere "viceroy." In 1784 as in 1762, then, *The Tempest* speaks specifically to Georgian anxieties about the legitimate workings of parliamentary monarchy. Prospero's struggle to assert his status as rightful and benevolent patriarch and to manage his disaffected island subjects provided the eighteenth century with a site of allegory, almost a diagnostic tool, through which to broach the problem of understanding and defining the constitutionality of royal power.

Equally, *Reynard's Hope,* like the earlier anti-Bute print, invokes the image of Prospero's island at a postwar moment when Britain's territorial borders were in flux, and prevailing ideas about its nascent imperial identity were being rewritten. In the background of Dent's design, close to the shore, lies the wreck of the *Royal George,* its splintered mast afloat in the ocean alongside it. The largest gunship in the fleet when it was launched in 1756, the *Royal George* had seen action in the Seven Years' War and, more recently, during the British victory at Cape St. Vincent in 1780. Its sinking while docked at Spithead in August 1782, just months after the Commons had conceded defeat in America by voting to end the war, was for many an all-too-apt sign of Britain's imperial decline. In Dent's parody of *The Tempest* the shipwreck portends the destruction of the island rather than of its enemies. The storm conjured by a king to overcome those who fail to acknowledge his rule has here caused irrevocable damage to the very nation it was summoned to protect.

Foxite Allegories

Reynard's Hope is the first of four caricatures that harness *The Tempest* as a means of satirizing the Foxite Whigs. But before I look in detail at the other three such prints, all of which are by Isaac Cruikshank and were published in the second half of the 1790s, I want to consider why the majority of caricature's appropriations of *The Tempest* during this period specifically broach

Fox and his parliamentary associates. What is it about this particular play that—as the consistency of graphic satirical parody certainly implies—ties it so closely to this particular political faction? The answer to this question, I want to suggest, lies both in its text and the material and ideological contexts of that text's performance during the last quarter of the eighteenth century.

First, *The Tempest* offers a paradigmatic political narrative in which rebellion against the legitimate patriarch is simultaneously described and neutralized. The political agency that Caliban, Trinculo, and Stephano believe themselves to possess is a drunken delusion, and they never seriously threaten the status quo; conspiracy is comedy. Indeed, the reassuring absurdity of this rebellion is central to the reading of *The Tempest* that under-lies the Dryden-Davenant adaptation of 1667, which excises the character of Sebastian, removes the subplot in which he and Antonio conspire to assassi-nate Alonso, and depicts both usurping dukes as penitent even before they are shipwrecked. Concomitantly, Stephano and Trinculo are made to speak the vocabulary of Parliament—"full Assembly," "free election," "settled Government"—as they assert rival claims to the rule of the island and the allegiance of two new characters, Mustacho and Ventoso.[19] Carefully expunging all reference to political intrigue within the court, Dryden and Davenant displace discussion of insurrection onto the lower-class dramatis personae and rewrite the play's comic scenes as a ribald satire of Cromwellian republicanism. Their *Tempest* thus sought to offer Restoration era audiences a compensatory spectacle in which the rhetoric of political rebellion, of contractualism, was insistently belittled and negated by its transposition on to a dramatic register (comedy) and a social stratum (the servants and slaves) in which, according to the circular logic of hegemony, its terms could have no real meaning. Though this adaptation dropped out of the repertory in the 1750s, graphic satires of the Foxites as Caliban, Trinculo, and Stephano none-theless recycle its comic strategy of equating Whiggism with a clownish working-class disaffection, a satirical ploy that gains even greater traction in the 1790s, when the Foxites' broad support of the French Revolution led them to be repeatedly caricatured as ragamuffin sans-culottes.[20] *The Tempest,* via Dryden and Davenant, provided caricaturists such as Dent with a sani-tized syntax of opposition to the Crown, an allusive framework that could enable a print at once to figure resistance to the royal prerogative and in the same moment evacuate the ideological substance and political menace of that resistance.

Yet these images also presume and draw upon their audience's knowledge of the specific political coding of the performance space that claimed *The Tempest* almost as an exclusive possession during the last decades of the eighteenth century. Throughout this period—in which the Tory administration of William the Pitt the Younger, son of the former prime minister, held power uninterrupted from the late 1783 until 1801—the rivalry between the two patent playhouses, Drury Lane and Covent Garden, was understood by many contemporaries to have a distinctly political inflection. Covent Garden was run by Thomas Harris, a friend of the treasury secretary, and was considered to be the progovernment theater. By contrast, from 1776 until 1809 Drury Lane was managed and in part owned by the playwright and Whig MP Richard Brinsley Sheridan, one of Charles Fox's closest and most prominent parliamentary allies. As a consequence, it came to be regarded as the Whig opposition's house, not least by George III, who refused to attend performances there between 1795 and 1799.[21] The importance of this context becomes clear once we recognize that *The Tempest* was, in practice, the repertorial property of Drury Lane throughout the eighteenth century, for it staged all but forty-four of the play's 354 performances in London between 1701 and 1800 (it was common for stock dramas to be produced at just one of the two royal theaters).[22] Indeed, Sheridan mounted a spectacular new production of *The Tempest* during his very first season at Drury Lane—itself a move to reassert that theater's "ownership" of the play, which Covent Garden had staged for the first time in the century earlier the same season. In total, across the twenty-four seasons spanning Sheridan's arrival as manager to the end of the century, the Drury Lane company produced the play eighty-seven times compared to just seven performances at Covent Garden (all of which occurred between 1776 and 1779). If Drury Lane became during the 1780s and 1790s the Foxite's playhouse, then it is easy to see how some, not least culturally and politically adroit graphic satirists such as William Dent, might regard *The Tempest* as a Foxite drama.

Two contemporary documents certainly suggest that the play accrued precisely this political charge. The first is the epilogue to John Philip Kemble's new adaptation of *The Tempest* of October 1789, which reintroduced from the Dryden-Davenant version the characters of Dorinda, Miranda's sister, and Hippolito, the man who has never seen a woman. The epilogue, which was tellingly written by the Whig MP and veteran of the American campaign General John Burgoyne, and spoken by Elizabeth Farren as Dorinda, chides men of the professional classes and the gentry for their effeminacy and obesity, respectively, before offering a portrait of the heroic, virtuous masculinity embodied by the king's sons and the Prince of Wales in particular:

> See one who leads—as mutual trials prove—
> A band of brothers to a people's love:
> One, who on station scorns to found control,
> But gains preeminence by worth of soul.
> These are the honours that on reason's plan,
> Adorn the Prince, and vindicate the man.
> While gayer passions, warm'd at nature's breast,
> Play o'er his youth—the feathers of his crest.[23]

When Farren spoke these words in October 1789, apparently gesturing to the prince's box as she did so, there was an urgent need to "vindicate the man." "The daily prints teemed with abuse of the Prince of Wales, and both his brothers, who were characterized as confederating with a set of political profligates, against their august Parent," wrote one royal biographer of the context for this epilogue.[24] During the Regency Crisis precipitated by George III's lapse into apparent madness in October 1788 the prince and his Foxite supporters had openly maneuvered for power, and upon the king's recovery in February 1789 they were widely castigated for unfeelingly exploiting the situation for their own political ends. Spoken at the close of a play in which an aging monarch is restored to his throne and another patriarch (Alonzo) is reunited with his heir (Hippolito), Burgoyne's idealized depiction of the prince as a man of feeling who eschews the distinctions of power and social rank was an unequivocal public relations exercise—one undoubtedly orchestrated by Sheridan, both the prince's confidant and the pro-Regency campaign's press manager, as a means of reviving support for the heir and his Foxite associates.[25]

Nor was this the first time that *The Tempest* had been conscripted to valorize the Prince of Wales. In January 1785, the publisher John Bell's new edition of *The Tempest* was embellished with an illustration of act 3, scene 1 by John Keyse Sherwin (fig. 3.3). The image shows Ferdinand and Miranda sat on a cluster of logs; she looks directly at her lover, asking, "Do you love me?" while, glancing upward and with arms outstretched, he exclaims, "O heaven, O earth, bear witness to this sound" (3.1.67–68). Directly above the

Fig. 3.3. John Keyse Sherwin, illustration of act 3, scene 1 of *The Tempest* (London: John Bell, 1784). By permission of the Folger Shakespeare Library.

oval design in which this moment is depicted is a large representation of the prince's insignia ("the feathers of his crest") that radiates light of such intensity that it illuminates the Shakespearean scene below. With the illustration and its frame bleeding into one another, Ferdinand's upward gaze seems in fact to be directed at the royal feathers, asserting an equivalence between the prince and Ferdinand as equally virtuous royal heirs. The image is, in this way, a panegyric to the patron, and political outlook, that the printer and artist shared.[26] Bell was bookseller to the prince, to whom his latest edition of Shakespeare's works (1785–88)—of which *The Tempest* was the first volume—was dedicated; Sherwin, as he announces at the edge of his design, was "Engraver to his Majesty" (a new appointment that year) and "His Royal Highness the Prince of Wales."[27] In August 1784, just months before the publication of Bell's *Tempest*, Sherwin had even contributed to the illuminations that celebrated the prince's birthday by adorning the front of his premises in St. James's Street with "a large plume of feathers, in lamps of buff and blue."[28] Bathing the prince's crest in the official Whig party colors, Sherwin offered a spectacular affirmation of his own, and his patron's, political affiliation—an affirmation he repeats in his *Tempest* illustration, where a similarly illuminated plume presumably radiates light of the same political hues.

Sherwin's depiction of the Prince of Wales as the virtuous Ferdinand offers a counterappropriation of *The Tempest* to Dent's caricature of the prince as Trinculo. If these divergent allegorizations mark the extent to which the political values read into and grafted on to *The Tempest* were always contested, then they both nonetheless testify to the tight association between the play and Foxite Whiggism in the final decades of the eighteenth century. Certainly, the satirical work performed by Dent's and, as we'll see, Isaac Cruikshank's parodies of the play becomes far clearer, and also more politically cogent, once we understand that by appropriating *The Tempest* they are offering political readings of both its text and this text *in performance;* that is, they are implicitly but actively inverting *The Tempest*'s contemporary Whig coding.

The force of this counterallegorization of the play was only renewed in the wake of the French Revolution, which fractured the Whigs and politically marginalized the Foxites. Fox's closest allies, if not always Fox himself, reiterated their commitment to moderate reform in response to the events of 1789, and from 1793 the Foxites also vociferously opposed Britain's war with the new French republic. But the large band of more conservative Whigs led by the Duke of Portland were alarmed by revolutionary proceedings across the Channel and in the summer of 1794 joined Pitt the Younger in a new wartime coalition ministry, leaving the Foxites an alienated and ineffective, if still highly vocal, opposition (think back to Gillray's image of a floundering and isolated Fox in *The Slough of Despond*).[29] It is within this context that, eleven years after William Dent's depiction of the beginnings of rebellion (act 3, scene 2), Isaac Cruikshank forecast its final failure in a parody of act 4, scene 1, where the would-be rebels are distracted by a fine wardrobe and pursued by spirits in the form of hounds. *Shakespeare's Prophecy, the Last Act but One in the Tempest* of February 1795 (fig. 3.4) shows Edward Thurlow (the deposed lord chancellor), Fox, and Sheridan—that is, Caliban, Trinculo, and Stephano, respectively—fleeing the treasury in their borrowed finery. Thurlow has regained the chancellor's robes, mace, and great seal; Sheridan sports a long gown; while Fox, still the man who would be king, wears the royal mantle and clutches the scepter and orb. They are hunted down, and evicted from the seat of power, by the ministerial hounds

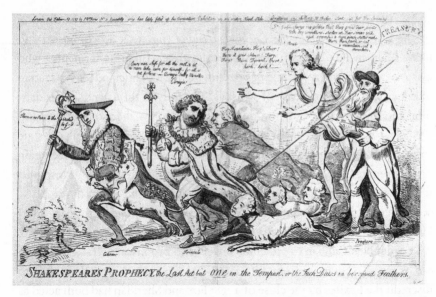

Fig. 3.4. Isaac Cruikshank, *Shakespeare's Prophecy, the Last Act but One in the Tempest, or the Jack Daws in borrowed Feathers* (S. W. Fores, 19 February 1795). BMC 8618. Courtesy of The Lewis Walpole Library, Yale University.

of George III and Pitt in the guise of Prospero and Ariel—characters here explicitly introduced into the graphic satirical repertoire for the first time. If Caliban and company once again offer readily identifiable figurations of (failed) rebellion, then Shakespeare's sorcerer-patriarch provides a seemingly stable idealization of sacral monarchy, and Ariel—described in the Dryden-Davenant (now Kemble) adaptation as Prospero's "aiery minister"— completes this typology of power relations as a model of delegated, prime ministerial authority.[30] Costuming marks the difference between political inside and outside in Cruikshank's print; in an ironic twist, it is those figures who most completely embody their Shakespearean personae that here represent governmental power (Pitt is portrayed as a winged fairy, while George III is shown with a long beard, staff, and book). Fox, Sheridan, and Thurlow, by contrast, conspicuously fail to take part in the drama; their very robes of state paradoxically signify their political marginalization—the men are identifiable as specific *Tempest* characters only by the labels Cruikshank provides.

In the pair of *Tempest* satires that Cruikshank published on 6 December 1798, however, the inefficacy of the Foxite opposition is depicted in the shape of impotent monstrosity, with Fox now cast as Caliban. In the first of the prints, *A Scene in the Enchanted Island* (fig. 3.5), a bedraggled and hairy Caliban-Fox staggers arm-in-arm with Sheridan as Trinculo, who clasps a bottle of sherry, while beside him the Irish politician Henry Grattan guzzles the contents of a cask of whisky. "The folly of this Island!" Sheridan-Trinculo mutters in a verbatim quotation, "They say there's but five upon this Isle—we are three of them; if the other two be brain'd like us the state totters," while at the right of the satire an eavesdropping Pitt, once again Ariel, prepares to report the drunken scene to the king, stating, "This will I tell my Master" (3.2.4–7, 117). In the companion print, a parody of act 1, scene 2 entitled *Prospero and Caliban in the Enchanted Island* (fig. 3.6), a similarly ragged, beastly Fox is chastised by an imperious Pitt, now Prospero, who orders his Caliban to "fetch us fewel" and promises to "rack thee with old cramps" should he refuse (1.2.368–73). Events conspired doubly to discredit the Foxites by the close of 1798: Fox and Sheridan had both acted as character witnesses for the Irish revolutionary Arthur O'Connor at his treason trial in May that year, only to be embarrassed by the publication of O'Connor's confession just months later; while news of Horatio Nelson's victory at the Battle of the Nile, which reached Britain in late September, confounded Foxite criticisms of the validity and management of the war and gave renewed force to antiopposition satires that denounced their politics as unpatriotic. Thus, in Cruikshank's two prints of late 1798, sold separately but published on the same day, *The Tempest* is no longer appropriated as a narrative of rebellion; rather it offers, in the shape of Caliban, a syntax of aberrance and powerlessness. "I must obey," Fox resignedly declares in the second of the satires.

The body of this Fox-Caliban, covered in thick stubble, is not just a grotesque physiognomic exaggeration (five o'clock shadow is Fox's most identifiable feature in caricatures of the period); it reifies ethical and sexual degradation. Cruikshank transforms the infamously promiscuous and dissolute statesman into a figure of barbarous, excessive virility who threatens to people the island with his progeny.[31] But in these prints, Cruikshank also maps sexuality onto political and class ideology: savage, rapacious masculinity operates as a hieroglyph of plebeian radicalism, of an all-too-corporeal politics. Depicting his Fox-Caliban as a Francophile republican—he wears the revolutionary's bonnet rouge in *A Scene in the Enchanted Island* and a tricolor sash in *Prospero and Caliban*—Cruikshank harnesses the rhetoric of

Fig. 3.5. Isaac Cruikshank, *A Scene in the Enchanted Island* (M. Allen, 6 December 1798). BMC 9276. © The Trustees of the British Museum.

Fig. 3.6. Isaac Cruikshank, *Prospero and Caliban in the Enchanted Island* (M. Allen, 6 December 1798). BMC 9275. © The Trustees of the British Museum.

monstrosity most cogently deployed by Edmund Burke, for whom the French Revolution was as a "monstrous tragi-comic scene" in which an animalistic lower class, "a swinish multitude," sought to consecrate a "monster of a constitution."[32] Nor was Cruikshank the first to use Caliban as a symbol of the aberrance of revolutionary enthusiasm. In 1792 William Cusack Smith, a friend of Burke's, denounced the "anarchy and desolation" of "Canibals (I should say Calibans) of France,"[33] while another commentator compared the French people, "grown drunk with the fumes" of their National Assembly, to the inebriated Caliban's worship of Trinculo.[34] In 1795 John Whitaker even described republicanism as "that Caliban of Man's own creation."[35] For these pamphleteers, as for Cruikshank, Caliban's particular embodiment of insurrectionary monstrosity—for all his regicidal proclivities he remains "tamed" and enslaved by the patriarch's far superior power—offered a means simultaneously of acknowledging and othering the force of revolution, relegating it to a disturbing but ultimately pliable alterity.

Prospero Triumphant?

More acutely than during the constitutional entanglements of 1762 and 1784, the war with revolutionary France was a historical juncture at which Britain felt both its physical borders and not just the prerogative but the very existence of its monarchy to be threatened. In 1798 especially, the tropological connection between nationhood and islandness was placed under unprecedented pressure: it was a year punctuated by an invasion scare, as reports of the French fleet preparing to cross the Channel caused widespread alarm; by the bloody rebellion across the Irish Sea that would ultimately compel the Pitt administration to press for legislative union between Britain and Ireland (a crisis foregrounded in one of Cruikshank's "enchanted islands" in the figure of Grattan, staunch advocate of Irish independence); and, finally, by British victory over Napoleon in Egypt. That three caricature parodies of *The Tempest* were published in just this one critical year demonstrates the extent to which the play's typology of island sovereignty was reflexively understood to allegorize the nation's territorial, constitutional, and cultural identity.

The potential of this allegory to offer a prophylactic projection of the robust monarchical state is made especially clear by the anonymous print *Prospero on the Enchanted Island* (fig. 3.7), published in November 1798, a

Fig. 3.7. *Prospero on the Enchanted Island* (William Holland, 8 November 1798). Courtesy of the Yale Center for British Art; Yale University Art Gallery Collection.

month before Cruikshank's diptych. Here, a victorious George III, as Prospero, stands atop the cliffs of "Albion" beside a flag that bears the Hanoverian coat of arms; he tramples a torn tricolor under his feet, holds out his magic book—the pages of which are inscribed "Justice" and "Integrity"—and points his staff across the English Channel in the direction of an impish revolutionary Caliban, who, in marked juxtaposition to the king, stands beside a broken flagpole, crushes Paris beneath his feet, and is partly engulfed in flames. The Prospero of this print safeguards his island by orchestrating not a storm but a naval rout: beneath his outstretched staff, British warships can be seen towing captured French vessels across the Channel. Where, in Dent's 1784 print, the wreck of the *Royal George* signified the end of empire, the mastless French ships here articulate an imperial confidence freshly renewed by the victory at the Battle of the Nile.

　　This caricature not only distills the military, ideological, and affective intricacies of Continental war to a strikingly simple and one-sided face-off between magician-king and monster; more significantly, it projects an image of Shakespearean nationhood. While Caliban announces that "these lands are mine by Sycorax my mother" (1.2.334), Prospero-George III declares: "Yea all which it inherit shall dissolve & like the baseless Fabric of a Vision leave not a Wreck behind." This might look like a misquotation, an easy pun on "rack"/"wreck"; in fact it is a verbatim citation of the lines featured on the Shakespeare monument in Westminster Abbey, where a life-size bard points to a scroll on which is painted a revision of Prospero's "Our revels now are ended" monologue (4.1.146–63). As Michael Dobson's detailed exegesis of this memorial (installed in 1741) has shown, William Kent's design offers an encomium to sacral monarchy.[36] First, it reinscribes what was by the mid-eighteenth century a well-rehearsed reading of Prospero as authorial surrogate, and of the character's most famous speech as Shakespeare's own pronouncement on his art. Second, the carved heads of Elizabeth I, Henry V, and Richard III, which form the base of the pedestal on which the statue leans, serve to enshrine the politics implicit in this surrogation: Shakespeare as Prospero is Shakespeare as monarch, or, as Dryden's prologue had put it in 1667, "Shakespear's pow'r is sacred as a King's."[37]

Such was the cultural impact of the monument's apotheosis that by the early 1770s acting texts of *The Tempest* used the adapted version of Prospero's monologue included on the abbey memorial, in which "the baseless fabrick of a vision" occupies the line position of "this insubstantial pageant faded," and "rack" becomes "wreck."[38] Though the 1777 Drury Lane production restored the original line, Kemble's adaptation of 1789 again returned the monument's inscription to the acting text.[39] There is no more striking demonstration of Joseph Roach's conception of the enactment of the effigy—the capacity of performances to "provide communities with a method of perpetuating themselves through specially nominated mediums or surrogates"—than the staging of *The Tempest* in the second half of the eighteenth century.[40] Each performance of Prospero gave flesh to the body of the Shakespeare-king as the guarantor of British cultural integrity. Few words were as instantly recognizable, carried more political and cultural charge, or performed more ideological work in the eighteenth century than the lines spoken by the king in *Prospero on the Enchanted Island*. The print offers an image not just of George III as Prospero but of George III as Shakespeare, who repels the nation's enemies and maintains public consensus (as suggested by the shouts of "huzza" and "God save the King" that penetrate the left edge of the design). Like Kemble's *Tempest,* which tellingly placed the memorial's lines at the very close of the play, this print responds to the threat of revolutionary France by invoking the body of the Shakespeare-king to uphold—indeed *as*—the body politic of an unassailable Britain.

This strategic deployment of *The Tempest* as an allegory of British supremacy can also be seen in two dramas written either side of the turn of the century that respectively offer a sequel and a prequel to Shakespeare's play. In Francis Godolphin Waldron's unperformed *The Virgin Queen* of 1797, which charts the fortunes of the characters once they leave the island, Prospero is shown to have renounced his necromantic powers in favor of an unmistakably Protestant piety. In an imperialist reworking of the Job narrative, this faith is put to the test when Caliban plots with the spirit of his mother, Sycorax—a "native of dark Africk's clime"—to entrap and kill Prospero, who remains steadfast in his belief in "righteous Providence" and is therefore saved at the last moment by his "guardian angel," Ariel.[41] So the divinely anointed king defeats his untamable colonial subject by the practice of Christian fortitude rather than magic. In similar terms, John Fawcett's spectacular two-act ballet *The Enchanted Island*—which was produced at the Haymarket in 1804 in the midst of yet another invasion scare—quickly establishes its protagonist as a proxy George III, beloved by his "loyal subjects" and chiefly relishing the simple pleasures of domestic life.[42] Here, at the end of a first act set twelve years before the action of Shakespeare's play, the arrival of Prospero on the island builds toward a choreographic moment supercharged with racial overtones as, out of gratitude for Prospero's dispersal of the evil spirits that harass him, Caliban "kneels to him, and strokes his legs, and places Prospero's foot on his head." Recycling the gestural vocabulary of one of the most iconic scenes in *Robinson Crusoe*—in which Friday marks his willing subjection to Crusoe by performing precisely this act—Fawcett's drama follows Waldron's in explicitly racializing Caliban's alterity, and now fuses the island/shipwreck typologies of Shakespeare and Defoe in order to posit Prospero-the-colonizer as a figure of and for British global mastery.[43]

And yet, just as Whig appropriations of *The Tempest* were contested in the 1780s by a print such as *Reynard's Hope,* so the very years in which the play was marshaled with particularly chauvinistic verve as an allegory of the cultural and racial authority of Britain's Shakespearean empire were also those in which the authorized political interpretation of the play on which these deployments rested first came to be questioned. Though, like reactionary discourses of the period, Isaac Cruikshank's prints utilize Caliban as a trope of governable monstrosity, they by no means invest in the kind of political and cultural dichotomy so bellicosely deployed by *Prospero on the Enchanted Island*. That is, Cruikshank's Prosperos are not straightforward valorizations of patriarchal power, cultural privilege, or colonial logic. In *Shakespeare's Prophecy*, as Bate has noted, the eviction and pursuit of the Foxites is given a more disturbing complexion by the words of Pitt-Ariel as he calls to the hounds:[44] "Hey Mountain, Hey! Silver! There it goes Silver! Fury, Fury! there Tyrant, there! hark, hark!" This is a direct quotation—in the play the lines are divided between Prospero and Ariel (4.1.254–5)—but in February 1795, within the specific matrix of reactionary phobia and the repression of radical activism in Britain, the word "Tyrant" would have carried significant political charge. The treason trials of the previous November and December had seen the prosecution, and ultimate acquittal, of key radical figures, and in the new year the Pitt administration further extended the suspension of habeas corpus, in place since May 1794. Speaking in the House of Commons a month before Cruikshank's print was published, Sheridan castigated Pitt for instituting a culture of surveillance and oppression that "fettered and shackled" the population and "destroys all confidence . . . between the governors and the governed."[45] *Shakespeare's Prophecy*, I'd suggest, is similarly critical of government authority. Prospero and Ariel, king and prime minister, here gleefully wield a power that is both violent and absolute. Both in this caricature, and in his later *Prospero and Caliban in the Enchanted Island*, Cruikshank's careful choice of quotations equates the language of authority with that of torture. The Prospero-George III of the first print commands his "goblins" to "grind their joints with dry convulsions: shorten up their sinews with aged cramps" (4.1.256–58), while the Prospero-Pitt of the second threatens to "rack" Caliban "with old cramps" (1.2.368–73). For all their lampooning of the political impotence of the Foxites, Cruikshank's caricatures offer an implicitly radical reading of *The Tempest* as a drama of absolutism.

Further still, Cruikshank's very decision to cast Pitt, rather than George III, as Prospero in one of his 1798 prints implies that the prevailing metonymy by which the sorcerer-patriarch stood for the king, for Shakespeare, and for Shakespeare-as-king was beginning to lose its cultural purchase at the end of the eighteenth century. If *Prospero on the Enchanted Island* is an emphatic enunciation of this surrogation, it is also one of the last. When *The Tempest* reappears in political caricature in May 1827, almost thirty years later, it is again the incumbent prime minister, George Canning, who takes the role of the Prospero. Published just a month after Canning became premier, the progovernment print *The Tempest or Prospero Triumphant* (fig. 3.8) recycles and recalibrates the iconography of *Prospero on the Enchanted Island*. Holding his staff before him, Canning stands atop the "Rock of Integrity," directs the storm, and—with the aid of his new ministers, who navigate the tumult in sailboats—overcomes his drowning adversaries: the prominent high Tories (Lords Eldon and Melville and the Duke of Wellington) who refused to serve in his ministry, unhappy with Canning's liberal sympathies and support of Catholic Emancipation.

Almost seventy years after the Wilkesite parody of *The Tempest*, this print remains concerned with both islandness and the defense of colonial borders. On the opposite shore the national personifications of Erin, contentedly strumming her harp, and John Bull, who has a large pack labeled

Fig. 3.8. *The Tempest or Prospero Triumphant. A Sketch from the Picture lately Exhibited at the National Gallery* (George Humphrey, 6 May 1827). BMC 15384. Courtesy of The Lewis Walpole Library, Yale University.

"National Debt" strapped to his back and a "Petition for Reform" slipping from his pocket, personify the two island states that the victorious Canning will, this print presumes, politically resuscitate. Moreover, as is suggested by the print's subtitle, "a sketch from the picture lately exhibited at the National Gallery," the caricaturist invokes the vocabulary not just of Shakespeare's play but of a particular painting—John Singleton Copley's *Defeat of the Floating Batteries at Gibraltar* (1791).[46] A spectacular restaging of the climax of the failed Spanish siege of the Gibraltar peninsula in 1782, Copley's picture shows the governor-general George Augustus Eliott directing defenses from the coastal battlements while in the harbor below Spanish ships burn, sailors struggle in the water, and the British relief fleet makes a dramatic entrance. Though not in fact shown in the National Gallery (opened in 1824 and here a punning reference to Parliament), the striking compositional correspondences and, more crucially, the presence in the print of Copley's son and namesake—the newly appointed lord chancellor, shown in a small boat with a sail inscribed "The Copley"—firmly establish the allusion.

Like Fawcett's ballet, then, *Prospero Triumphant* interweaves the choreography of two colonial dramas in order to reinforce the political binary it imagines. It is almost as if, by the early nineteenth century, *The Tempest* is no longer a sufficiently stable syntax of legitimate and effective authority, an adequate idealization of secured borders, to be deployed independently and without the supplemental support of a second level of citation. Within the heroic idiom of the print, Canning is as much Governor-General Eliott as Prospero; he acts at the behest of, not *as*, the king. Prospero might still be the embodiment of British virtue and indomitability, but he has manifestly lost his sovereignty. Indeed, the caricaturist tellingly harnesses an entirely different symbolic register in his depiction of the two royal figures in the print. On the right of the design and at the water's edge, the Duke of Clarence—the king's brother and heir (subsequently William IV)—makes an imposing appearance, impervious to the destruction around him, as the triton-bearing sea god Neptune, a reference to his recent appointment as lord high admiral. And where in *Prospero on the Enchanted Island* the sun smiles down on the victorious George III, in *Prospero Triumphant* George IV becomes that sun. Such iconographic readjustment suggests the extent to which this stridently proroyal print (published by the loyalist George Humphrey) works hard to separate the king and duke from—we might say, to inoculate them against—its own Shakespearean parody.

The exigencies that underwrite this careful circumscription of allusion come into better focus once we recognize that *Prospero Triumphant*'s deployment of *The Tempest* as a language of political panegyric is exceptional within its historical moment. In the 1820s, and in the years surrounding the Catholic Relief Act of 1829 especially, readings of Prospero as an arbitrary patriarch—the characterization that quietly informs Cruikshank's satires in the 1790s—become almost rhetorically commonplace. For instance, at a public anti-Emancipation meeting held in Hereford the very same month that *Prospero Triumphant* was published, the Reverend Arthur Matthews took to the podium to denounce Canning as "this modern *Prospero*" who "wield[s] the creative wand of eloquence with magical effect, and seems to subdue every thing to his will," and whose storm threatens to "founder" the "vessel of the state."[47] The following year, in a speech that notably approaches the Irish question from exactly the opposite political angle, Shakespeare's sorcerer-patriarch was again deployed as a symbol of malevolent and repressive power. Speaking in support of Daniel O'Connell, the leader of the campaign for Catholic Emancipation, at the hustings during the crucial by-election in County Clare in July 1828, the playwright Richard Lalor Sheil declared of his candidate: "The rod of oppression is the wand of this potent enchanter of the passions, and the book of his spells is the penal code. Break the wand of this political Prospero and take from him the volume of his magic, and he will evoke the spirits which are now under his control no longer."[48] Prospero might be a radical here, but the source of his power to agitate, Sheil assures his auditors in a revisionist reading of *The Tempest*'s colonial drama, is Britain's subjugation of Ireland.

Performance and political appropriation histories remain entwined at this moment. Until William Charles Macready restored Shakespeare's "original" play to the stage at Covent Garden in 1838, the acting text of *The Tempest* was still based on Kemble's adaptation, in which Prospero essentially remained the creation of Dryden and Davenant. As Katharine Eisaman Maus has argued, this Restoration father-king exhibits far more "repressive tendencies" than his Shakespearean prototype; he repeatedly demands strict obedience from Miranda, Dorinda, and Hippolito (keeping Hippolito in the solitary confinement of a cave) and is so enraged when Ferdinand seemingly kills Hippolito that he summarily condemns Ferdinand to death and promises to "chain" Ariel in "the burning bowels of Mount Hecla."[49] As Dobson observes, this Restoration adaptation was "self-evidently better suited to

Kemble's right-wing purposes than Shakespeare's original text."[50] At the start of a revolutionary period in which the very institution of monarchy was resolutely challenged, Kemble's reinstitution of an autocratic Prospero was part of his wider program of deploying Shakespeare's plays as a dramaturgy of conservatism.[51] Perhaps in 1789 this Prospero's vestigial brand of Filmerian patriarchalism could indeed still offer Kemble and his audiences a compensatory theater of political nostalgia. But by the 1820s the political landscape in Britain had been dramatically altered by the Peterloo Massacre of 1819, when the yeomanry charged a peaceable crowd of around sixty thousand people gathered in St. Peter's Fields, Manchester, killing eleven and injuring hundreds; by the Six Acts, the repressive legislation passed in response to Peterloo and the public outrage it had generated; and then by the Cato Street Conspiracy of 1820, when a plot to assassinate the cabinet was exposed by government agents provocateurs and its leaders were executed. In the aftermath of these events, the coercive apparatus of the state became a lightning rod of political debate, and the onstage persistence of the Restoration's absolutist Prospero was at once a political anachronism too obvious to pass unnoticed and all too resonant of contemporary governmental repression. "*Prospero* in the piece before us is a testy old gentleman, arbitrary and jealous of his power," noted the *Examiner*'s reviewer of Covent Garden's new production of *The Tempest* in 1821.[52]

Moreover, the troping of Prospero as tyrant that was common to Matthews's and Sheil's speeches at the end of the decade discloses the palpable gap that had opened up by the reign of George IV between *The Tempest*'s configuration of island sovereignty and the self-image of the British polity as a parliamentary and imperial democracy. The royal prerogative was a defunct party-political concern, while George IV, the prince that Dent saw fit to depict as Trinculo in 1784, was a famous debauch and the most unremittingly satirized royal in history, not least during his regency (1811–20).[53] Alongside the Irish question it was the fiercely contested issue of parliamentary representation that drove the politics of the 1820s. Equally, the ideology of nationalism was now shaped by a very different geographical imaginary. In place of the specter of invasion, the sense of border fragility so prominent in 1762, 1784, and 1798, were the fantasies of cultural and racial supremacy stimulated by the ever-broadening horizons of empire. To posit Prospero's isle as modern Britain thus involved an increasingly impossible—implausible—kind of surrogation.

Nowhere is this obsolescence of national allegory more clearly shown than in the period's final graphic satirical appropriation of the *Tempest*. Published in January 1829, just two months before Parliament finally passed the Catholic Relief Act, Henry James Richter's anti-Catholic print, simply entitled *The Tempest* (fig. 3.9), transforms Prospero into the pope. Sat on a throne crawling with small serpents, this Prospero casts a Machiavellian glance at the dragonlike Caliban, who sits attentively to his right, while on his left a haloed but barely clothed Miranda looks with incestuous longing at her father and plays suggestively with a cord that hangs down from his papal tiara. According to the print's engraver, John Sartain, Miranda and Caliban respectively represent "the Church and the Devil."[54] Reminding its audience that the Duke of Milan is a Catholic patriarch, Richter invokes the age-old English correlation between Catholicism and absolutism, and also foregrounds the play's subtextual engagement with sexual violence and perversion. Richter's Prospero is a tyrant who courts demons and his own daughter in equal measure, a phobic inversion of those institutions most

Fig. 3.9. John Sartain, after Henry James Richter, *The Tempest* (W. Roberts, 29 January 1829). © The Trustees of the British Museum.

ideologically constitutive of modern Britain: the Protestant church, the balanced constitution, the heteronormative family.

Sartain noted that this pictorial polemic generated considerable controversy. "The print was displayed in the window of a print shop in Gracechurch Street," he wrote, "and attracted such a crowd of excited persons who angrily inquired what was meant by it, that it had to be removed from the window for fear of trouble."[55] Such furor only makes sense within, and perhaps as the culmination of, the history this chapter has unfolded, the history of the recurrent invocation and recalibration, from the mid-eighteenth century onward, of *The Tempest* as an allegory of the island state: its besieged borders, constitutional limits, and monarchical paternalism. The likes of Isaac Cruikshank, in 1795–98, and of Sheil, in 1828, may have cast Prospero as an oppressor, but they did not finally rupture the fundamental metonymy of this allegory. *The Tempest,* in their appropriations, is still a cogent means of politically mapping Britain. But Richter's satire forcefully resists this allegory. With disturbing, discriminatory audacity, it exposes the increasing redundancy of the long-standing correspondence between Shakespeare's enchanted island and Protestant, imperial Britain. And in doing so, it also reveals the precariousness of political caricature's repeated negotiations between Shakespeare and topicality—something we'll continue to explore in the coming chapters. The prints at which we've been looking seize on *The Tempest*'s narrative and characters to give sense and structure to the political moment, but as an image like *Prospero on the Enchanted Island* suggests, they nonetheless work to preserve the power of "Shakespeare" as a cultural and ideological abstraction even as they put his plays to topical use. As the embodiment of aesthetic and political ideals that are (must be) for all time, Shakespeare remains the totem of a high literary canon removed from historical contingency even as his plays help to plot what Terry Eagleton calls the "sordidly historical."[56] Richter's print recognizes this logic precisely because it so flagrantly violates it in order to press home a particular political point. Here, feared incursion is articulated in the very act of appropriation, in the explicit catholicization of the play and its author. The print provocatively imagines and enacts the invasion of Shakespeare; it takes *the* image of British high culture and reveals it to be all too susceptible both to the influence of foreign beliefs and practices and to the vagaries of historical circumstance. No wonder it so angered the printshop crowd.

4. *Macbeth* as Political Comedy

We need only call to mind two well-known allusions to Macbeth's murdering of sleep (2.2.34–39)—Edmund Burke's attack in his *Reflections* on the French National Assembly for offering Louis XVI not " 'the balm of hurt minds' " but "the cup of human misery," and William Wordsworth's description in *The Prelude* of a revolutionary Paris haunted by the cry " 'Sleep no more!' "—to understand the rich and often uncomfortable political charge of *Macbeth* at the end of the eighteenth century.[1] And given both its resonant depiction of regicide and its sensational conjoining of the political and the fantastical, it is to be expected that *Macbeth* was a recurrent source for the period's graphic satirists (as it remains for their counterparts today).[2] Between 1754 and 1835 at least sixty-two political prints cite the play in some manner: thirty-seven do so in extended or elaborate ways, and many others engage with it by means of brief but often complex intertextual gestures of the kind exemplified in Isaac Cruikshank's *Near in Blood, The Nearer Bloody* (see fig. 1.1). Given this number, and in contrast to my method in the previous chapter, I consider here only the largest and most prominent cluster of *Macbeth* prints, that is, parodies of the weird sisters. The manifest benefit of such a tight focus is that it offers the opportunity to navigate well-trodden critical and historical ground in a productively different way.[3] First, the weird sisters—in their dramatic function, relationship to Jacobean demonology, and sexual and ideological significance—have long been the subject of scholarly fascination, but when looked at through the political and parodic lens of graphic satire their history and status seems suddenly less familiar. Second, the work of Mary Jacobus, Jonathan Bate, and Matthew Buckley has made us

well aware of the profound extent to which romantic writers and commentators invested in Shakespeare's play as a syntax of regicide, atrocity, and criminality that could bring some sense and structure to the experiences of the
French Revolution and its aftermath.[4] Yet, while visual parodies of Shakespeare's witches by no means refute or displace this history of political
appropriation, they do reveal another dimension to the political valency of
Macbeth, one that at once complements and countervails the narrative we
already know.

In particular, graphic satire takes us beyond the terms *romanticism,*
revolution, and most especially *tragedy* that usually provide the conceptual
armature for discussions of *Macbeth* in the period. With regard to the first
two of these terms, we need to recognize the political currency of Shakespeare's play across the long eighteenth century and well before the events
of 1789. Take, for instance, the broadside *The Magical Installation or Macbeth
Invested* of 1762 (fig. 4.1), where—as in the print *The Tempest or Enchanted
Island* (see fig. 3.1)—*Macbeth* is readily mobilized by a Wilkesite satirist

Fig. 4.1. *The Magical Installation or
Macbeth Invested* (September 1762). BMC
3896. Wellcome Library, London.

both to traduce Lord Bute as a usurper and to play upon pervasive midcentury Scotophobia.⁵ Responding to Bute's simultaneous appointment as first lord of the treasury and investiture into the Order of the Garter in late May 1762, the satire folds two scenes into one image. On the right, in a parody of act 2, scene 1, Bute gazes upward toward a scepter that hovers before him and exclaims: "Is this a Scepter that I see before Me? The handle tow'rds my Hand—Come, let me clutch thee!" (adapting 2.1.33–34). On the left, meanwhile, in a travesty of act 1, scene 3, Bute is greeted by three witches who respectively hail him as "Knight," "King hereafter," and "more than King." Yet while the print castigates the new prime minister's delusions of grandeur and warns the public of his fondness for arbitrary rule, it also engages in a predication its own, for the witch closest to Bute tellingly holds a noose. The satirist embeds an allusion to the play's close in a parodic reimagining of its opening, thereby reminding the reader that Macbeth's rise to power will culminate in his death and the restoration of the legitimate regime. Here, the weird sisters are an especially powerful device for the political parodist in part because their prophecies press together beginning, middle, and end. Bute's rise and fall collapse into each other; coronation becomes execution.

Jump forward almost sixty years, to *The Cauldron—or Shakespeare Travestie—1820* (fig. 4.2), and not much has changed. Now the witches are themselves ministerial: the minions of George IV-cum-Macbeth in a satire that takes aim at the cabinet's efforts to end the royal marriage by parliamentary decree and so strip the king's estranged wife, Caroline, of her title as consort. At the center of the caricature, the titular cauldron is tended by the cloaked, broomstick-wielding figures of Lords Liverpool, Sidmouth, and Castlereagh—respectively the prime minister, home secretary, and foreign secretary—and satirically emblematizes the elaborate institutional plot to discredit the queen. Into this bubbling pot a winged demon empties the contents of an "Infernal Green Bag," including a cluster of legal documents that read "Lies," a reference to the two sealed green bags presented to Parliament in 1820, in which the evidence amassed against Caroline by the government was deposited. Like *The Magical Installation*, the caricature's appropriation of *Macbeth* hinges on the thematics of prophecy. Where, at the right of the print, Frederick, Duke of York, the heir presumptive, confidently asserts, "I'll do!—I'll do!—I'll do!" (1.3.9), the king, on the left, anxiously inquires of the ministerial witches whether he is to obtain the

Fig. 4.2. *The Cauldron—or Shakespeare Travestie—1820* (John Fairburn, August 1820). BMC 13787. © The Trustees of the British Museum.

annulment that will allow him to remarry, produce an heir, and block his brother's succession: "Tell me ye d——n'd infernal Hags of Night, shall Fr[ederic]k reign?" (citing 4.1.117–18). This juxtaposition is reaffirmed by two blue devils, the first of which exclaims to George, "All hail Macbeth! thou'rt now the cause of laughter," while the other kneels to Frederick, saying, "All hail Macduff!! that shall be K——g hereafter—" (1.3.48). Conscripting Shakespeare's play as a drama about royal accession, the caricature's casting of the king as Macbeth forecasts that his crown and scepter, which lie at his feet, will be "fruitless" and "barren" (3.1.62–63).

   As is well suggested by these two examples, there are remarkable continuities to the manner in which satirical prints make use of *Macbeth* across the period. Eminently adaptable to the particularities of political circumstance, the play was deployed just as often as a drama of sinister governmental conspiracy as of radical collusion. Its appeal to graphic satirists, who we've seen to be in the business of plotting futurity as much as tracing the present, evidently resided in part in its theater of prophecies and portents, which makes palpable the human need to "feel now / The future in the instant," as

Lady Macbeth puts it (1.5.56–57). At the same time, however, and to turn to the notion of *tragedy,* the last and most entrenched of the keywords I want to trouble here, the performance history of the weird sisters offers another, still more significant reason why satirists were so compulsively drawn to the play. Attention to this history—one increasingly divergent from that of the play's critical reception as the century wore on—requires us to recognize that *Macbeth* was a source of comedy and the grotesque as well as of tragedy and that in mining it caricaturists were often seizing upon a readily available repertoire of comic scenes and characters. Graphic satirical parody therefore enables us not only to track the ever-mobile political codings of a text such as *Macbeth* but also to apply critical pressure to its generic status.

In part this approach is a matter of registering the historical contingency both of the generic identity of any given text and, of course, of genre itself. But it is also a question of approaching genres as what Peter Seitel calls "frameworks of expectation" or, more precisely, what Frederic Jameson regards as "literary *institutions* . . . social contracts between a writer and specific public."[6] Parody invariably makes explicit the terms of this contract because it depends upon and plays with not only readerly familiarity and expectation but also the reader's sense of responsibility to engage with a text according to an established set of interpretative and affective protocols. Yet, the caricatures we're looking at here also require us to adjust Jameson's definition, for in drawing upon prevailing theatrical practices and critical orthodoxies they remind us that authors and authorial intentions need not always figure in the agreement that genre represents. Rather, precisely because genre's contract is *social* it might just as easily set the terms for a relationship between a writer's self-appointed proxies (actors, impresarios, or critics, say) and a specific public. So, where for Buckley *Macbeth* reveals how far the romantics found tragedy to be "a genre bound inextricably to revolutionary experience," parodic prints disclose a rather different politics of literary form. Indeed, they suggest that across the long eighteenth century the play's political (and sexual-political) charge resided at least in part in the willful slippage between tragic and farcical modes that marked its life on stage.[7] That is, the contract between the actors and audiences of *Macbeth* at this time was one that mandated not only pity and terror but also grotesquery and even laughter.

This concern with comedy animates the first part of this chapter especially, where I consider some of the many prints that cast the weird sisters as conspiratorial figures whose clandestine rituals threaten to distort or jettison the established constitution, whether in the name of revolution or the preservation of the status quo. The power wielded by a group, be that a government or an opposition, a cabal or a rebellion, is an obvious representational challenge in a medium of such economy as the satirical etching. Yet, in the "hell-broth" the witches together concoct, and in the dance they make around their cauldron, caricaturists found an especially compelling—and necessarily comic—motif of collective political action and intrigue. The second part of the chapter then returns once more to the matter of the politics of sight and concerns the satirical conscription of the weird sisters—or, in one important exception, Lady Macbeth—as the purveyors and embodiments of hazardous forms of (sexual) ambiguity and delusion in parodies that trouble the very grounds on which politics might be seen and known. In working my way through this material, moving back and forth across the period as I go, I build on the cultural interfaces I identified in my history of *The Tempest* and remain especially attuned to the intricate nexus of satire, theater, and criticism. It is by repeatedly overlaying these discourses, I hope to show, that the matters of form and genre at the heart of this discussion come into focus and can be seen anew. As a coda to this chapter I then pull back from *Macbeth* to address, briefly, the complex relationship between Shakespearean parody, cultural literacy, and political engagement that emerges through and is reinforced by the prints considered in this chapter and the last. Through a reading of Gillray's *Shakespeare-Sacrificed* (1789), a satire acutely concerned with questions of literary proprietorship and the politics of cultural consumption, I ask what kind of readership these Shakespearean prints may have invited, and I problematize easy assumptions that they advance or embody any form of popular Shakespeare.

Laughing, not Shuddering

In William Heath's 1810 caricature *The Last Recorce or Supernatural Committee Employ'd* (fig. 4.3) a desperate prime minister looks to the dead for help. At the time, Spencer Perceval's government was in crisis. Radical MP Sir Francis Burdett had stoked the fires of opposition by printing in William Cobbett's *Political Register* a speech in the Commons in which he had accused Parliament of acting unconstitutionally in incarcerating popular orator John Gale Jones. Violent riots then ensued when attempts were made to apprehend

Fig. 4.3. William Heath, *The Last Recorce or Supernatural Committee Employ'd* (Elizabeth Walker, 12 May 1812). BMC 11555. © The Trustees of the British Museum.

Burdett, who was found to be in breach of parliamentary privilege. In the midst of this debacle, Heath's print shows Perceval, as Macbeth, in consultation with the weird sisters, who respond to his plea for assistance—"I Conjure you by that which you profess, Answer me!" (abbreviating 4.1.66–67)—by raising the specters of three recently deceased statesmen: Charles James Fox, Pitt the Younger, and Edmund Burke. Emerging through the thick smoke of the witches' cauldron, this strange coalition of the dead offers Perceval robust counsel on how to manage Burdett and the radical threat, all of which excerpts the prophecies spoken by the apparitions that appear to Macbeth in act 4, scene 1. Fox instructs the prime minister to "be Bloody bold & Resolute"; Burke advises that he "Laugh to Scorn the Power of Man"; and Pitt tells Perceval to "Be Lion mettled proud and thak [sic] no Care—who Chases, who frets or where Conspirers are" (4.1.95–96, 106–7). Heath's parody satirizes Perceval for lacking the strength of conviction possessed by his political forebears and, like *The Magical Installation*, envisages the ultimate demise of the incumbent government; at the far left of the image,

Charles Abbott, the speaker of the House and the man responsible for issuing the warrant for Burdett's arrest, quotes Macbeth's battlefield speech: "They have tied me to a stake, I cannot fly but bear-like must fight the *cause*" (adapting 5.7.1–2). Yet this print also traces a more profound disjunction between the political past and present, implying that Burdett's new brand of radicalism, one that works from within the precincts of the Commons, threatens to render the prevailing ideologies of the previous political generation all but obsolete. In summoning the spirits of the late eighteenth century's most prominent parliamentarians, the witches of *The Last Recorce* present Perceval with the respective traditions of Pittite Toryism, Foxite Whiggism, and Burke's counterrevolutionary conservatism. The question, this print seems to ask, is whether any of these ideologies can offer cogent solutions to the nineteenth-century political problems that confront Perceval's ministry.

It's tempting to broach a parody such as this one in terms of its marshaling of the supernatural and the uncanny. As Ian Haywood has shown, graphic satire of this period delights in spectral tropes, and *The Last Recorce* certainly reaffirms his contention that the power of such images resides in their harnessing of a syntax of fantasy "to de- and re-mythologise regimes."[8] However, before we align the politics of the paranormal in *Macbeth* parodies such as Heath's with either Jacques Derrida's notion of "spectropolitics" or the entwined modes of romanticism and gothicism—conceptual moves upon which Haywood insists—we need to keep in mind that eighteenth-century theatrical practice invariably posited the weird sisters as buffoonish and transvestite figures whose performance register was one of insincerity and even farce. William Davenant famously transformed Shakespeare's play into a spectacular pseudo-opera to suit the tastes and technologies of the Restoration stage, refashioning the sisters as all-singing and all-dancing in the process, and though in 1744 Garrick returned the performed version of *Macbeth* to something resembling the folio text ("as written by Shakespeare," read his advertisement), he nonetheless retained Davenant's witches.[9] Throughout the century, the weird sisters, and also the character of Hecate, were played by male actors who specialized in physical comedy, such as John Quick at Covent Garden (from 1770 to 1780) and Richard Yates (1745–65), John Moody (1769–96), and William Parsons (1770–86) at Drury Lane.[10] Occasional attempts were made to bring a greater sense of gravity, if not tragedy, to their scenes, notably by Charles Macklin in 1773 and John Philip

Kemble in 1794, but it was not until the mid-nineteenth century that the weird sisters were staged as figures of genuine occult terror.

This stage history makes itself readily felt in Heath's *Last Recorce,* in which at least two of the witches appear to be performed, as it were, by men. In particular, the pronounced musculature and long cat's whiskers of the one who stretches out a serpent-coiled arm toward Perceval presents us with an awkward and manifestly stagey androgyny in which the semiotics of horror give way to those of the ludicrous. This print imagines a collision between the political past and the political present that unfolds within a theatrical idiom that pushes the supernatural toward low comedy rather than the sublime. And by the time Heath published this caricature satirical prints had been making use of the sisters as figures of farce and slapstick humor for a good half-century. In *The Gypsy's Triumph* (1754; BMC 3214), a satire on the controversial abduction case of Elizabeth Canning and the first political print to cite *Macbeth* directly, Crisp Gascoyne—lord mayor of London and the judge who overturned the conviction of Canning's supposed kidnapper, Mary Squire—is hailed and held aloft by four witches, one of whom exclaims, "I'll give thee wind" (1.3.10), as she farts in his direction. Similarly, in *The Blessings of Peace* of 1783 (fig. 4.4), a response to Britain's loss of its American colonies, a witch repeatedly farts the word "Peace" as she flies above an anxious conference of king and ministers, while in *Hecate; or, The Voyage of Discovery* of 1831 (fig. 4.5) the Whig lord chancellor Henry, Lord Brougham is caricatured as a witch festooned with tricolor ribbons, preposterously mounted on a bubble inscribed "Reform," and dressed in a corset and skirt. Published by Tory stalwart George Humphrey during the election that saw Brougham take his reform mandate to the polls, the print recasts the unsettling prospect of parliamentary reform as a spectacle of empty idealism and transvestism in which political principle is shown to be nothing more than bizarre role-play.[11] Far from converting political tragedy into political comedy, these graphic parodies of the weird sisters work with scenes that are already comic and with characters that are already discernibly carnivalesque.

While audiences, as the actor-turned-bookseller Thomas Davies tells us, "were pleased with the comic dress which the actors gave to the witches," critics complained vociferously about such willful generic confusion.[12] Horace Walpole opined that the weird sisters were "by the folly of the actors, not by the fault of Shakespeare, represented in a buffoon light" and costumed

Fig. 4.4. *The Blessings of Peace* (M. Smith, 16 April 1783). BMC 6212. Courtesy of The Lewis Walpole Library, Yale University.

"like basket women and soldiers' trulls," while on going to see Kemble's production of *Macbeth* in the 1790s German writer Jacques-Henri Meister was shocked to see the weird sisters portrayed with "meanness and false taste": "you might be led almost to imagine," he observed in a telling comment, "that the actors wished to burlesque them."[13] For the romantics, ever quick to express their contempt for the contemporary stage, such performance conventions were tantamount to sacrilege. Samuel Taylor Coleridge denounced the theatrical rendering of the witches as a "vulgar stage errour," and an acerbic William Hazlitt, remarking that they appeared "ridiculous on the modern stage," doubted that "the furies of Aeschylus would be more respected."[14] For Samuel Johnson, at least, the problem went deeper than the issue of staging. Written and performed in the reign of a king who took an active interest in demonology, *Macbeth* addressed an audience for whom "the Doctrine of Witchcraft [was] at once established by Law and

Fig. 4.5. *Hecate; or, The Voyage of Discovery* (George Humphrey, 21 May 1831). BMC 16684. © The Trustees of the British Museum.

by the Fashion, and it became not only unpolite but criminal to doubt it."[15] If the witches were risible on the contemporary stage, Johnson therefore noted, they were so because such belief had long since faded. Or as the politician Maurice Morgan put it in his *Essay on the Dramatic Character of Sir John Falstaff* (1777), the weird sisters were "a machinery which, however exquisite at the time, has already lost more than half its force; and the Gallery now laughs in some places where it ought to shudder."[16] Quite simply, the witches were out of their time, and Heath's print seems consciously to take up and politicize this sense of anachronism. Offering Perceval only a dialogue with the past, they draw the prime minister away from the present rather than enabling him more effectively to encounter it.

This understanding of the play as a victim of historical change reminds us that the critical discomfiture elicited by performances of the weird sisters was symptomatic not only of the increasingly antitheatrical tenor of much literary criticism at this time, of the growing compulsion to sequester Shakespeare from the realities of theatrical embodiment, but also of the extent to which the witches rubbed uncomfortably against the empirical sensibilities of Enlightenment modernity. For many, *Macbeth* seemed to indulge in forms of superstition that were antithetical to an avowedly Protestant and politely commercial Britain. Francis Gentleman articulated this concern with particular vehemence: "exhibiting such personages and phantoms as never had existence but in credulous or heated imaginations," he argued in his *Dramatic Censor*, "tends to impress superstitious feelings and fears upon weak minds." For this reason, Gentleman concluded, *Macbeth* was "improper for young, unexperienced spectators."[17] However comic they might be, the witches were nonetheless an unsavory holdover from a violent and ignorant past. Such a view goes some way toward explaining the almost reflexive association in graphic satire between the necromantic practices of the weird sisters and the rituals and paraphernalia of Catholicism, symbolic logic that was only strengthened by *Macbeth*'s connection with the Jacobean court and, by extension, the Gunpowder Plot of 1605. In Heath's *Last Recorce,* for instance, Burke, so often accused of crypto-Catholicism, wears a Jesuit's biretta; in Thomas Rowlandson's *Pit of Acheron* (January 1784; BMC 6364), the three witches conjure the spirits of Fox, Lord North, and Burke by throwing into a blazing cauldron not only papers that read "deceit" and "rebellion" but also a set of rosary beads and a crucifix; while in his ballad sheet *The "No Popery!" Cry* (1826; BMC 15125), published during a general election dominated by the Catholic question, C. H. Perring turns this entrenched trope on its head by imagining the anti-Emancipation Tories as Shakespeare's witches, recoding their cauldron dance as an emblem of government scaremongering rather than Catholic mysticism.

More important, what in equal measure repelled Gentleman and fascinated Johnson—who pursued Shakespeare's engagements with the supernatural with uncommon scholarly passion—was the control that the weird sisters exercise over the course of the play's action.[18] This was, on their rather different accounts, a drama that seemed to cede human agency to forces of a more spectral kind. "*Macbeth* strongly inculcates power of prediction," Gentleman complained, "even in the worst and most contemptible agents; inculcates a supernatural influence of one mortal being over another."[19] Romantic criticism was certainly more receptive to the poetic efficacy of supernatural phenomena, as Jonathan Bate notes; Coleridge, for one, considered the witches to be "awful beings" who "blended in themselves the Fates and Furies of the Ancients with the sorceresses of the Gothic and popular superstition."[20] But the romantics' difference from earlier commentators lay in their willingness once more to embrace folklore and fantasy, not in the degree of structural agency their readings ascribed to the weird sisters. In fact, the most popular interpretation of *Macbeth* throughout the eighteenth century—that it charts the fall of a heroic man who is seduced by malevolent forces and succumbs to his own sublime but fatal ambition—placed special emphasis on the role of the weird sisters as "the instruments of dire events."[21] For Elizabeth Montagu, Macbeth was a man of "kindness" and "honour" who found himself caught in an overwhelming vortex of otherworldly power: "The agency of the witches and spirits," she wrote, "excites a species of terror that cannot be effected by the operation of human agency or by any other form or disposition of human beings."[22]

Just as much as the play's stage history, these critical contours intersect with and are made visible in contemporaneous caricatural parodies of *Macbeth*. That is, if prints work with the comedy of witchcraft, then they also, like so much criticism of the play, engage with and seek to interrogate the particular kind of political agency—an agency at once illegitimate, surreptitious, and emphatically corporate—that the weird sisters embody. Indeed, for a satirical form driven in part by the imperative of political containment, these maneuvers were necessarily intertwined: to cast certain politicians as the weird sisters, as a number of prints do, was a move that depended for its satirical efficacy on the sisters' double status within the period as figures of both conspiratorial agency and ribald comedy. For all that the witches offered the parodist a useful paradigm of political intrigue, of the group rather than the individual, the matrix of theatrical performance was needed to keep at bay their potential to evoke exactly the "species of terror" that gripped readers of the play such as Montague.

We can track the workings of this strategy in William Dent's *Revolution Anniversary or, Patriotic Incantations* of 1791 (fig. 4.6), which depicts dissenting preachers Joseph Priestley and Joseph Towers, along with Charles James Fox and Richard Brinsley Sheridan, dancing around the cauldron of liberty and working together both to summon what Towers hails as "Spirits of discord" and also to exorcize the monarchy from the British state, with the rising smoke of the cauldron, inscribed "French spirits," expelling an upturned crown. All four men were thought to be sympathetic to the political tenets of the French Revolution, though only Towers attended the dinner held at the Crown and Anchor tavern on the Strand on 14 July 1791 to

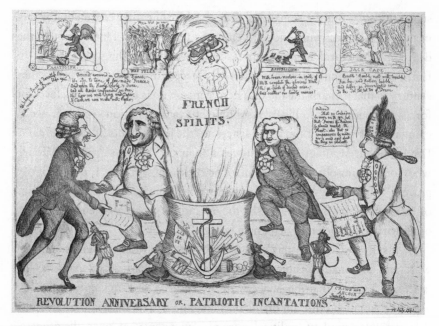

Fig. 4.6. William Dent, *Revolution Anniversary or, Patriotic Incantations* (12 July 1791). BMC 7890. © The Trustees of the British Museum.

celebrate the second anniversary of the fall of the Bastille—the immediate subject of Dent's caricature.[23] On the one hand, Dent's travesty of *Macbeth* suggests just how conducive the witches are to satires concerned less with a particular public figure than with the identities and underhand machinations of parties, factions, or coalitions. In appropriating the cauldron scene Dent offers his readers an ironic portrait of the opposition and equates Franco-phile Whiggism and radicalism with the gleeful malevolence, subversion, and clandestine practices of Shakespeare's weird sisters.[24] His Sheridan, dismissing George III's crown as a mere trinket, punningly sings, "Bauble! Bauble melt with trouble! / Fire burn, and Nation bubble," while Fox adds: "Around! around in Chaotic Dance, / We step to tune of free-made France; / And when the Hurly-burly's done, / And all Ranks confounded in One" (parodying 4.1.10–11, 59–60). The ring dance of the witches, as Fox's words intimate, figures not only the perverse collectivity of revolutionary action but also the erasure of social difference at which such a politics ultimately aims; the anarchic choreography of witchcraft becomes the emblem of egali-tarian ideology.[25] On the other hand, however, this dance is manifestly comic.

Where Priestley carries a copy of Thomas Paine's *Rights of Man*, Sheridan, the politician and theater manager in one, clutches a volume inscribed "Drury's Prompt Book. Cauldron Scene Macbeth." As Bate suggests, the print "may thus be imagined as simultaneously representing a production at Drury Lane and the radicals' preparations of an infernal broth to be consumed at their forthcoming dinner."[26] This reference to the staging of the play establishes the scene as one of farce; these supposed radicals are the all-singing, all-dancing witches conceived by Davenant rather than Shakespeare. There is no revolution here, only a comedy of political agitation that comforts far more than it disconcerts.

Macbeth, as we know, was in many ways *the* go-to text during the 1790s. During a performance of the play in May 1792 the slippage between radical politics and theater imagined by Dent became something of a reality, with sections of the audience at Sheridan's playhouse reported to have struck up a rendition of the revolutionary anthem "Ça Ira."[27] Equally, in his *Political Dictionary* of 1795 the radical Charles Pigott mischievously glossed definitions of the words "lie" and "neck" with apposite quotations from the play.[28] More often, though, the tragedy resonated for those who looked with alarm at events unfolding across the English Channel. In the wake of Louis XVI's execution, Charles James, an officer who had witnessed the outbreak of the Revolution in Lisle, wrote that the bloody scenes of *Macbeth* "should be perpetually before" the public, and throughout the Terror that followed the regicide comparisons of Robespierre to Macbeth were almost commonplace.[29]

At this highly charged moment, as Dent's print suggests, the witches offered an obvious admonitory model of willed sociopolitical disorder and the rule of the disenfranchised. Thomas Ford's *Confusion's Master-Piece: or, Paine's Labour's Lost*, a parody of *Macbeth*'s supernatural scenes, converted the weird sisters into conniving Parisian citizens—"When shall we Three meet again, / And thundering rail against this Reign?" asks the first of them—while a writer of the *Antigallican* described the regicidal French government as having "culled the most anarchical ingredients from the most Democratic Colonies, which they mingled together as the witches of Macbeth, to make 'a deed without a name.' "[30] As is so often the case in late-century political discourse, the origins of this trope can be traced back to Burke. Addressing the Commons in May 1791, he deplored the spread of revolution to the French colonies of St. Domingo and Guadeloupe, where "anarchy, confusion and bloodshed . . . was a general summons for 'Black spirits and white, / Blue Spirits and gray, / Mingle, mingle, mingle.' "[31] Burke's adapted quotation of one of *Macbeth*'s incantatory songs (4.1.44–45), itself interpolated into the 1623 folio text from Thomas Middleton's play *The Witch*, not only demonizes insurrectionary politics but also, as Marcus Wood rightly notes, sutures the perils of miscegenation and Jacobinism.[32] In Burke's racialized reading of the play, one bereft of comedy, the weird sisters threaten to collapse differences of both class and skin color.

These post-1789 allusions and appropriations offer further confirmation, if it were needed, of the familiar account of romantic era *Macbeth* as a typology of revolutionary trauma. But this narrative makes sense only when placed within a broader matrix of comic political appropriation, for the conception of Shakespeare's weird sisters as an archetype of radical collusion dates back to Davenant's adaptation of *Macbeth* in 1663–64, which gave a distinctly Restoration inflection to the play's politics by transforming the witches into grotesque caricatures of the regicides responsible for Charles I's death in 1649. Davenant's witches actively aim at Duncan's assassination and fashion songs from an avowedly republican language, exclaiming, "We should rejoice when good Kings bleed," and "We gain more life by *Duncan*'s death."[33] As in his subsequent reworking of *The Tempest* with Dryden—where the rhetoric of parliamentarianism is given to the oafish, lower-class characters precisely as a means of at once acknowledging and neutralizing it—Davenant's *Macbeth* employs comedy as a vehicle of ideological exorcism and assurance. In giving expression to a regicidal vocabulary only in scenes, and songs, that manifestly eschew the tragic register of the rest of the play, Davenant both staged and disarmed the lingering imaginative purchase of revolutionary politics in the very same theatrical moment. In its exhibition of grotesque bodies in continual, raucous motion, the performance idiom of witchcraft in his adaptation was certainly carnivalesque, but it was so on the terms described by Terry Eagleton rather than Mikhail Bakhtin. That is, the carnival of the weird sisters gave expression to an entirely licensed theater of transgression, "a permissible rupture of hegemony" that reinforced that which it contravened, and not to any kind of destabilizing play.[34] It was this version of the Shakespearean supernatural, in which comedy and conspiracy were tightly imbricated, that the eighteenth century inherited and that graphic satirists readily plundered. The long political history of the weird sisters that lies behind Dent's *Revolution Anniversary*, where the comedy of radical inversion seemingly evacuates the power of the very discord it figures,

begins to come into focus once we understand that the witches were still gleefully singing of bleeding kings at Drury Lane in 1794—and still evoking
laughter for such song.[35]

Perhaps the more surprising dimension to this history—one, again,
that makes more sense when we recognize Davenant's witches as caricatures
of the Civil War parliamentarians—is that satirists of the eighteenth century
coopted the weird sisters just as often to delineate sinister forms of governance as they did to give legible shape to a particular group of recalcitrants.
Even in the 1790s, a moment at which the counterrevolutionary exegesis of
the play was almost irresistible, the antiwar pamphleteer John Fenwick imagined "the people of Great Britain" as a well-intentioned Macbeth duped into
military conflict by the empty prophecies of the Pitt ministry: "Like the
witches that betrayed Macbeth, the minister hailed you by the successive
names and titles with which you were to be adorned. Deliverers of France,
arbitrators of the fate of Europe, and preservers of the peace and social order
of the human race . . . Which of your titles have you worn?"[36] Fenwick's
extended conceit of the British public as Macbeth, which looks back to Elizabeth Montagu's reading of the play as a tragedy of the good man deceived by
malignant power, is somewhat exceptional; but his invocation of the weird
sisters as agents of corrupt institutional power is not. As early as 1743, Horace
Walpole published a verse parody, *The Dear Witches*, that excoriated the
patriot ministers responsible for ousting his father, Robert, from office by
depicting them as the three witches.[37] Similarly, if now also in unequivocally
antiestablishment terms, the Wilkesite parody *The Three Conjurers, a Political
Interlude* (1763) cast as the witches the statesmen who orchestrated John
Wilkes's imprisonment for his scathing criticism of the ministry and Crown
in *North Briton* No. 45. In this parody, George Grenville and the Earls of
Egremont and Halifax work covertly to keep Wilkes incarcerated and to aid
Macboote's (Bute's) endeavors to "Cancel and tear to pieces that great bond
/ Which keeps me pale! that fatal *M——g——a Ch——ta*" (adapting
3.2.50–51).[38] There is a precise politics of literary form here. Unapologeti-
cally confessing on the title page that his piece is "Stolen from Shakespeare,"
the writer posits his parody's seizures from the national poet as an ironic
reflection of the power that Bute and his confederates have unconstitutionally snatched from Parliament and the public. As in Richter's *Tempest*, this is
parody that willfully distorts the integrity of Shakespeare, as embodiment of
the English canon, for the purposes of topical application, and that then

offers its own breach of cultural decorum as a satirical analogue of contemporary political crisis.

Yet the laughter that these satirical prints elicit is invariably shadowed by something much darker. On stage, the sisters might have been figures of comedy, but they inhabited a world that remained stubbornly tragic. In this way, *The Blessings of Peace* invokes *Macbeth* twice over: first in the scatological presence of the farting witch and again in an epigraph that, borrowing Ross's lament, strikes a far more somber note: "Alas poor country! / Almost afraid to know itself" (4.3.167–68). The humor of the carnivalesque body collides with tragic syntax of political catastrophe. Equally, in the parodic incantations of *The Cauldron—or Shakespeare Travestie* Lord Liverpool sings that to "make great Macbeth single" the trio must "mingle" the "Earth of Snuffy from the grave" with the "Blood of Radicals," while Lord Sidmouth chants:

> Cats, that draw the Soldiers blood,
> Chains, that bind the brave and good,
> Tongue of slander, Eye of hate,
> Mix—and now our charm's complete.

Even as the outlandish, brightly cultured accouterments of the statesmen-cum-witches maintain a tone of farce, the concatenation of disquieting images here—decomposition, execution, flagellation (Sidmouth also clutches the "cats"), incarceration—unfolds a picture of an administration that routinely trades in pain and suffering. "Old Snuffy" was the soubriquet of Queen Charlotte, George's mother, who had died in 1818, while the radicals to whom Liverpool refers were Arthur Thistlewood and the four other Cato Street conspirators executed in May 1820 (a man hanging limply from a gallows can be seen amid the cauldron's flames). In the strange, necrotic entwining of royal and radical bodies enacted in Liverpool's song, the satirist of *The Cauldron* overlays sardonic references to the ministry's victimization of a popular queen and to its suppression of democratic radicalism, reading both policies as confirmation of the government's ruthless fortification of the political establishment. As these prints suggest, it was finally *Macbeth*'s interpolation of comedy into tragedy that made it such a fertile source for graphic satire, a form, after all, that routinely plays at the boundary between the sublime and the ridiculous. In political prints that often hinge on the constitutive friction between tragedy and comedy, *Macbeth*'s scenes of witchcraft offer a theater of farce nested at the center of high political drama.

It is in Dent's *Revolution Anniversary* that the comedy of conspiracy is most conspicuously freighted, and complicated, by the sense of tragedy—and history. At the back of this scene hang four pictures, each one a gloss on the figure at that moment dancing before and below it. Priestley and Towers stand under images of "Fanaticism" and "Republicanism," while the pictures above Fox and Sheridan, respectively, show Wat Tyler, leader of the 1381 Peasants' Revolt, addressing a mob and Jack Cade, head of the rebellion in 1450, overseeing the slaughter of a retreating crowd. Comic capering here juxtaposes a history of popular uprising; the farce of present revolution clashes with the bloody scenes of plebeian rebellions past; radicalism is comically neutralized only to be aligned with a history of violence that once more renders it unsettlingly possible.[39] In prints such as Dent's we find distilled both the complex generic status of *Macbeth* in the eighteenth century and the political valency of its specific, awkward kind of tragicomedy.

"Unreal Mockery": Nation, Gender, and the Comedy of Vision

Each of the *Macbeth* parodies at which we've looked thus far claims to disclose otherwise concealed, or at least not clearly apprehended, political alliances and stratagems. The weird sisters are, after all, figures whose influence finally resides in deception and illusion. They wield authority only over those who are too quick to accept promises and appearances that are, as Francis Gentleman worried, "well calculated to mislead credulity."[40] Yet, on occasion, graphic satirists engage at a far deeper and more critical level with *Macbeth*'s texture of doubt and equivocality by appropriating the play specifically as a drama about the manifold difficulties of seeing, judging, and knowing in a world of eroded certainties, ghostly presences, and sexual ambiguity. Here, I consider just three such prints, two by Gillray and a much later one by Theodore Lane. Some two hundred years before scholars such as Huston Diehl understood the play to be "centrally concerned with the problematics of vision" and as "presenting all kinds of ambiguous 'sights,' " these caricatures satirically harness *Macbeth*'s exploration of illusion and spectacle, and they do so in ways that register the intricate political relations between visuality, gender, and nationhood, both in Shakespeare's text and in their own cultural moment.[41]

I begin with Gillray's 1803 caricature *A Phantasmagoria;—Scene— Conjuring up an Armed Skeleton* (fig. 4.7) because at first glance, as another

A PHANTASMAGORIA ;— Scene *—Conjuring up an Armed-Skeleton .*

Fig. 4.7. James Gillray, *A Phantasmagoria;—Scene—Conjuring up an Armed Skeleton* (Hannah Humphrey, 5 January 1803). BMC 9962. By permission of the Folger Shakespeare Library.

parody of act 4, scene 1, it takes us to what is now recognizable satirical territory. A mordant response to the fiscal and cultural costs of the Peace of Amiens, the treaty that brought a brief cessation of hostilities between Britain and France in 1802–3, Gillray's print depicts Prime Minister Henry

Addington, Foreign Secretary Lord Hawkesbury (later Lord Liverpool), and Charles Fox, who endorsed the peace from the opposition benches, as the three witches. The melancholic Hawkesbury wantonly casts into the fire papers inscribed with the names not only of the territories from which Britain had withdrawn its troops (Egypt) or ceded its claims (the West Indies, Malta, the Cape Colony) in accordance with the treaty, but also those of further regions—the British Isles, Ireland, Gibraltar, the "Dominion of the Sea"— that, Gillray suggests, have been left critically vulnerable to Napoleonic attack by the excessively generous terms of the peace. Addington, meanwhile, spoons guineas from a sack labeled "To make the Gruel Thick & Slab" (4.1.32) into the cauldron, where they join the dismembered limbs of the British lion, the lifeless head of which lies discarded in the foreground, where it serves as a perch for a French cockerel. This infernal stew generates a thick billow of smoke, which reads "PEACE," through which the skeletal specter of Britannia, armed with her trident and shield, rises up. The government, this print contends, has willfully sacrificed the nation—boiling down its fiscal and military capacities, its cultural identity—to create the conditions for peace. Ministerial and radical readings of the witches are here folded into one image, for the three statesmen all sport tricolor ribbons: Addington is at once the premier who conspires against his people and the Francophile radical bent on treasonously undermining the British state.

Both the comic transvestism of this scene—the statesmen are all dressed as old woman—and its particular symbolic economy of cauldron, fire, broth, and conjured spirits are familiar to us, but Gillray significantly complicates such parodic conventions in his introduction of a second strand of cultural citation. The phantasmagoria was an electrifying new mode of theatrical spectacle brought from Paris to London, and specifically to the Lyceum Theatre, by its creator, Paul de Philipsthal, in October 1801. Employing an arrangement of lenses and mirrors, Philipsthal projected on to a transparent screen a sequence of images that appeared to materialize, move, and vanish before astonished spectators.[42] This magic lantern show was an immediate success, but Philipsthal was all too aware of the concerns that invariably shadowed spectacular performances in the period, in particular that they enthralled or seduced audiences into experiences of sensory over-load and so negated their potential for rational—and ethical—engagement.[43] Such anxieties were only amplified in cases of gothic spectacularity, with its dependency on a repertoire of ghosts and demons, as is suggested by

Gentleman's objections to *Macbeth* on the grounds that it tended to overwork the imagination and "impress superstitious feelings and fears upon weak minds." Philipsthal thus sought to forestall criticism along these lines by positing his phantasmagoria as a form of theater that instructed as much as it amused. As an advertisement in the *Morning Post* averred:

> This and every Evening will be Opened to the Public the Grand
> CABINET of OPTICAL and MECHANICAL EFFECTS; in which will
> be produced the Phantoms or Apparitions of the Dead or Absent,
> in a way more completely illusive than has ever been offered to
> the eye in a public Theatre, as the objects freely originate in the air,
> and unfold themselves under various forms and sizes, such as imagi-
> nation alone has hitherto painted them. . . . This SPECTROLOGY,
> which professes to expose the practices of artful imposters and
> pretended Exorcists, and to open the eyes of those who still foster an
> absurd belief in GHOSTS, or DISEMBODIED SPIRITS, will, it is
> presumed, afford also the spectator an interesting and pleasing
> Entertainment.[44]

In conjoining the seemingly antithetical vocabularies of popular entertainment and Enlightenment empiricism, this description reminds us of the porous distinction between the experimental scientist and the popular conjuror that, as Barbara Maria Stafford has shown, so troubled this period. Knowingly juxtaposing a new, sophisticated technology of "complete illusion" with outmoded shibboleths that upheld the reality of a spirit world of specters and ghouls, the advertisement maintains that the convincing and immersive fantasy of the phantasmagoria operates as an effective antidote to such fallacious beliefs, exposing the means by which the eye and the mind might be tricked into taking fiction for reality.[45]

Gillray makes complex use of this new cultural form. On one level, his parody of *Macbeth* visually equates the politics of peace with superstition and necromantic practices and, in turn, like many satirists before him, derisively likens such pagan ritual to the supposed peril of Catholic doctrine and ceremony; as Stafford points out, the link between Catholicism, magic tricks, and the occult was a deep one at this time.[46] In the foreground of the caricature William Wilberforce—in fact, an Evangelical—is shown dressed in a monk's cowl, kneeling before the apparition, and clutching a book from which he recites a "Hymn of Peace." The Treaty of Amiens, Gillray implies, is a disturbingly sacrificial rite that gives up the nation's material possessions in an attempt to grasp at something utterly chimerical. But this scene is only one part of the caricature, for beyond the bounds of its oval frame Gillray give us the flat, monochrome surface of a brick wall. The central image is revealed to be no more than a phantasmagoric projection. Like Philipsthal, the satirist pits the modern against the archaic or illusory, first taking up *Macbeth* to cast the peacemakers as witches and then, through his invocation of the phantasmagoria, exposing these witches as figures of obsolescence and fraud. Gillray shows peace to be little more than a sham that is "well calculated to mislead credulity."

On this reading, Gillray posits caricature as a modern technology of viewing akin to the phantasmagoria. Both media purport to "open the eyes" of their consumers, teaching them to parse the visual world more adeptly and cautiously. As Joseph Monteyne argues, eighteenth-century graphic satire repeatedly employs the motif of the magic lantern in ways that elicit comparison between the caricature and the light show as commensurate modes of image presentation, modes that draw attention to their own materiality and representedness.[47] Yet, for this very reason, Gillray's phantasmagoric framing of his *Macbeth* travesty can be read not only as a means of debunking the Peace of Amiens as a dangerous delusion but also as a gesture that troubles his own satire by calling upon its readers to recognize caricature as but one more distortion of reality. In other words, by revealing the print's central image to be a projection—or, further still, a simulacrum of a projection— Gillray fosters a hermeneutic of suspicion that applies as much to the terms of his own Shakespearean parody as to the politicians that this parody lampoons. The relationship between the two theatrical events that this print appropriates, *Macbeth* and the phantasmagoria, suddenly becomes one of tension rather than complementarity.

And this friction is crucial to the print's satiric operations. Shakespeare was *the* national poet, the epitome of British cultural values and supremacy; Philipsthal's phantasmagoria, by contrast, was understood to pose a threat to the native tradition of serious drama, both as a French import and as a form of popular, illegitimate spectacle, of "degenerate taste," as one contemporary prologue put it.[48] The satirical ploy here is similar to that of Richter's provocative caricature of Prospero as a Machiavellian pope and *The Three Conjurors'* announcement of its own theft of Shakespeare. In superimposing the phantasmagoria onto *Macbeth,* and so destabilizing the network of

meaning established by this Shakespearean reference, Gillray's print ironically enacts the very incursion of French culture and ideology into British
society—an incursion facilitated by peace—that it cautions its audience
against. In permitting Shakespeare to be contaminated by that which is
culturally other (the foreign, the popular, the commercial), *A Phantasmagoria* seems to stage a kind of literary vandalism in order to signal the cultural
damage that peace will involve. I use the word *seems* here because readers of
the print are finally deprived of any secure position from which to make
sense of Gillray's satire. Does it discredit the peace, reading the treaty as a
mere fantasy orchestrated by buffoonish crossed-dressed politicians, or does
it rather debunk that very reading of events, outing the parody it embeds as
a clever but misleading picture? Ultimately, I'd suggest, it is precisely on this
irresolvable ambiguity that Gillray's overarching satirical point hinges. To
this extent, even as he muddies the cultural boundaries between high and low,
native and foreign, Gillray looks to Shakespeare rather than Philipsthal for
his master trope. *A Phantasmagoria* rejects the claim to clear-sightedness, the
confident investment in the efficacy of vision, that underwrite Philipsthal's
"spectrology." Just as *Macbeth*, in Stuart Clark's words, "offers visual uncertainty *itself* as an accompaniment to political treason and moral turmoil," so
this print thematizes equivocation and corrosive doubt as themselves the
corollaries of a pacificatory political regime.[49]

In Gillray's earlier *Wierd-Sisters; Ministers of Darkness; Minions of the
Moon* (fig. 4.8), surely the best known of all eighteenth-century print parodies of *Macbeth*, this use of uncertainty as a structuring satirical device is
played out through the language of gender. A late response to the Regency
Crisis, the caricature shows the home secretary Henry Dundas and the lord
chancellor Edward Thurlow on either side of Pitt the Younger as the witches
of Henry Fuseli's iconic painting of act 1, scene 3 (1783), as Gillray again
offers a highly intermedial parody that approaches Shakespeare through and
alongside a further cultural form. Conspiratorial alliance remains the dominant motif. *Wierd-Sisters* suggests that the ministerial trio seek self-servingly
to safeguard George III's throne, and thus guarantee their own parliamentary ascendancy, regardless of the constitutional ramifications of the king's
fragile mental health. Two further details satirically gloss this political expediency. First, extending his network of allusions still further, Gillray cites
Falstaff's distinction in *1 Henry IV* between "gentlemen of the shade, minions
of the moon" and "men of good government" (1.2.26–27), the inference

Fig. 4.8. James Gillray, *Wierd-Sisters; Ministers of Darkness; Minions of the Moon* (Hannah Humphrey, 23 December 1791). BMC 7937. Courtesy of The Lewis Walpole Library, Yale University.

being, as Bate observes, that the three statesmen are "thieves, men of bad government."[50] Second, Pitt's yellow hood, caught by the wind, clearly resembles a jester's cap. The gibe is not simply that the prime minister's conduct is imprudent but perhaps also, implicitly, that he performs the Fool to George III's mad Lear.

What interests me, though, is the particular complexity generated by the caricature's epigraph, which quotes Banquo's description of the weird sisters' ghastly appearance: "They should be Women!—and yet their beards forbid us to interpret,—that they are so" (1.3.43–45). The quotation directs the reader's attention to the faces of Pitt, Dundas, and Thurlow, yet Gillray has given each of them no more than a few, barely visible tufts of hair around the mouth; they are shown to be stroking beards that do not exist. This discrepancy between word and image insinuates that the ministers *are* women or, rather, that they are neither quite male nor female. As in *A Phantasmagoria,* we, the audience, are confronted with a series of allusive gestures that are deliberately and constitutively misaligned and that seem designed to disorient us. As we've seen, Gillray is no by means the only caricaturist of the period to mine the satirical potential of the witches' androgyny or theatrical transvestism, but he does politically code this performance of gender in a new way. Here, their liminal sexuality is not merely comic; it is also an analogue of political breakdown, of a government that works for its own interests rather than those of the nation. Opponents of Pitt, who never married, routinely insinuated his homosexuality, but *Wierd-Sisters*, like so many other parodies of *Macbeth*'s witches, is concerned with diagnosing the problems of the group or institution, not those of the individual.[51] Gillray's satire calls into question the traditional Whiggish paradigm of parliamentary masculinity that rested on the classical republican understanding of virtue and disinterestedness as the prerequisites of high political office and civic responsibility. Of course, as Martin Myrone notes, this understanding was besieged from all sides in a century of social change and commercialization (think back to the macaronis of Chapter 2), but this matrix of cultural contestation only makes Gillray's marshaling of gender as a language of political crisis all the more resonant.[52] In *Wierd-Sisters* the inefficacy or illegitimacy of policy renders its architects, absurdly and disturbingly, less than men.

Gillray takes his cue in this regard not only from the cross-dressing antics of the witches on the contemporary stage but also from their circulation within the discourse of the gothic, which toward the end of the century both looked to the Shakespearean canon for legitimizing antecedents and also renewed interest in the supernatural scenes of plays such as *Macbeth* and *Hamlet* as moments of genuine terror and irrationality. For Madame de Staël, writing in 1800, the weird sisters were "phantoms of the imagination" who showed that there was "always something philosophical in the supernatural employed by Shakespeare."[53] Both *A Phantasmagoria* and *Wierd-Sisters* are doubled parodies: they engage satirically not only with *Macbeth* but additionally with a specific manifestation of gothic culture—Philipsthal's spectacular light show, Fuseli's painting—and their political thematization of ambiguity is part of this parodic dialogue with gothicism. Gillray's mock dedication at the top of *Wierd-Sisters* explicitly acknowledges this dimension of his satire: "To H: Fuzelli Esqr this attempt in the Caricatura-Sublime, is respectfully dedicated." I will consider the rich suggestiveness of this coinage, "Caricatura-Sublime," in the next chapter; what's important here is that the dedication evinces Gillray's commitment to comically—and critically—repurposing the visual syntax of Fuseli's Shakespeare paintings, which are populated with unreal, equivocal, and strangely sexualized beings.

Reviewing Fuseli's *Weird Sisters* in 1783, the *Morning Post* commented on the artist's "success in pieces of *deformed nature*," and it is exactly this facet of Fuseli's art that Gillray seizes upon.[54] Politically parodying Fuseli's disorienting aesthetics of liminality and sexual aberrance, and mischievously colliding word against image, Gillray once more leaves viewers of his ministerial witches, like Macbeth, "smothered in surmise" and knowing only that "nothing is / But what is not" (1.3.140–41).

Moreover, Gillray's concern with manliness, or rather the lack thereof, is entwined with his interest in transgressive femininity. In the print, Pitt, Dundas, and Thurlow gaze anxiously toward the illuminated crescent of the moon, which carries the profile of Queen Charlotte and in turn encloses the darkened, slumbering head of George III. Gillray at once visually puns on the king's "lunar-cy" and implies that his consort now controls the throne. This was an allegation repeatedly voiced by the opposition in 1788–89; Burke, for one, was convinced of "the power and predominance of the Queen in this province."[55] The emasculation of the three politicians is thus an ironic reflection not only of their failure to adhere to the ideals of statesmanship but also of their willingness to subject themselves to female rule, to serve as "minions of the moon." And in depicting the queen as the moon, Gillray associates her with Hecate, the goddess of witchcraft and the moon who twice appears in *Macbeth* (likely in interpolations by Middleton); a mythological dictionary of 1779 states that Hecate is so called only "in the infernal regions" and that she is "Luna in heaven, and Diana on earth."[56] For all its troping of equivocality, *Wierd-Sisters* is quiet but insistent in its exposure and castigation of female political influence. Both in this print and in *A Phantasmagoria* political crisis is imagined in terms of emasculated statesmen subordinating themselves to female figures that are decidedly otherworldly and grotesque. Where the decayed Britannia of the later print inverts the allegory of the female form, replacing the beautiful female body as symbolic of national strength with the putrid corpse as symbolic of national dissolution, the Hecate-like Charlotte of the earlier caricature threatens to place the feminine at the center of the political world as something more than just an abstraction.[57]

The misogyny implicit to the satire of *Wierd-Sisters* is not without precedent in parodies of *Macbeth*. *The Gypsy's Triumph* of 1754 couples femininity and criminality by depicting the alleged abductor Mary Squires as a witch who also recites lines spoken by Tamora in *Titus Andronicus,* while anti-Bute satires of the early 1760s cast the Dowager Princess of Wales as a witch (*The Tempest and Enchanted Island*) or as Hecate (*The Three Conjurers*) to her beloved "Macboote."[58] Yet, given the ferocity with which graphic satirists of the eighteenth century policed the gendered boundaries of the public sphere—the excoriation of the Duchess of Devonshire for canvassing on behalf of Fox in 1784 stands out—it's somewhat surprising that *Macbeth* was not more regularly coopted as a typology of political womanhood.[59] Lady Macbeth, in particular, is conspicuously absent from the intertextual vocabulary of eighteenth-century political satire. In 1768 a Massachusetts patriot cited her as the unnatural mother that Britain, in its treatment of the American colonies, had come to resemble, and in 1798 Richard Polwhele indirectly quoted her in the title of his poem *The Unsex'd Females,* a reactionary bludgeoning of Mary Wollstonecraft's radical feminism.[60] But no political parody of the period, graphic or textual, goes so far as to cast an identifiable woman as Lady Macbeth.

This was to change in 1821 when Theodore Lane represented Queen Caroline as Lady Macbeth in *The Whole Truth, or John Bull with his Eyes Opened* (fig. 4.9), a caricature published by George Humphrey, the loyalist print seller then mounting a concerted satirical campaign against the queen, who had returned to London in 1820 to claim her title as consort. Like Gillray's two *Macbeth* parodies, Lane's *Whole Truth* takes up Shakespeare's play as a political exploration of the vicissitudes of sight, but in distinct contrast to *Wierd-Sisters* and *A Phantasmagoria,* his satire rests firmly on the prospect of efficacious vision. In a travesty of the sleepwalking scene (5.1), Lane shows Caroline standing in the middle of a city street, clutching a candle, and exclaiming:

> Out damned spots, I say!
> One, two, ——— fie! fie!
> All the perfumes of Arabia will not sweeten me!
> Abroad! Abroad! What's done can't be undone! (adapting 5.1.33,
> 48–49, 65)

These "spots" are not imaginary bloodstains but rather the pictures that adorn her nightgown and that represent the men with whom she stood accused of having sexual liaisons.

Lane casts Queen Caroline as a political woman of ruthless ambition, a character whose willful "unsexing" of herself in pursuit of power and privilege disturbed the period's critics; Shakespearean editor George Steevens

Fig. 4.9. Theodore Lane, *The Whole Truth, or John Bull with his Eyes Opened* (George Humphrey, 1 Feb. 1821). © National Portrait Gallery, London.

described Lady Macbeth as "depraved," while the playwright Richard Cumberland thought her "the auxiliary of the witches."[61] But, more precisely, Lane's composition evokes the many images of Sarah Siddons in this scene, most especially the illustration included in John Bell's 1784 edition of the play and often reproduced thereafter (fig. 4.10). Siddons retired from the stage in 1812 but, in her early sixties, made a brief comeback as Lady Macbeth in 1816–17, at the request of Princess Charlotte (Caroline's daughter). Critics such as Hazlitt considered her return an unmitigated disappointment. "We certainly thought her performance inferior to what it used to be," Hazlitt wrote in the *Examiner:* "She speaks too slow, and her manner has not that decided, sweeping majesty, which used to characterise her as the Muse of Tragedy herself."[62] Cast not simply as Lady Macbeth but more specifically as Siddons's Lady Macbeth, Caroline is a woman who has outstayed her welcome on the public stage, a figure who no longer possesses the requisite "majesty" to play a queen; like the witches, she is out of her time. Shadowed by the figure of Siddons, Caroline is the would-be tragic heroine who now inhabits a comedy born of her own awkward posturing.

Act 5.   MACBETH.   *Line 33.*

J.Rhamberg del.   *Delattre fc.*

Mrs SIDDONS in LADY MACBETH.

"Yet here's a Spot."

Printed for John Bell, British Library London: Aug.t 26.1784.

Fig. 4.10. Jean Marie Delattre, after J. H. Ramberg, *Mrs Siddons in Lady Macbeth* (John Bell, 1784). © Victoria and Albert Museum, London.

The Whole Truth locates its readers at a specific point in the play's action: Lady Macbeth's *final* scene. It is the moment not only at which she is psychologically crushed by the guilt of her past crimes but, more tellingly, of her last appearance before the audience, and Lane presses this point home by closing the lines at the foot of his print with the ironic stage direction, "Finale. Exit with a Flourish!" As in satires such as *The Cauldron,* Lane's engagement with *Macbeth* is animated by questions of emplotment and prophecy, but this print is as much about the future of its public as it is about the future of the queen. Behind Caroline, emerging from a shop called "Time & Common-Sense Occulists," the figure of John Bull observes the scene of shame before him with manifest horror. His lines, again given beneath the caricature's title, recycle Hamlet's exhortation to Ophelia—"To a Nunnery Go! To a Nunnery! a Nunnery!" (*Hamlet,* 3.1.141)—and so both mobilize a second Shakespearean image of female hysteria, one that will likewise prove fatal, and also invoke Ophelia's innocence and chastity as an ironic counterpoint to Caroline's supposed promiscuity. Equally, Bull's position at the rear of this scene, seeing but unseen, aligns him with the Doctor in *Macbeth,* who understands that "unnatural deeds / Do breed unnatural troubles" (5.1.68–69). In this imagined moment of political anagnorisis John Bull, and the public he embodies, has his "eyes opened" and at last recognizes the popular Caroline for what she truly is. Like *A Phantasmagoria, The Whole Truth* aligns its own satire with a modern technology of vision that promises to correct defective vision and, as a corollary, faulty judgment; unlike Gillray's caricature, however, this self-alignment is not made within a space of proliferating ironies. "NB. Films expeditiously removed," proclaims the sign above the oculist's shop. Enjoining its audience to look more carefully, Lane's caricature overwrites the pervasive epistemological doubt of *Macbeth* with the binaries of right and wrong, of man and woman; it reads the play as modeling a politics of clear-sightedness in which—contra Gillray—seeing is knowing and the male gaze will always finally discern the dangers of aberrant womanhood. It is, as recent cartoons of Hillary Clinton and Cherie Blair as Lady Macbeth readily attest, a version of Shakespeare's play, of *Macbeth* as comedy, that continues to haunt our own political discourses.[63]

Coda: Caricature, Shakespeare, and Popular Culture

In their sheer number, the graphic satirical parodies of *The Tempest* and *Macbeth* discussed in this chapter and the last can leave us in no doubt that, as Frans De Bruyn puts it, "Shakespeare had become an indispensable part of the political lexicon" by the close of the eighteenth century.[64] Yet the question of what constituency or constituencies of readers were likely conversant in this language remains difficult, if not impossibly vexed, and it is for this reason that I've deferred consideration of it until now. I make no claims here to resolve the historical and conceptual conundrums encompassed by the topic of Shakespeare and popular culture, but I do wish to make something of an intervention in how we understand the changing status and cultural transmission of Shakespeare in the later eighteenth century and, more especially, how we position Shakespearean caricatures in relation to that broader cultural trend.

The already thorny issue of caricature's readership is particularly complicated in the case of Shakespearean prints. Miltonic caricatures, as we shall see shortly, often assume a depth of knowledge of *Paradise Lost*—and also of the poem's role as a formative text in the development of aesthetics and literary criticism—that only the most well-read could have possessed. By contrast, as I suggest in Chapter 6, satirical prints that take up *Gulliver's Travels* mine a text that had a significantly dispersed presence across the hierarchies of print and that, at least in its first two parts, lent itself to striking and ostensibly simple visual juxtapositions of a kind appreciable by a wide range of readers. Shakespeare, though, straddles seemingly opposed cultural and ideological domains; he is at once the embodiment of high cultural values and a writer and icon who has shaped, and continues to shape, various formations of popular culture in profound ways.[65] Such doubleness was especially pronounced in the eighteenth century, for this was the period in which a discernably modern "Shakespeare" and a recognizable Shakespeare industry were being vigorously constructed. In navigating the textual and performance archives of the Georgian era, Shakespeare often seems less an individual author than an entire field of cultural contestation. We find ourselves confronted, as Michael Dobson notes, by "a series of alternative Shakespeares."[66]

What is beyond dispute is that the audience for Shakespeare was expanding from the second half of the century onward. By the first decades of the nineteenth century, and with more affordable copies of the individual plays available, Shakespeare's works began to permeate popular culture in increasingly dynamic ways. Jane Moody has drawn our attention to the rise of "illegitimate" Shakespeare at this time, as the minor playhouses, which were legally prohibited from staging the canon of spoken-word drama, used music, pantomime, and spectacular dramaturgy to mount Shakespearean adaptations that self-consciously struck at elite practices and values and that brought the bard to a wider public.[67] Shakespeare burlesques were, as Richard Schoch's study of the form makes clear, a rich and even virtuosic manifestation of late Georgian and Victorian popular culture.[68] By the tercentenary of his birth in 1864, Andrew Murphy tells us, Shakespeare had gained a genuinely working-class readership.[69]

But, from the vantage point of the material under consideration in this book, most of these developments—or at least their consolidation—lie ahead, and it would be a mistake to regard Shakespearean political caricature as a meaningful manifestation of this efflorescence of popular Shakespeare, let alone as one of its most distinctive markers.[70] The prints of *The Tempest* and *Macbeth* at which we have looked generally require far more than a passing familiarity with the scenes invoked and parodied. It's worth restating the distinction between allusion and parody I offered early in this book: where the first, which is by definition brief and local, may often be missed by a reader without significant detriment to her or his reading experience or understanding, the second demands comprehensive recognition of the text it ironically inhabits and distorts. The success of anthologies such as William Dodd's *Beauties of Shakespeare* (1752) goes some way toward explaining the increasing quotability of Shakespeare in the eighteenth century, but this kind of anthologization serves to decontextualize lines and phrases; it runs counter to the imperatives of parody, which relies precisely on a reader's appreciation of entire scenes or works.[71] In the case of plays, this appreciation might be acquired as much by watching as by reading, and we have seen just how far caricatures of the weird sisters assume knowledge of stage conventions, of the performed text as much as the printed text. Yet in the 1780s or 1790s the cheapest seat at Drury Lane cost a shilling, a day's pay for many laborers, and would have been within the regular means of only the most affluent artisans. Writing in 1825, John Clare lamented that "the common people" knew of "the name of Shakespeare as a great play writer" only because they had seen it on "the bills of strolling-players."[72]

Ultimately, in their detail, irony, and political exegesis, the Shakespearean parodies of graphic satire are no easier to read or decode than the plays themselves. Even against a backdrop of increased readership, these prints delight in interpretative games and expect a level of cultural literacy that would have limited their audience. This is not to claim them to be wholly elitist—an argument as flawed as its opposite—but it is soundly to reject the conception that Shakespearean political caricature is somehow Shakespeare for everyone. Given the absence of empirical data we cannot know how many people knew *The Tempest* from first to last line in Georgian Britain; nor can we know how many people looked at and understood graphic satirical appropriations of that play. But rather than moving from the acritical and ahistorical assumption that caricature is a popular cultural form and that Shakespearean caricature therefore is popular Shakespeare (an argument that all too quickly becomes circular), we might legitimately point to the extent and complexity of Shakespearean parody in later Georgian graphic satire as a striking indication of how caricature quite self-consciously occupies the domain of high culture.

Let me offer two important, if fairly obvious, qualifications. First, to speak of Shakespeare's works in general is itself a simplification. Just as the different plays, and scenes, carried different political associations, so too did they vary markedly in their cultural prominence. Act 3, scene 2 of *The Tempest*, which is closely parodied in William Dent's *Reynard's Hope* (see fig. 3.2), would not have been as widely recognized as the cauldron sequence of *Macbeth*, which was regularly represented in illustrations and paintings of the period.[73] Second, understanding is, of course, a matter of degrees. A reader might well register that a print such as *The Cauldron—or Shakespeare Travestie* invokes *Macbeth* (not least because the title prompts such recognition) without necessarily grasping the finer nuances of the satire's engagement with and inversion of the textual moment in question.

To get a better purchase on these issues we can helpfully turn to the example of Alderman John Boydell's Shakespeare Gallery, along with Gillray's well-known critique of that project in his 1789 print *Shakespeare-Sacrificed;—or—The Offering to Avarice* (fig. 4.11). Boydell, a successful print seller, engraver, and three-time lord mayor of London, opened his gallery of Shakespeare paintings—which included works by the likes of Joshua Reynolds, Henry Fuseli, and James Barry—in Pall Mall in 1789. The ambitious scheme largely rested on a plan to publish by subscription a lavish, multivolume edition of the *Works* that was to be embellished with engravings of the gallery's paintings, and these prints were also to be sold separately. Boydell's venture was a commercial failure, not least because European war depressed the Continental print market, and his collection of paintings was sold by lottery in 1805, but scholars generally agree that the Shakespeare Gallery is significant for the manner in which it consciously sought to democratize both exhibition culture and Shakespeare. "The formulation of the Shakespeare Gallery as an egalitarian space . . . pervaded the press criticism," writes Rosie Dias: it "came increasingly to be seen as a democratic space indicative of English liberty."[74] For now, I want to put aside the important matter of this Shakespearean nationalism, a topic I return to in my final chapter. Here, I'm rather interested in the Shakespeare Gallery as a turn-of-the-century project that was manifestly concerned with questions of cultural access and audience. Boydell's Shakespeare, as Christopher Rovee and others have argued, was very much a Shakespeare for the bourgeoisie; Boydell's appeal to the middle classes "seemed downright revolutionary" in 1789.[75] The Shakespeare Gallery provided educated bourgeois Londoners with a site in which they could mimic—acquire—the cultural habits and capital of their social betters. And the exhibition catalog, compiled by Humphry Repton and given to all admitted to the gallery, provides an insight into just how familiar these consumers likely were with the Shakespearean canon, for the descriptions of the pictures were accompanied by lengthy excerpts, often extending

Fig. 4.11. James Gillray, *Shakespeare-Sacrificed;—or—The Offering to Avarice* (Hannah Humphrey, 20 June 1789). BMC 7584. Courtesy of The Lewis Walpole Library, Yale University.

to two or three pages, from the scenes depicted in the paintings.[76] The catalog was a kind of anthology. Certainly this practice brings into the foreground the ekphrastic nature of Boydell's enterprise, and more work needs to be undertaken to probe the verbal-visual play (and tension) that must have constituted a central part of the gallery's viewing experience. But, on a mundane level, the apposite portions of text served a utilitarian function: the catalog was a necessary hermeneutic aid for a public who by and large were not so deeply familiar with Shakespeare's plays that they could encounter cold a series of paintings that operated at a precise, scenic level.[77]

Consumers of Shakespearean political caricatures had no such help. In the comforts of their own home they might certainly consult an edition of the *Works*, presuming they owned one, but it's clear that the prints we have examined expect their readers to be able immediately to recall not just lines but entire scenes. Occasionally, prints facilitate this process of recollection and recognition by noting the act and scene numbers in question, and, of course, prints provide mnemonic cues for readers by way of textual (mis)quotation. However, it remains the case that, in contrast to the patrons of the Shakespeare Gallery, who moved through its space with Repton's catalog in (and on) hand, graphic satire's audience had comparatively little support to facilitate their recognition of a particular parody's moment of choice—and this in a medium that, unlike the Boydell paintings, actively distorts the plays, comically maps them onto the contemporary political landscape, and sometimes travesties multiple scenes (even multiple plays) within the discursive space of a single image.

In his excoriation of Boydell, Gillray denounces the strident commercialism that lay, thinly veiled, beneath the gallery's rhetoric of artistic patronage, literary prestige, and patriotism. But at the same time, *Shakespeare-Sacrificed* elicits the difficulties of reading that attend caricature's parodic architecture and predilection for cultural citation and suggests how such difficulty could be harnessed as part of a strategy of cultural demarcation. Gillray shows the alderman burning Shakespeare's plays as an oblation to Avarice, a grizzled, impish creature who is perched atop a giant, upright volume labeled "List of subscribers to the Sacrifice." Avarice carries two bulging sacks of cash under his arms, while a young boy with a peacock-feather headdress, symbolizing Vanity, stands on his shoulders and blows a bubble of "Immorality" from a pipe. In the center of the image, the conflagration of texts sends up plumes of smoke that partly obscure the Westminster Abbey monument to Shakespeare, only the bottom half of which is visible; the profit imperative effaces the bard. The thick swirls of smoke at the periphery of the print, meanwhile, are populated by an abundance of Shakespearean characters as they appear in the Boydell paintings. Gillray isolates and exaggerates specific details of the pictures; decontextualized and tightly juxtaposed, they appear absurd. Above the alderman, Bottom and Lear, both from Fuseli's contributions, are crushed together with Reynolds's depiction of the death of Cardinal Beaufort (*2 Henry VI*) and James North-cote's portrayal of Queen Elizabeth cradling the newborn prince (*3 Henry VI*); at the top of the print, Gillray reproduces figures and limbs from John Opie's rendering of act 2, scene 2 of *The Winter's Tale*, with the infant Perdita accompanied by a floating helmet and an equally disembodied arm of Leontes; and on the right, *Henry VI*'s Earl of Warwick (after Josiah Boydell), the Ghost of Hamlet, and the weird sisters (both Fuseli) all jostle for atten-tion. The presence of the witches suggests that, in its ironic depiction of dark rites, we might read this print as an elaborate allusion to, and certainly inspired by, *Macbeth*'s cauldron scene.

This satire has rightly been understood as personal. Gillray still harbored aspirations as a fine-art engraver and had tendered his services to Boydell in 1788 only to be embarrassingly rebuffed.[78] Yet the print is far more than an act of revenge. As Jonathan Bate has shown in an extended close reading of the caricature, Gillray's cast of Shakespearean figures forensically spoofs the muddled aesthetic codes of the gallery and recycles its visual tropes precisely in order to expose the derivativeness of the pictures on show. Gillray not only borrows from Boydell's exhibition but also organizes these local details within a compositional frame that travesties and inverts Robert Edge Pine's 1784 painting *Garrick Delivering His Ode to Shakespeare*, which was engraved by Caroline Watson in a print published by Boydell. *Shakespeare-Sacrificed*, Bate contends, must thus be seen as "a parodic history painting which argues that the Shakespeare Gallery is a parody of true history painting."[79]

To this persuasive interpretation I would add that Gillray's print works hard to distinguish the cultural grammar and audience of its own form, parodic caricature, from those of the Shakespeare Gallery. Bate's lengthy and erudite exegesis, which runs to seven pages and even includes a diagram, high-lights the challenge that confronts the readers of *Shakespeare-Sacrificed*. Gillray expects his audience to parse multiple planes of allusion—to the plays, to the various Boydell paintings, to Pine's picture of Garrick—and to register confluences and frictions across these planes. Certainly, its early readers strug-gled with the print's bewildering citational density. The caricature had origi-nally been issued only as an uncolored etching, and in 1800 John Sneyd wrote to the satirist, asking: "Would it not (now that Boydell's 'Shakespeare' is more familiar) be well to have coloured impressions from that plate?"[80] Sneyd's parenthesis is telling and reminds us that *Shakespeare-Sacrificed* first appeared at a time when comparatively few could have visited Boydell's Pall Mall venue, then only recently opened, or have seen reproductive engravings of the paintings exhibited there. Gillray's response to a cultural project that was emphatically public in its orientation is a satire that constitutes almost a private joke, one that no more than a select number of highly informed consumers could have read with any precision or understanding.

And the print is manifestly concerned with the issue of cultural exclusion. Gillray's Boydell stands within a magic circle marked with the Greek words "ΟΥΔΕΙΣ ΑΜΟΥΣΟΣ ΕΙΣΙΤΩ" (Let no stranger to the Muses enter), the motto inscribed above the entrance to Royal Academy's rooms at Somerset House. The rise of exhibition culture in the second half of the eighteenth century—part of what Peter de Bolla understands as the emergence of a broader "culture of visuality"—generated considerable anxiety among the artistic and social elites about the constitution and boundaries of the public. The Royal Academy inscription testified to this concern about the demographics of taste, that most resonant of Georgian keywords, as did the academy's one-shilling admission charge, which was levied expressly "to prevent the Rooms being filled with improper Persons."[81] Again, the thrust of Gillray's satire here is at least partly personal. He had trained, alongside William Blake, at the Royal Academy Schools, but the academy did not admit engravers to its membership, and at the bottom left of *Shakespeare-Sacrificed* a boy carrying paintbrushes and a palette is shown preventing a second boy, who clasps a burin, from crossing into the magic circle.

At the same time, the ironic quotation of the motto equates Boydell's gallery, which also charged an entry fee of a shilling, with the Royal Academy; neither, Gillray's print suggests, are the bastions of taste, fine art, or civic virtue they purport to be. Luisa Calè reads this satirical collapsing of the difference between the Shakespeare Gallery and the Royal Academy as both exposing the commercialism masked by academy's supposed civic humanism and rebuffing the gallery's claims to inclusiveness. So, in this way, she finds in Gillray's satire confirmation of her own Bourdieuian analysis of Boydell's literary venture as appealing to "an audience fit though few" in its identification of "spectators as readers."[82] Calè rightly registers the critical pressure that Gillray applies to Boydell's conception of the "public," but it needs to be emphasized that *Shakespeare-Sacrificed* is not by any means undertaking such an exposure in the name of inclusivity. Rather, the print works hard to define a space of refined taste that stands apart from institutions it regards as culturally debased. While folios of "modern masters" prop up Boydell's giant-sized list of subscribers, an abandoned album of "Ancient Masters" lies conspicuously in the foreground, beyond the bounds of the circle. It is thus precisely what falls outside Boydell's magic circle that Gillray valorizes. The caricature draws a line in the sand: on the one side, vulgar commercialism and cultural desecration; on the other, true artistic standards and a concomitant humanistic appreciation for the cultural achievements of the past. It is in this latter space, one in which the old masters are located, that Gillray positions his own art (engraving, including graphic satire) and thus, by extension, his own audience. We have, in a rhetorical sense, returned to the image of the printshop window and its careful adjudication between those viewers who do and do not possess the requisite cultural capital to count as members of the graphic satirical public. In lambasting a commercialized bardolatry that disguised itself as a public good and as a project of national celebration, Gillray's print works proprietorially to claim cultural ownership of Shakespeare for the more discerning patrons of Hannah Humphrey's printshop. Once more we are in the presence of topical satire that paradoxically seeks to inoculate high literary culture against the vulgarizing force of the popular and everyday.

Of course, Gillray's caricature is certainly open to the charge of hypocrisy. At the foot of the print a mock advertisement for Boydell's first volume of "Shakespeare Illustrated" notes acerbically that the edition will be priced at an expensive "One Guinea," but Gillray's folio-sized caricature was hardly cheap at a cost of five shillings uncolored. The business of graphic satire is business still. Yet in its considerable size and cost *Shakespeare-Sacrificed* reminds us once again of the clientele for whom Gillray was working, of the affluent and educated consumers who would understand the complex jests and critical engagements of this print. Gillray's Shakespeare, and perhaps graphic satire's Shakespeare more generally, is certainly not for everyone. What at first glance might look like a wry inversion of high cultural ideals rather functions to safeguard those ideals against the encroachments of indiscriminate commercialization and an ever-expanding public. That is, for all their arch irreverence and pronounced topicality, the Shakespearean parodies of graphic satire might be seen to protect an "authentic" Shakespeare by insisting that his plays continue to be located away from the crowd and within a fairly narrow cultural space of knowingness.

5. *Paradise Lost,* from the Sublime to the Ridiculous

Sustained critical efforts across the eighteenth century worked to remove *Paradise Lost* from the internecine ideological struggles of the seventeenth century and to refashion Milton the republican as a figure of, in Lucy Newlyn's words, " 'deified' authority."[1] In particular, Joseph Addison's eighteen essays on the poem, serialized in the *Spectator* in 1712, both established *Paradise Lost* as a monument of English literature and crafted a new critical taxonomy—centered on the terms *epic* and, more especially, *the sublime*—in order to enact this cultural elevation. In doing so, Addison not only used Milton to nurture a discourse of aesthetics (as it would come to be called) but also deployed this new discourse as a means of sequestering poem and poet from the disconcerting political radicalism and religious enthusiasm of the preceding century. Addison shaped a version of *Paradise Lost* that sat comfortably beside and even embodied the cultural agenda of his urbane and commercial Whiggism.

Of course, successful though this venture certainly was, it did not and could not entirely occlude Milton's troubling regicidal credentials; as Dustin Griffin has shown, a "prominent and enduring tradition" continued to denounce Milton as a traitor.[2] *The History of King-Killers* (1719) placed him on a list of 365 "Hellish Saints"; the *Critical Review* of 1758 reminded its readers that Milton had served as "secretary to the usurper and tyrant Cromwell" and even "insulted the ashes of his murdered king with calumny and reproach"; while Samuel Johnson chidingly described the poet as "an acrimonious and surly republican."³ Nor was the political exegesis of *Paradise Lost* the invention of such romantic polemicists as William Blake. Both Newlyn and Jackie DiSalvo note the heated partisan exchange that played out in the *London Chronicle* in 1763–64, as correspondents offered opposing political interpretations of Milton's Satan—a debate to which I will return later.⁴ But the most compelling evidence that the poem remained important to the way Georgian political culture thought about the matters of executive power and insurgency is to be found in graphic satire from the early 1780s onward. Despite the prevailing Addisonian mood of Enlightenment literary criticism, the prints I consider in this chapter testify to *Paradise Lost*'s continued cultural purchase as a text that undertook, as John Toland wrote in 1698, "to display the different Effects of Liberty and Tyranny."⁵

More precisely—for this insight alone is hardly new—I want to suggest that attention to the many graphic satirical parodies of *Paradise Lost* discloses the workings of two different political readings of the poem, readings that respectively function to attenuate and foster rather different conceptions of the Miltonic sublime. The first, and more familiar, regards Milton's epic as an anti-Whig allegory that warns readers of the dangers of opposing the constitutional authority of the sovereign. This interpretation has a long history, but its climactic moment certainly arrives in the years 1782–84, a period of acute parliamentary upheaval and successive governmental change that was defined by the standoff between George III and Charles James Fox as Crown and Commons wrestled for control of the state. During these years, caricaturists turned to *Paradise Lost* for the first time and with unprecedented frequency. Put simply, no other moment in British parliamentary history, before or after, was as extensively and elaborately processed by contemporaries through recourse to one particular literary narrative. Milton's poem became *the* text through which the vicissitudes of the Foxite campaign against the royal prerogative were understood and satirically framed.

What we are dealing with here, then, are exercises in mock-epic. As a mode that engineers a collision between the everyday and the culturally sacrosanct in which the damage incurred is all on the former side, mock-epic must have had an immediate appeal for caricaturists who, as we've seen, often sought to reinforce the opposition between high culture and the topical or popular, even as they insistently read across these domains. Yet the jeopardy of mock-epic is always that the comparison it sustains might inadvertently elevate the ideas and characters of the mundane world to the prestige of myth, and this risk is especially evident in the analogy between Fox and Milton's Satan that became so commonplace in caricatures of the early to mid-1780s. This ironic equivalence in part took its cue from the terms of the Whig leader's own impassioned rhetoric, but it nonetheless brought with it distinct problems for Tory satirists, who by proffering such a comparison perforce risked counterproductively advertising the charisma of the very Satanic politics they sought to warn their public against. The danger was that mock-epic might all too easily look something like epic.

In contrast to this reading of *Paradise Lost*, one that looks to it as a political allegory of and for the present, a different and still more complex approach to the poem emerges in a number of Gillray's mature caricatures. In the second part of this chapter I offer a sustained analysis of these Miltonic prints as intricate exercises in mock-epic and generic play that are deeply engaged in the century's critical debates about the formal registers and status of the poem. In a manner that is highly idiosyncratic, Gillray seems less interested in conscripting Milton's text as a cautionary tale of rebellion or in mining the well-rehearsed parallel between Fox and Satan—a correspondence he helped establish—and more concerned with exploiting the generic peculiarities of *Paradise Lost* for satirical and political effect. For Gillray, Milton's poem is a text that germinates forms of the ludicrous within its very epic construction. As in the previous chapter, then, I'm especially interested in the way graphic satirical parodies excavate the contours of literary genre and apply critical pressure to the supposed formal coherence of the text they take up.

In what follows it is important to keep in mind the difficulty of *Paradise Lost*. It has often been claimed that after the Bible and Bunyan's *Pilgrim's Progress* it was the most widely read book of the eighteenth century.[6] True though this may be, the poem's tremendous popularity across the period needs to be set against repeated efforts, of varying success, to abbreviate or rewrite Milton's masterpiece so as to render it readily accessible to a larger and more diverse readership.[7] *The State of Innocence: And Fall of Man* (1745) translated Milton's blank verse into prose; in 1773 the grammarian John Buchanan offered a parallel text edition of the first six books of the poem with the "Words of the Text being arranged, at the bottom of the Page, in the same natural Order with the Conceptions of the mind," an exercise designed to be of service to "our most eminent Schools" and "private Gentleman and Ladies"; while in his *Extract from Milton's Paradise Lost* (1763; reprinted 1791) John Wesley conceded that the poem was "unintelligible to an abundance of

Readers: the immense learning which [Milton] has every where crowded together, making it quite obscure to persons of a common Education," and excised close to two thousand lines on the grounds that he "despaired of explaining [them] to the unlearned."[8] Taken together, such attempts not only acknowledge the difficulty of Milton's Latinate syntax and dense allusions to classical and Renaissance texts but also suggest pervasive pedagogical—we might say, ideological—anxieties that *Paradise Lost* was failing to reach the broader audience demanded by its literary merit and Christian temper. In his memoir, Thomas Cooper—poet, Chartist, and, in his youth, apprentice to a shoemaker—recounts having found *Paradise Lost* "above my culture and learning," though impressively he went on to memorize books 1 to 4.[9] And it wasn't just the laboring classes who struggled. "I cannot possibly read our countryman Milton through," the Earl of Chesterfield, a quintessential man of letters, confessed to his son: ". . . the characters and speeches of a dozen or two of Angels, and of as many Devils, are as much above my reach as my entertainment."[10] The satirical prints to which I attend here thus work with a text that makes considerable demands on its reader. Of course, even an illiterate viewer might recognize the figure of the devil (though correctly identifying Charles James Fox would be another matter), and one would certainly expect most literate viewers to have registered a reference to a poem as widely known and admired as *Paradise Lost*. However, as we'll see, these prints, and those of Gillray more than any, engage with the poem in a detailed manner that especially rewards those with a deep and local knowledge of Milton's epic, and often also of the critical industry that enshrined it. In 1800 the *True Briton,* adapting Hamlet's words, described Henry Fuseli's Milton paintings as "caviare to the Million"; the same might perhaps be said of many of the Miltonic parodies I consider here.[11]

The Devil's Party: Fox and the Whigs, 1782–1784

JOHNSON. "And I have always said, the first Whig was the Devil."
BOSWELL. "He certainly was, Sir. The Devil was impatient of subordination; he was the first who resisted power:—'Better to reign in Hell, than serve in Heaven.' "[12]

In March 1782, having held power for twelve long years and overseen the ultimately disastrous military campaign in America, Lord North's ministry

finally fell. It marked the beginning of a dizzyingly turbulent phase of political history, which was to see four changes of government in a little over two
years and a near constitutional crisis.[13] We have touched on this period
already, in Chapter 3, so far as it concerned the Fox-North coalition (the
main players of which William Dent, you will recall, so dexterously cast as
Caliban, Trinculo, and Stefano). However, it is necessary here to provide
a somewhat more detailed summary of events in order fully to understand
the satirical prints that respond to them, as well as the significant role that
Paradise Lost plays in this response.

North was succeeded as prime minister by the increasingly frail Whig
grandee the Marquess of Rockingham. His new government was tasked with
negotiating the end of hostilities in America in the wake of Britain's crushing
defeat at Yorktown, but found itself crippled by deep divisions within the
cabinet. With Rockingham too ill to take an active role, it fell to Lord Shelburne and Charles James Fox, as home secretary and foreign secretary,
respectively, to lead the ministry, and these men disagreed frequently and
bitterly—over the issue of American independence especially. George III
was unsure of Rockingham and stridently distrustful of Fox, and Shelburne
seems to have served as the king's agent within the cabinet; Fox, for one,
considered him to be obstructing the Rockinghamite agenda expressly at the
monarch's behest.[14] In early July Fox resigned in exasperation, and at the
same moment Rockingham died, leaving Shelburne to form a ministry and
conclude the terms of peace. Yet this government was toppled just eight
months later when Fox joined forces with Lord North, the long-term parliamentary adversaries now united by their opposition to the details of the peace
treaty negotiated by Shelburne. Their coalition, nominally headed by the
Duke of Portland, came to power in March 1783. Such an alliance of interest
was, historians point out, entirely consonant with the realities of eighteenth-
century politics; most of the period's ministries had been coalitions of some
kind.[15] In time, though, many contemporaries came to view the coming
together of two men who had spent so many years hurling abuse at each
other across the floor of the Commons as an unpalatable case of hypocritical
expediency.

The king despised the coalition. He sought assiduously for alternatives
before finally accepting that the majority commanded by Fox and North left
him no choice other than to permit them to form a government. Already
scornful of Fox, George III was further angered to find himself, contrary to

established practice, shut out of the process of appointments to the cabinet and other government offices, and he made little secret of his determination to oust the new ministry at the first opportunity. That chance presented itself in December 1783, in the form of the controversial India Bill, which proposed much-needed reform of the East India Company by instituting a board of commissioners to oversee its administration. Opponents accused Fox of attempting to seize control of the company's patronage and to appropriate the Crown's power to appoint officials, and though it passed in the Commons, the bill was rejected by the Lords after the king worked behind the scenes to pressure bishops and peers to vote it down. Within hours of the defeat George III summarily dismissed the ministry and installed William Pitt the Younger, aged just twenty-five, as his new prime minister. Though nick-named the "mince-pie" administration because it was not expected to survive Christmas, this minority government clung to office until the end of March 1784, when Parliament was at last dissolved and an election called. In one of the most bitterly contested campaigns in British history, the Foxites found their support eroded and Pitt gained a sizable majority; he was to remain in power for the next seventeen years.

For all the merry-go-round of appointments, the years 1782–84 are defined by the extended struggle between two men, Fox and George III, in what was a fight not just for political supremacy but also, as John Cannon writes, "between rival views of the constitution."[16] At stake was whether the country was ultimately to be ruled by the executive or the legislature. From Fox's perspective, the king's use of Shelburne to undermine the Rockingham ministry in 1782 and, far more flagrantly, his engineering of the coalition's downfall confirmed his long-held opinion that George III wielded his royal prerogative unconstitutionally and conspired to diminish the influence of the Commons. The Revolution Settlement of 1689 was in jeopardy. "We shall certainly lose our liberty," protested Fox in December 1783, "when the delib-erations of Parliament are decided—not by the legal and usual—but by the illegal and extraordinary exertions of Prerogative."[17] For the king and his supporters, however, this cry of freedom rang hollow; rather than the man of the people, as he claimed, Fox was understood to be the belligerent head of an aristocratic faction (as the Foxites undeniably were) whose spurious rhet-oric of liberty concealed a determination to monopolize the system of patronage and establish an oligarchy of noblemen. On this view, George III's actions were those not of a tyrant but rather of a monarch legitimately using his executive power to thwart Fox's efforts to topple the mixed constitution.[18] And it was very much in the service of this latter, Tory reading of events that satirists conscripted *Paradise Lost*. No fewer than ten visual political parodies of Milton's poem were published in the period just outlined, and all of them, without exception, execrate Fox. Literary historians have long associated *Paradise Lost* with the radicalism of the 1790s and what Peter Schock terms "Romantic Satanism" (think especially of Blake's contention that Milton was "of the Devil's party without knowing it").[19] Yet the efflorescence of political appropriations of the poem in the years of the French Revolution was nothing to that of the period 1782–84, when it became the go-to text for critiques of Fox and his party, not just in satirical prints but also, as we'll see, in the columns of the daily newspapers.

The print that set this trend in motion—indeed the first of the century to parody Milton's poem—is James Sayers's *Paradise Lost* (fig. 5.1), which was published on 17 July 1782, thirteen days after Fox announced his resignation from the cabinet and sixteen after the death of Rockingham. In a comic reworking of the frequently illustrated "Expulsion from Paradise" scene of book 12, Sayers depicts Fox and Burke (who had resigned as paymaster of the forces) joined in inconsolable grief before the gates of paradise, or government. At the foot of the print Sayers quotes the following lines:

> ————————— to the eastern Side
> Of Paradise so late their happy Seat
> Waved over by that flaming Brand, the Gate
> With dreadful faces throng'd and fiery Arms
> Some natural Tears they dropt, but wiped them soon
> The World was all before them where to chuse
> Their Place of Rest and Providence their Guide
> They Arm in Arm with wandring Steps and slow
> Thro' Eden took their solitary Way.[20]

As Sayers expects his readers to register, these are, with a few minor changes, the final lines of Milton's poem. This print is concerned with ends. As in Theodore Lane's *Whole Truth* (see fig. 4.9), the conclusion of a narrative arc, the exit of key protagonists, is given political charge. In Sayers's ironic version of the poem's close, however, there is no sense of ambivalence, of *felix culpa;* there is nothing fortunate about the fall of Fox and Burke and no promise of future redemption. And this Miltonic finale enables Sayers to read events in a

Fig. 5.1. James Sayers, *Paradise Lost* (Charles Bretherton, 17 July 1782). BMC 6011. Courtesy of The Lewis Walpole Library, Yale University.

particular way. Where resignation implies agency, these two statesmen have been forcibly ejected from office.[21] The trope is, of course, expulsion.

Sayers is alert to the specifics of the image unfolded in the lines he quotes. The "dreadful faces" that "throng" the gate become in this satire the countenances of the reshuffled cabinet: Shelburne, now prime minister, who grins with unabashed satisfaction; John Dunning, Baron Ashburton, who continued as chancellor of the Duchy of Lancaster; and Colonel Isaac Barré, who was promoted to the post Burke had vacated. Equally, at the top right of the image a hand plunges down into the frame wielding the "flaming brand," which is inscribed "Commission to the Lord of ye Treasury" (that is, Shelburne). But this motif also shows Sayers parodically channeling the illustrative tradition that, from the late seventeenth century, rapidly developed around Milton's poem, for his rendering of the fiery sword is striking similar to that carried by Michael as he drives Adam and Eve from Eden in the plate of the Expulsion included in the first illustrated edition of *Paradise Lost* in 1688 (fig. 5.2). This pictorial resonance extends to the figure of Burke, who in tucking his hand inside his waistcoat repeats Eve's gesture of placing her hand across her chest (a motion of modesty and shame). If Charles Fox is the Adam of this parody, then Burke, his seeming subordinate, takes on the role of Eve.

Throughout the period 1782–84 Sayers was the most consistent and effective satirist of Fox. Sayers's depiction of him as the self-appointed mogul Carlo Khan is the most enduring and politically damaging image of the Whig leader of these years, and in an age in which the partisan allegiances of satirists were highly mobile, Sayers remained a firm propagandist for Pitt the Younger throughout the 1780s and 1790s, loyalty that earned him a government sinecure.[22] He was, moreover, as Lord Eldon wrote in 1829, "an excellent classical scholar," and a conscious delight in learning, a pride in one's cultural capital, pervades Sayers's prints, where literary references, as well Latin phrases and mottos, appear in abundance.[23] It should not be surprising, then, that the first graphic satirical parody of Milton's poem came from Sayers's hand. And as one of his earliest political prints, *Paradise Lost* is

Fig. 5.2. Hendrik Eland, illustration to Book 12 for the seventh edition of *Paradise Lost* (London: Jacob Tonson, 1705), after Michael Burghers's engraving for the fourth edition of 1688. © The Trustees of the British Museum.

also a manifesto of sorts for Sayers's own educated and urbane brand of graphic satire, for he adorns the gate of paradise with the faces not only of Shelburne and his ministers but also of satyrs. The implication is that satire (then often spelled "satyr" and associated etymologically with this mythological figure) will work in tandem with Fox's adversaries to exclude him from office. Sayers's print posits his mode of satire as, quite literally, a gatekeeper of power.

Two years after Sayers's caricature, Fox returned as Milton's Adam in a pair of prints published in the *Rambler's Magazine* in July and August 1784, in the wake of the general election. Georgiana, Duchess of Devonshire canvassed openly on behalf of Fox during the campaign, and amid rumors that she was trading kisses for votes, satirists repeatedly denigrated her as a whore; female incursion into the male sphere of politics was made legible through the vocabularies of promiscuity, prostitution, and perversion.[24] The two Miltonic parodies published by the *Rambler's Magazine* continue this smear campaign by casting Fox and the duchess as Adam and Eve. In the first, *The D——ss and the Man of the Peo—— in buff tho' not in blue* (fig. 5.3)—a title that puns on the Whigs' party colors—the pair are shown standing in a grandly furnished room and naked but for their fig-leaf girdles. "We are driven out of *paradise* by the *young serpent* of the *back stairs*," opines the duchess in the accompanying text, a reference not just to Pitt but also to the back-channel aid he received from the king. In the sequel to this etching, *The D——ss of D——v——e tasting forbidden fruit* (fig. 5.4), Fox and Georgiana, again in a state of undress, now embrace beneath a tree in Eden, where they are watched over by North and, in serpent form, Burke.[25] Though these prints ostensibly appropriate *Paradise Lost* as a narrative of transgression and suggest the dangerous codependency of Fox and the duchess, it is unquestionably the erotic potential of Milton's Eden that is of particular appeal. The *Rambler's Magazine* undertook, as its subtitle unabashedly declared, "to furnish the man of pleasure with the most delicious banquet of amorous, bacchanalian, whimsical, humorous, theatrical and polite entertainment." There was nothing polite about it. Images of naked women in sexually compromising scenarios were a staple feature of the magazine's unwholesome brew of salacious gossip and crude humor; it was, in James Boswell's words, "a vehicle of licentious tales."[26] In distinct contrast to Sayers's suggestive close reading of the expulsion scene, *Paradise Lost* is here little more than a pretext for soft pornography.

Fig. 5.3. (left) *The D——ss and the Man of the Peo—— in buff tho' not in blue* (*Rambler's Magazine*, July 1784). BMC 6656. © The Trustees of the British Museum. Fig. 5.4. (right) *The D——ss of D——v——e tasting the forbidden fruit* (*Rambler's Magazine*, August 1784). BMC 6651. © The Trustees of the British Museum.

Nonetheless, the *Rambler's Magazine* does at least gesture toward a political application of Milton's poem that contemporaries found to be far more compelling. "I am now one of the fallen angels, but not a despairing one," Fox insists in the dialogue that glosses the first of the prints, "I shall, like another Lucifer, Try 'What may be yet *regain'd* in heaven, / Or more *lost* in hell' " (quoting *Paradise Lost*, 1.269–70). This use of Satan as an analogue of Charles Fox was almost ubiquitous by the summer of 1784. Other parallels were also common—to Oliver Cromwell, Cataline, and Indian moguls (Carlo Khan), not least—but in both graphic satire and the daily press it was as Milton's Satan that Fox most frequently appeared. I want to interrogate in some depth the precise appeal of this political analogy, the diagnosis of personality and party that it adumbrates, the longer cultural history on which it draws, and the problems that inhere in it. Before I do so, though, it's

important to understand the remarkable escalation of this anti-Foxite deployment of Milton's Satan from 1782 onward.

The first print to mine the correspondence between Fox and Satan was
Gillray's *Gloria Mundi, or—The Devil addressing the Sun* (fig. 5.5), which was
published less than a week after Sayers's *Paradise Lost* in July 1782. As his
title acknowledges, Gillray splices two different sources, reworking and
inverting the satirical iconography of George Townshend's 1756 caricature
Gloria Mundi (BMC 3441), which had skewered the Duke of Cumberland, by
adding to it a parody of Satan's resentful address to the sun as he approaches
Eden (4.32–112). In Townshend's print the haughty Cumberland stands atop
the globe, his swollen body radiating light; in its absurd hyperbole, the satire
offers, as its original annotation put it, "An ironical Complement [sic] paid to
a great Commander."[27] In his adaptation, Gillray also stands his target on the
world, but this figure, Fox, is now both indigent—his pockets having been
emptied at the E.O. table that here serves as his pedestal—and also a political
outcast. Rather than shine himself, he gazes with a mixture of envy and

GLORIA MUNDI,
or—*The Devil addressing the Sun*

Fig. 5.5. James Gillray, *Gloria Mundi,
or—The Devil addressing the Sun*
(William Humphrey, 22 July 1782).
BMC 6012. Courtesy of The Lewis
Walpole Library, Yale University.

dejection toward the bright sun, which encircles the bust of a smug Shelburne, and rasps:

> To thee I call,
> But with no friendly voice, & add thy name,
> Shelburne! to tell thee how I hate thy beams,
> That bring to my remembrance from what state I fell: &c. &c. &c
> (adapting 4.35–39)

Townshend's mock panegyric becomes an image of bitter political alienation.

Together, Sayers's *Paradise Lost* and Gillray's *Gloria Mundi* gained the attention of the newspapers, with the *Morning Post* commending their "satirical effect."[28] In fact, *Gloria Mundi* takes up a hint first expressed in the pro-Shelburne *Morning Herald* on 13 July, which noted that "Mr. Fox's fall, and Mr. Pitt's rise [Pitt had been appointed chancellor of the exchequer in the new ministry], may not improperly be compared to the excommunication of Satan:—nor are the words which Milton puts into the mouth of the Devil, when he addresses the rising sun very inapplicable—'*I hate thy beams!*' "[29] This was a joke of which the anti-Foxite newspapers never tired. In October 1782, the *Herald* printed a mock "List of New Publications" that included "Satan's Address to his infernal subjects, after his dismissal from heaven, a patriotic poem, by the Hon. *C. Fox*"; at the end of March 1783, as Fox and North readied themselves for government, the *Public Advertiser* published a poem that imagined Fox "In Pandæmonium thus midst Flames of Fire / His Eye balls flashing with tremendous Ire" and rallying his "black infernal crew" with the refrain, "To reign is worth Ambition e'en in Hell" (reworking 1.193–94, 262); while in the run-up to the general election a year later an article in the *Advertiser* implored "Britons [to] *read* and *judge* of the COALITION ADMINISTRATION," asserting that "Satan and his Fiends were not more intent in Rebellion against their Almighty God, than these two Satans and their Fiends are for hurling Perdition upon the best of Constitutions, and the best of Sovereigns."[30]

If such partisan polemic testifies to the extent to which the Tory press worked to embed the image of Fox as Milton's archfiend within the collective imagination of the political public, then it also suggests the gradual intensification of this trope between the resignation of Fox in 1782 and the rancorous election contest of 1784. The Fox of *Gloria Mundi* is hardly menacing. Gillray repeats the easy visual pun through which Fox, like his father, was so often identified satirically (his legs and tail are vulpine), and the overarching design of the print, like the original hint in the *Morning Herald*, emphasizes Fox's impotence. He may recite Satan's speech, but there is otherwise little of the devil about him. The same is true of Gillray's return to *Paradise Lost* in December 1782. *"Aside he turn'd for envy, yet with jealous leer malign, Eyd them askance"* (fig. 5.6; quoting 4.502–4) cites the scene in book 4 of Milton's poem in which Satan, secreted in Paradise, beholds the contentment of Adam and Eve (now Shelburne and Pitt) with an acute sense of envy. Apart from the bucolic backdrop there is no attempt to illustrate the poem; Fox-Satan again cuts a forlorn and even benign figure, painfully aware of the juxtaposition between the satisfaction of those who enjoy divine (read royal) favor and the irrevocable acrimony of his own fallen position. Compare this

Fig. 5.6. James Gillray, *"Aside he turn'd for envy, yet with jealous Leer malign, Eyd them Askance"* (Hannah Humphrey, 12 December 1782). BMC 6044. Courtesy of the Beinecke Rare Book and Manuscript Library, Yale University.

rendering of Fox to that offered by the verses and article published in the *Public Advertiser* in 1783–84, with their thunderous pseudo-Miltonic register, and the contrast could not be starker. Once Fox leagued himself with Lord North and became a genuine threat to the king and his parliamentary allies, the tenor of political parodies of *Paradise Lost* changed fundamentally. As Milton's Satan, Fox was now a malevolent and highly dangerous rebel.

Once more it was James Sayers who led the way among graphic satirists in adapting *Paradise Lost* to the political moment and, more especially, in turning it to the Pittite agenda. His *Pandemonium* (fig. 5.7) was published on 12 January 1784, the day the Commons reconvened after the Christmas recess and thus the first occasion on which Fox and North sat in the House at the head of a majority opposition. Sayers tellingly bifurcates the title of his print with the coat of arms of Rockingham (to which he adds a skull and crossbones), the implication being that the present political crisis is a direct consequence

Fig. 5.7. James Sayers, *Pandemonium* (Thomas Cornell, 12 January 1784). BMC 6372. Courtesy of The Lewis Walpole Library, Yale University.

of the earl's death. But it is Fox who dominates the scene, and he positively glowers with menace as his colleagues—North, Burke, Lords Derby, Carlisle, and Cavendish, and Admiral Augustus Keppel—huddle around him. Where Gillray's Fox-Satan is the pariah, Sayers's is commander in chief of the disaffected. This point is made emphatically clear by the nine lines from the poem quoted at the foot of the print, which describe the "Down cast and damp" fallen angels regrouping around Satan and finding "some glimps of joy" in beholding his "wonted pride" (1.522–30). Though defeated and ejected from government, Fox and his supporters are "not lost / In Loss it self," Sayers informs his audience; they remain a constitutional threat even in opposition.

Ten days later, and evidently inspired by Sayers, an anonymous print took this depiction of Fox further still. In a parody of the insurrection in heaven reported by Raphael in book 5 of the poem, *Satan harangueing his Troops previous to Action* (fig. 5.8) shows a cloven-hooved Fox rallying the massed ranks of his rebel army, labeled "Majority." To his side, and holding his arm, stands the Prince of Wales, who flattens his motto "Ich Dien" (I serve) beneath his feet. Having publicly sided with the Foxite Whigs, this prince would, it seems, sooner reign than serve. Each of Fox's four standard-bearers—the Duke of Portland, North, Burke, and Keppel—is also cast as

Fig. 5.8. *Satan harangueing his Troops previous to Action* (William Humphrey, 22 January 1784). BMC 6383. Courtesy of The Lewis Walpole Library, Yale University.

one of Milton's fallen angels, and as attentive readers of this print would have understood, the satirist draws these parodic parallels with care. In the character of Belial, who in book 2 of *Paradise Lost* recommends "ignoble ease, and peaceful sloath" (2.227), Portland is dismissed as a political passenger of the Foxite cause (he had been the nominal head of the coalition). As Mammon, North is castigated as a statesman more concerned with "riches" than principles (1.682). Asmodeus, the demon who can be repelled by "fishie fumes" (alluded to at 4.166–71), is an apt satirical cipher for Keppel, whose credibility as a naval officer was wrecked by his controversial defeat at the Battle of Ushant in July 1778. Finally, the casting of Burke as the "Moleck the Sublime & Beautiful," described by Milton as a "horrid King besmear'd with blood / Of human sacrifice" (1.392–93), triangulates allusions to *Paradise Lost*, the *Philosophical Enquiry*—particularly its conceptual linkage of "barbarous" modes of worship with obscurity and sublimity—and Burke's supposed crypto-Catholicism (once more he wears a Jesuitical biretta).

Published on 22 January 1784, the day after the opposition had forced Pitt to postpone the second reading of his India Bill "partly as a show of strength and partly to embarrass" the prime minister, this print warns of the constitutional ramifications of a majority opposition to the king's government.[31] Yet the Miltonic narrative ultimately tempers this concern, for we well know the outcome of the celestial battle here shown in its infancy. In parodying the war in heaven, *Satan harangueing his Troops previous to Action* plots the future trajectory of Fox's struggle with the king and Pitt and forecasts Fox's downfall even as it gives pictorial expression to his vigorous resistance and temerity. Indeed, following Pitt's electoral triumph in early summer 1784 the anonymous graphic satirist was quick to offer a sequel entitled *Satan Haranguing his Troops after their Defeat* (fig. 5.9). Fox and his confederates, who appear in various postures of dejection and embarrassment, now inhabit the "Hell of Disappointment"; their standards have been inverted, and a "Paper Crown" slips into oblivion at the bottom right. Fox places his right foot on a stone that reads "To reign is worth Ambition e'en in Hell" (1.262) and declares: "What tho' the Field be lost all is not Lost / th' Unconquerable Will & Study of Revenge" (1.105–7). In the face of such resounding political defeat, all that remains for the Foxites are the dubious pleasures of festering resentment and futile parliamentary intransigence.

Along with Sayers's *Pandemonium*, this pair of *Satan Haranguing* prints suggests just how successful anti-Foxite satirists were, in 1784 especially, at

Fig. 5.9. *Satan Haranguing his Troops after their Defeat* (William Humphrey, March 1784). BMC 6482. © The Trustees of the British Museum.

mapping the political present onto Milton's narrative arc. Most obviously, and like the parodic images of Fox as Caliban that we've already seen, these satires find in *Paradise Lost* a means of allegorizing Fox's opposition to the royal prerogative. In the anonymous *Satans Journey from Hell* (fig. 5.10), for instance, Fox is even shown flying through the infernal region in the company of a manifesto inscribed "A Method to Dethrone the K——g AD 1784." Such depictions of Fox in fact invoke and reinvigorate a longer tradition of reading Milton's Satan as "the first Whig," to borrow Samuel Johnson's phrase, that was first given cogent expression in John Dryden's *Absalom and Achitophel* (1681), a Tory satire published at the climax of the Exclusion Crisis, as Charles II and his supporters fought off a Whig campaign to divert the line of succession from the Catholic Duke of York. As critics have long recognized, Dryden channels Milton's archfiend in his portrayal of the Earl of Shaftesbury, leader of the Exclusionists, as Achitophel, a smooth-tongued statesman who stands "at bold Defiance with his Prince" and tempts Absalom (proxy for the Duke of Monmouth, Charles's illegitimate but favored son) to rebel against his royal father.[32]

SATANS *Journey from hell*

Fig. 5.10. *Satans Journey from Hell*
(1784). Courtesy of The Lewis
Walpole Library, Yale University.

For the persistence of this hermeneutic into the mid-eighteenth century
we need look no further than the debate played out in the *London Chronicle* in
1763–64 against the backdrop of the constitutional entanglements of the
early years of George III's reign. An essay published in the newspaper in
November 1763 considered "who were Whigs, who Tories," in Milton's
narrative and argued that "in shewing us the fatal effects of disobedience"
Paradise Lost was itself an exercise in political apostasy, a confessional allegory of the wrongs of the revolution its author had formerly championed: "I
consider this poem as a confutation of the error of his own pen, and a confession of the guilt of his own actions. Indeed, how could he better refute the
good old cause he was such a partisan of, and such an advocate for, than by
making the rebellion in the poem resemble it, and giving the same characters
to the apostate angels, as were applicable to his rebel-brethren?"[33] In contrast
to the later Blakean reading of *Paradise Lost,* and like the anti-Foxite caricatures of 1784, Satan is in this arch-Tory exegesis an unequivocal villain, the

cautionary embodiment of a would-be regicide. This interpretation did not, however, go uncontested. The following year the *London Chronicle* printed rebuttal essays possibly written by Dissenter and radical Whig Thomas Hollis.[34] The second of these articles sought "to retrieve the glory of Milton" by arguing that "the true motive of the infernal serpent, which was not to level but to control, not to create a democracy in heaven . . . but to set himself highest on the eternal throne." In this way, the essay concluded, "the Tory plan, where man assumes a right of dominion over man, was nearer related to Satan's aim."[35]

As this long view makes clear, the Satan-as-Whig reading of *Paradise Lost* insists that the poem cannot be understood outside of the context of Milton's own republicanism. The first correspondent in the *London Chronicle* actively conjures the specter of the seventeenth-century regicides in his admonishment of the Whig opposition to the Crown, and the same rhetorical strategy is implicit in the prints of Fox in 1784. Fox was often satirized as a second Cromwell at this time, and just a week after *Pandemonium* James Sayers depicted the Whig leader as the lord protector in *A Mirror of Patriotism* (20 January 1784; BMC 6380). In part these caricatures respond to the heated terms of Fox's rhetoric. After the fall of the coalition, Fox's denunciations of the prerogative became increasingly impassioned and unguarded, and he freely alluded to the constitutional debacles of the previous century. Speaking in January 1784, for instance, he maintained that "a majority of the House of Commons" had "almost from time immemorial, governed the country" and asked, with more than a hint of threat: "Was it not in clashing with this radical and primary principle that so many calamities had happened in some of the reigns prior to the Revolution?"[36] As Boyd Hilton observes, this "attempt to drink from the well of seventeenth-century Whiggism proved disastrous" in that it all too readily recalled the bloody republicanism of the English Civil Wars.[37] The discernable darkening of the Fox-Satan analogy between 1782 and 1784—the emergence of an archrebel in place of a harmless malcontent—was thus a reaction to the intensification of Fox's incendiary language. Satirists turned to Milton not least because Fox injudiciously mobilized the conflicts of the seventeenth century as a meaningful political and discursive framework for understanding the contemporary crisis; visual parodies of *Paradise Lost* at this time show Fox to have become a prisoner of his own highly charged vocabulary.

In fact, *Paradise Lost* was very much in Fox's thoughts in these years, and on his reading of the poem, like that offered by Hollis (or Hollis's mouthpiece) in 1764, Satan represented a resonant model of insidious despotism. The MP George Selwyn observed in March 1782 that Fox "talked of the King under the description of Satan, a comparison which he seems fond of, and has used to others."[38] Evidently this trope had considerable currency within Foxite circles at this time, for just a few months later Richard Fitzpatrick, a close associate of Fox, privately fretted that the appointment of Shelburne as prime minister would signal "a total end of *Whig principles,* and everything more in the hands of *Satan* than ever."[39] The rival views of the constitution that underpin this period of political history were thus articulated through opposing presentist interpretations of *Paradise Lost,* or more precisely of the figure of Milton's Satan, and the victory of Pitt at the polls in 1784 is in some sense a testament to the triumph of the Tory account of the poem that was so assiduously promulgated, in newsprint and caricature, by the supporters of George III. That it was this version that prevailed, and imprinted itself upon the cultural memory, is in many ways unsurprising, for, though the king was by no means exempt from criticism and satire, to compare a reigning monarch to Satan in public would have been to court treason.[40] Equally, Fox's open advocacy of party politics made the Satan analogy especially compelling. "I have always acknowledged myself to be a party man," he exclaimed in 1783, "I have always acted with a party in whose principles I have confidence." Party, though, remained a suspect notion for many at the time—George III declared his outright detestation of it—and in the pair of *Satan Haranguing* prints it is Satan's marshaling of what Fox's critics called a "systematic and factious opposition" that gives the Miltonic parody such force.[41] Yet the ultimate irony is that the Tory satirists won out not only by invoking Satan as a figure of anarchic rebellion but also by successfully appropriating the Whig view of him as a tyrant in the making. In the guise of Satan, as in that of Cromwell, the "man of the people" is exposed as a fraud who harnesses the rhetoric of liberty only as a convenient means by which to "set himself in Glory above his Peers" (1.39).

And rhetoric was, somewhat problematically, at the heart of Tory concerns. Like Milton's Satan and Dryden's Achitophel, Fox was a highly effective orator, and the *Paradise Lost* prints of 1784 repeatedly and anxiously foreground the perils of his eloquence. The passage quoted in Sayers's *Pandemonium,* for instance, reminds the public that Satan's "high words . . . bore / Semblance of worth, not substance" (1.528–29), while the *Satan Haranguing* prints take Fox's speechifying as their express subject. Addressing

Fox on the terms of peace with America, the pamphleteer John King wrote: "The figure you made in the late debates on the peace, was such as would have startled an infernal assembly; for you reconciled contradictions; avowed defection of principle; proclaimed your necessities as reasons for your being employed, with an audaciousness that exceeded moral depravity: the House seemed to acquiesce under a torrent of vociferous words, and you was hailed as Satan on the burning lake, the leader of the next pestilential band, which is to pillage the indigent of this county."[42] King's excoriation of Fox perfectly articulates the critique of Whig rhetoric advanced in some measure by all public iterations of the Satanic analogy in the early 1780s, but the power evoked by his extended simile also discloses the risks that inhere in such elaborate appropriations of *Paradise Lost*. In the previous two chapters, I argued that satirists were careful to invoke literary archetypes of insurgency and agitation that were already in some manner neutralized. Allusions to Caliban's uprising and the weird sisters' confederacy present revolution as a reassuring comedy in which the would-be agents of change are grotesque and powerless. Milton's Satan, however, is a rebel of indubitable power and charisma. In his *Philosophical Enquiry* Burke famously cited the portrait of Satan in book 1 of the poem—"he above the rest / In shape and gesture proudly eminent / Stood like a Towr . . ." (1.589–99)—as an example of "sublime description" that lends the character "a dignity so suitable to the subject."[43] In comparing Fox to this Miltonic Satan, then, Tory satirists risked ennobling the very figure they set out to denigrate. Even in the ribald context of caricature, Satan might easily retain some of his "dignity," and his words possess exactly the allure that the satires sought to negate. Mock-epic threatened to lapse into epic.

This danger was perhaps especially acute in the years 1782–84 because the artist Philip James de Loutherbourg had given new cultural prominence to Burke's sublime Satan. Loutherbourg's Eidophusikon, which combined moving scenery and lighting effects to offer spectators a protocinematic sequence of kinetic pictures, first opened in Leicester Square in 1781, but it returned the following year with a new final scene: "Satan arraying his Troops on the Banks of the Fiery Lake, with the Raising of the Palace of Pandemonium, from Milton."[44] As a reviewer for the *European Magazine* wrote, this "grand climax" presented a "view of the Miltonic Hell, cloathed in all its terrors" and "all the grandeur bestowed by Milton."[45] That the years of the Eidophusikon are also those that witnessed the proliferation of political parodies of *Paradise Lost* is no coincidence. Though Loutherbourg sold the Eidophusikon in the summer of 1782, it reopened under new management in early 1784 in exhibition rooms in the Strand, and that year advertisements for the show and commentaries on Fox and the election routinely jostled side by side in the columns of the daily newspapers.[46] While there are a number of possible reasons for the sudden satirico-political interest in Milton's poem in the early 1780s—not least the explosion of Miltonic painting from the 1770s that has been charted by Marcia Pointon—the sensational success of the Eidophusikon, with its unprecedented visual staging of Satan's oratorical prowess, must surely have been a particular cultural stimulus.[47] The correspondences between Loutherbourg's depiction of Pandemonium and the title and composition of *Satan harangueing his Troops previous to Action* or, more especially, the image of Fox as "Satan on the burning lake" offered by John King, are thus both striking and paradoxical. If the Eidophusikon inspired satirists and polemicists to make analogic use of Milton's Satan, then it also conferred upon the character a magnetic appeal that made him an unstable political cipher.[48]

How, then, did graphic satirists draw attention to Fox's Satanic eloquence while simultaneously denying his words and arguments the power that might inadvertently recruit their public to the devil's party? In *Pandemonium*, Sayers achieves this difficult accommodation simply by refusing his Fox-Satan speech. Instead, as Lord Derby's exclamation of "Hear hear hear" indicates, Sayers depicts the moment immediately *after* Satan has spoken. *Satan harangueing his Troops previous to Action*, meanwhile, takes a more complex approach to this problem. Here, in a large speech bubble, Fox repeats Satan's address to his followers as they prepare for battle in heaven. I quote this passage in full, and from the poem rather than the print, because I want to highlight the satirist's strategic excision of certain lines (which are shown struck through below):

> Will ye submit your necks, and chuse to bend
> The supple knee? ye will not, if I trust
> To know ye right, ~~or if ye know your selves~~
> ~~Natives and Sons of Heav'n possest before~~
> ~~By none, and if not equal all, yet free,~~
> ~~Equally free; for Orders and Degrees~~
> Jarr not with liberty, but well consist.

> Who can in reason then or right assume
> Monarchie over such as live by right
> His equals, if in power and splendor less,
> In freedome equal? ~~or can introduce~~
> ~~Law and Edict on us, who without law~~
> ~~Erre not?~~ much less ~~for this to be our Lord,~~
> ~~And~~ look for adoration, to th' abuse
> Of those Imperial Titles which assert
> Our being ordain'd to govern, not to serve. (5.787–802)

These redactions are freighted with anxiety that Satan's (Fox's) words might carry a certain allure. In truncating this monologue by six lines, the satirist cuts Satan's claims both that "all" are "equally free" and that the law is an arbitrary, ex post facto invention to which the rebel angels have not consented. That is, the speech of Fox in *Satan harangueing* has been purged of a vocabulary, and an argument, that reads rather like a short-form version of Lockean contractualism and that is too carefully, too persuasively elaborated.

Finally, Thomas Rowlandson adopted Milton's own means of undermining Satan's charismatic authority. In *Preceptor and Pupil* (fig. 5.11), published in May 1784, Rowlandson depicts Fox as an enormous toad (with a vulpine brush) who, against an Edenic backdrop, squats beside the sleeping Prince of Wales and whispers seditious counsel into his left ear: "Abjure thy Country and thy parents And I will give thee dominion over Many powers," Fox mutters, "Better to rule in hell than Serve on Earth" (adapting 1.263). As is confirmed by a gloss below the image—"Not Satan to the Ear of Eve / Did e'er such pious Counsel give. Milton"—Rowlandson parodies book 4 of *Paradise Lost*, where Ithuriel and Zephon discover Satan

> Squat like a Toad, close at the eare of *Eve;*
> Assaying by his Devilish art to reach
> The Organs of her Fancie, and with them forge
> Illusions as he list (4.800–803)

This ironic adaptation effeminizes the prince, who, given his profligacy, resembles Eve in his susceptibility to temptation, but the more significant detail here is that Rowlandson takes his audience to a point in Milton's poem where the encroachments of corruption are, for the first time, written on the Satanic body. As Raymond Waddington notes, "Milton exploits a consistent

Fig. 5.11. Thomas Rowlandson, *Preceptor and Pupil* (George Humphrey, 18 May 1784). BMC 6585. Courtesy of The Lewis Walpole Library, Yale University.

level of irony through the idea that Satan thinks he is effectively disguising himself, while the disguises only reveal his nature more effectively to the judicious spectator."[49] Rowlandson's Fox-Satan is a comically and grotesquely debased figure—slimy rather than sublime.

Underlying these various satirical maneuvers are precisely the concerns—the heroic stature of Satan, the authoritarianism of God—that would come to dominate twentieth-century Milton criticism, most notably in the approaches of William Empson ("The reason why the poem is so good is that it makes God so bad") and Stanley Fish ("The reader who falls before the lures of Satanic rhetoric displays again the weakness of Adam").[50] Likewise recognizing that the political tenor of the poem hinges on the persona of Satan, these prints work hard to shut down the appeal of the very literary figure they invoke. But to some extent the ideological tension inherent in political parodies of Milton's Satan remains, for together the prints to which I have attended bespeak an undeniable fascination with the mythology of his character even as they deploy him as a symbol of political vice. Though the years 1782–84 certainly mark the climax of this anti-Whig reading of

Paradise Lost, prints such as John Doyle's *Satan alias the Arch Agitator* (1 December 1836), which casts the Irish political leader Daniel O'Connell as Satan, or texts such as "Satan Reformer," a poem of 1832 that imagines Satan goading the Whigs into backing parliamentary reform, show Tory satirists continuing to make use of Milton's syntax of rebellion and seduction through to the 1830s.[51] The allure of Satan endures.

Gillray and the Other Paradise Lost

The prints I've considered to this point carefully apply *Paradise Lost* to a particular set of parliamentary-political circumstances. Such images advance an interpretation of the poem that the critic John Upton aptly described in 1748 as "mystical and allegorical," for they are primarily interested in mining satirical equivalences and insist upon parsing Milton's narrative analogically.[52] But in Gillray's later Miltonic parodies of the 1790s and early 1800s we can see an attempt to read the same text in a manner that goes far beyond this mode of political allegory. *Paradise Lost* was, more than any other literary work, an imaginative and rhetorical touchstone for Gillray. Eight of his prints, beginning with the early *Gloria Mundi*, take up Milton's epic in an extended, parodic fashion, and at least a further nine quote from the poem either verbally or visually. Indeed, Milton's presence radiates across Gillray's entire body of work. The strident and cynical secularity of his prints is saturated in—and paradoxically emerges through—the residual forms and phrases of the sacred and supernatural. In what Vic Gatrell calls Gillray's "dreamscapes" we find a Manichaean structure, a symbolic play of light and dark, and a proliferation of demons and devils that often seems discernably (and distortedly) Miltonic.[53] When we consider late eighteenth-century artistic engagements with *Paradise Lost* the names that most readily spring to mind are Blake and Fuseli, but we ought also to think of Gillray.

If this is the first claim that I want to make in what follows, then the second and more central one is that Gillray's Miltonic parodies show him to be perhaps the foremost reader and practitioner of mock-epic in the later Georgian period. This insight is certainly not new—both David Erdman and, more recently, Ian Haywood have understood Gillray's prints in this way—but it is in need of greater elaboration because the constitution of Gillray's mock-epic form is unusually complex.[54] While, as we've seen, prints such as *Satan harangueing* aim at mock-epic effect in that they seek ironically to equate the great (the Miltonic cosmos) and the petty (Fox's campaign against the royal prerogative), Gillray contrastingly attends to *Paradise Lost* not simply as material that is ripe for political parody but as a text that is already in some sense mock-epic, or other than epic.

Of course, *Gloria Mundi* visually established the Satan-Fox parallel that proved so fruitful for later graphic satirists, but even in this very early work Gillray demonstrates a fascination with unusual scenes in *Paradise Lost,* including moments, such as Satan's address to the sun, for which there existed little or no antecedent pictorial tradition. This interest in sections of the poem that are marked by their formal and/or narrative peculiarity manifests itself again, and to crucial effect, in the mature caricatures, and in the rest of this chapter I want to consider three of these prints: *"An angel, gliding on a Sun-beam into Paradise"* (11 October 1791), *Sin, Death, and the Devil* (9 June 1792), and *End of the Irish Farce of Catholic Emancipation* (17 May 1805). My argument about these works, what I together regard as a sort of Miltonic triptych, is that they are united by a specific concern with those scenes from *Paradise Lost* that most troubled its eighteenth-century critics, scenes that were perceived to attenuate or jettison the imperatives of both the epic and the sublime. This approach of Gillray's is by no means static; I read the prints chronologically because they show the graphic satirist's developing interest in satirically excavating moments in Milton's poem where the sublime and the ridiculous seem to bleed into each other.

Addison's 1712 essays on *Paradise Lost* are key to this discussion, for they furnished eighteenth-century readers with a road map of the poem that identified certain passages as "beauties" and also, in the spirit of critical equanimity, acknowledged "the several defects which appear in the fable, the characters, the sentiments, and the language."[55] So, where Gillray's *Gloria Mundi* parodies a speech that Addison hailed as "very bold and noble . . . the finest that is ascribed to Satan in the whole poem," *"An Angel, gliding on a Sun-beam into Paradise"* (fig. 5.12) contrastingly takes up a passage that the critic had given short shrift.[56] In this later print a winged Elizabeth Juliana Schwellenberg, the keeper of the queen's robes, descends along the path of a sunray toward Hanover (shown as a distant fortification), carrying with her two swollen bags of money. The Miltonic scene that Gillray cites here is the archangel Uriel's descent into Eden to warn Gabriel of Satan's incursion:

Fig. 5.12. James Gillray, *"An Angel, gliding on a Sun-beam into Paradice"* (Hannah Humphrey, 11 October 1791). BMC 7906. Courtesy of The Lewis Walpole Library, Yale University.

> Thither came *Uriel*, gliding through the Even
> On a Sun Beam, swift as a shooting Starr
> In *Autumn* thwarts the night (4.555–57)

Of these lines, Addison writes: "*Uriel's* gliding down to the earth upon a sunbeam, with the poet's device to make him *descend*, as well in his return to the sun, as in his coming from it, is a prettiness that might have been admired in a little fanciful poet, but seems below the genius of Milton."[57] This assessment invokes a binary—"genius" on the one hand, "prettiness," littleness, and fancifulness on the other—that is implicitly gendered. In its gratuitous contrivance, Addison suggests, the feminine poetics of Uriel's descent compromises the robust and manifestly masculine force of epic. Gillray's *"Angel, gliding,"* then, employs a moment that already teeters on the cusp of absurdity. But rather than simply appropriating the passage as an instance of epic malfunction, Gillray's satire hinges on the comic disjunction between the elegance of the Miltonic scene he cites and the lumbering figure of Schwellenberg, who looks more like she is falling than flying. Like other satires of Schwellenberg, a notoriously difficult personality, Gillray both caricatures her corpulence and rehearses accusations that the queen was using her as a means of conveying presents and money into Hanover.[58] "Down thither, prone in flight,—Lo Schwelly speeds, & with her brings, the Gems, and Spoils of Heav'n," reads the gloss beneath the print's title, which splices Milton's account of Raphael's descent to earth (5.266–67), Eve's image for the starry night sky (4.649), and, tellingly, Satan's description of mankind as his "Heav'nly spoils" (9.151). This textual mosaic introduces ambiguity here: Is Schwellenberg in fact a fallen angel? Either way, and as is so often the case in Gillray's work, the framing/quoted text sits in ironic tension with the contours of the image, for his caricature of Schwellenberg does not (and cannot) "speed" and her celestial booty is no more than ready cash. Gillray's Uriel-Schwellenberg not only lacks due archangelic grandeur but fails even to meet the standard of "prettiness" to which Addison opposed true epic. Seizing upon a moment that already sits at the boundaries of epic propriety, Gillray pushes it into the openly bathetic.

My point here is not that Gillray is directly taking his cue from Addison, though it seems highly likely that he would have been familiar with the *Spectator* essays, given their influence in instituting a reading of the poem that formed the foundation of subsequent criticism and also their consistent popularity throughout the century. Rather, I'm arguing that Gillray carefully pinpoints and unravels moments in *Paradise Lost*—an angel surfing the sunlight into Eden, for instance—at which epic appears already fractured. Such is the case when, eight months after the publication of *"Angel, gliding"*, Gillray returns to Milton's poem in what is the best known of his *Paradise Lost* parodies, *Sin, Death, and the Devil* (fig. 5.13). The print responds to Edward Thurlow's dismissal as lord chancellor in June 1792, an event that represented the culmination of his increasingly strained relations with the Pitt ministry. Thurlow had played both sides during the Regency Crisis of 1788–89 in the hope of retaining the Great Seal whatever the outcome, and when in 1792 he denounced a number of government policies in the House of Lords, Pitt presented George III with an ultimatum: either Thurlow be removed or he would resign. The king kept his prime minister, of course. In an ironic political reworking of Satan's encounter with Sin (his daughter) and Death (the

Fig. 5.13. James Gillray, *Sin, Death, and the Devil* (Hannah Humphrey, 9 June 1792). BMC 8105. Courtesy of The Lewis Walpole Library, Yale University.

son born of their incestuous union) at the gates of hell (2.648–889), Gillray satirizes the circumstances surrounding the lord chancellor's ousting by depicting Thurlow as Satan and Queen Charlotte and Pitt as Sin and Death, respectively, with other major players in Pitt's cabinet—Henry Dundas, Lord Grenville, and the Duke of Richmond—shown as the three-headed Cerberus.

This caricature is usually, and rightly, discussed in terms of its targeting of John Boydell and Henry Fuseli; we encountered both Gillray's scathing critique of Boydell's Shakespeare Gallery and his travesty of Fuseli's gothicism in the previous chapter, and *Sin, Death, and the Devil* now enmeshes these satirical programs.[59] In September 1791 Fuseli and the publisher Joseph Johnson published their prospectus for an illustrated edition of Milton's works and accompanying gallery, and Boydell, whose commercial model they looked to replicate, published his own prospectus for a rival edition of Milton just days later.[60] Gillray's caricature responds directly and caustically to these projects, as a note along the inside bottom edge of the design makes clear: "NB: The above performance containing Portraits of the Devil & his

Relatives, drawn from the Life, is recommended to Messrs Boydell, Fuselli & the rest of the Proprietors of the Three Hundred & Sixty Five Editions of Milton now publishing, as necessary to be adopted, in their classick Embellishments." Gillray posits his print as an ironic audition for Boydell's and Fuseli's ventures, and though Fuseli's Milton Gallery did not open until 1799, Gillray may well have taken immediate inspiration for his satire from advertisements for William Sharp's forthcoming engraving of Fuseli's "Satan opposing Death, and Sin intervening."[61] At the same time, Gillray mischievously inserts himself into the longer tradition of artistic engagements with this scene from *Paradise Lost*, for he also parodies Hogarth's unfinished oil sketch (fig. 5.14), likely the earliest painting of any episode from the poem. *Sin, Death, and the Devil* is thus a palimpsest of parodic strata; it is as much concerned with the cultural mediation of Milton's epic as with the poem itself.

Indeed, Gillray's print frustrates and inverts the Miltonic sublime as understood by Burke and practiced by artists such as Fuseli. In his *Philosophical Enquiry*, Burke hailed Milton's description of Death as the epitome of a sublime that operates through obscurity:

> It is astonishing with what a gloomy pomp, with what a significant and expressive uncertainty of strokes and colouring, he has finished the portrait of the king of terrors:
>
> > *The other shape,*
> > *If shape it might be called that shape had none*
> > *Distinguishable, in member, joint, or limb;*
> > *Or substance might be called that shadow seemed;*
> > *For each seemed either; black he stood as night;*
> > *Fierce as ten furies; terrible as hell;*
> > *And shook a deadly dart. What seemed his head*
> > *The likeness of a kingly crown had on.*
>
> In this description all is dark, uncertain, confused, terrible, and sublime to the last degree.[62]

As W. J. T. Mitchell suggests, Burke's privileging here—as throughout the *Philosophical Enquiry*—of abstraction and ambiguity (the word) over clarity and precision (the image) adumbrates a theory that is fundamentally antipictorialist, and it is testament to its conceptual tenacity that in the early nineteenth century Coleridge would again look to this sequence of the poem to espouse the hierarchy of verbal over visual, attacking those painters who depicted Milton's Death as "the most defined thing that could be conceived in nature—A Skeleton."[63] Gillray's print offers a mordant riposte to such dismissals of the efficacy of pictures. As Luisa Calè rightly notes, where Fuseli's Milton canvases aspired to the Burkean sublime and sought to show that "painting can present the unpresentable," Gillray's *Sin, Death, and the Devil* stridently subverts this attempt to paint abstraction and is, by contrast, interested in " 'physiognomizing' the allegory, fixing the plot in its supposed real referent, and showing its actualization in the political realm."[64] That is, he takes up a scene that Burke and Fuseli posit as ineffably sublime and drags it, kicking and screaming, into the realm of gross corporeality and identifiable personae. His figures, he insists, are "drawn from the life." Like Burke, Gillray quotes from the description of Death, reproducing part of the passage at the top left corner of his print. But where Burke mistranscribes one of the lines—writing "black *he* stood as night" rather than "black *it* stood as night" (2.670) in a slip that indexes the gendering of his sublime— Gillray is in this instance faithful to the text. This is significant because his caricature of Pitt rests on the work performed by the pronominal confusion central to the mechanics of Milton's description and effaced by Burke. As Death, Gillray's Pitt is as much an "it" as a "he"; Pitt is here "uncertain, confused" only in respect to his genitalia, which are covered by the outstretched hand of the queen but given liminal presence by the large phallic shadow cast against the cloak between his legs. As in *Wierd-Sisters,* Pitt is but half a man. In a comic disarticulation of Burke's *Enquiry,* Gillray renders the syntax of obscurity the stuff of sexual jokes.

In this respect, Hogarth's precedent is important, for in the earlier artist's hands this episode already approaches mock-epic. As Ronald Paulson notes, Hogarth's *Satan, Sin, and Death* replays the compositional structure of his famous *Beggar's Opera* paintings and so gives the scene a "slightly comic" slant that may "have proved risible to the unsympathetic Burke."[65] But if Gillray amplifies this Hogarthian model, he also changes its emphases. Where his predecessor represents Sin as an attractive young woman, an embodiment of Beauty, Gillray's Queen Charlotte is a hideously caricatured figure; she looks up at Thurlow with haggard features, her flaccid breasts swinging before her. In the frame of his print, Gillray also quotes Milton's description of Sin but now makes a telling omission: where Milton depicts Sin as "Woman to the waste, and fair" (2.650), Gillray cuts the final two

SATAN SIN & DEATH *Paradise Lost Book II.*

Fig. 5.14. Samuel Ireland, after William Hogarth, *Satan, Sin & Death* (Molton and Co., 1788). Courtesy of The Lewis Walpole Library, Yale University.

words of this line. In his rendering of this scene there is neither beauty nor ambiguity, only the clarity of physical corruption.

Yet attention to this print's complex dialogue with Hogarth, Burke, and Fuseli alone has occluded the intricacies of Gillray's reading of Milton. What has passed largely without comment is that it satirically exploits by far the most critically contested of all the *Paradise Lost*'s scenes. Burke's reading of the meeting of Satan, Sin, and Death was, we must remember, an exercise in theoretical recuperation. In fact, the episode's interpolation of allegory into an epic poem persistently unsettled Enlightenment critics, before and after Burke. Addison wrote that, though "a very beautiful and well-invented Allegory," he could not "think that Persons of such a chimerical Existence are proper Actors in an Epic Poem; because there is not that Measure of Probability annexed to them, which is requisite in Writings of this kind."[66] Lord Kames made the same complaint: "The impression of real existence, essential to the epic poem," he contended in *Elements of Criticism*, "is inconsistent with that figurative existence which is essential to allegory; and therefore no means can more effectively prevent the impression of reality, than to introduce allegorical beings co-operating with those whom we conceive to be really existing."[67] And in his *Life of Milton* Samuel Johnson reaffirmed this view, opining that "Milton's allegory of sin and death is undoubtedly faulty. Sin is indeed the mother of death, and may be allowed to be the portress of hell; but when they stop the journey of Satan, a journey described as real, and when death offers him battle, the allegory is broken. . . . This unskillful allegory appears to me one of the greatest faults of the poem."[68] As Steven Knapp notes in *Personification and the Sublime*, a book that charts the trajectory of this critical debate through to Coleridge, what ultimately troubled these eighteenth-century critics was the sense, first, that Sin and Death both represented gothic interlopers in "the essentially realistic and classical world of the epic" and, second, that their presence collapsed "the boundaries between literal and figurative agency."[69]

If *Sin, Death, and the Devil* parodies Fuseli's Milton and augments Hogarth's mock-epic take on the scene, then it also appropriates a point of epic fracture in the poem. Gillray explores a point at which the requisite probability and "reality" of Milton's epic narrative are openly violated by the incursion, to quote Johnson's *Dictionary,* of "a figurative discourse, in which something other is intended, than is contained in the words literally taken."[70] The satirical thrust of the print rests, in part, on an understanding of the Miltonic scene's problematic intermingling of two different modes of representation. Jameson's definition of genre as a contract between writer and readers, one that assumes the status of an institution, is once more instructive here, for Gillray's use of this scene depends on our recognition that it involves a breach of exactly this contract. Here the negation of epic as a literary institution is equated with constitutional slippage.[71] Pitt was often accused both of assuming powers more monarchical than prime ministerial and also of intriguing with the queen, and Thurlow's downfall provided further evidence of Pitt's remarkable influence at court. As Death and Sin, Pitt and the queen—both savagely caricatured—are thus figures who intervene in a narrative in which they do not belong, who assume an agency that is not properly theirs. As Milton's Death, Pitt plays the (false) king; he wears "The *likeness* of a Kingly Crown" (2.673; my emphasis). By casting real political personalities in this Miltonic allegory, Gillray enhances precisely the formal dissonance that disconcerted the likes of Addison and Johnson; he presses together the literal (Thurlow, like Satan, *has* fallen) and the metaphorical (Pitt behaves *as if* he were sovereign and Charlotte *as if* she were Pitt's consort). The intrusion of allegory into epic here stands as an analogue of constitutional breach.

Readings of *Sin, Death, and the Devil* too often overlook its immediate political subject in their efforts to trace Gillray's dizzying parodic negotiations, but it is exactly his application of Milton's supposedly unwarranted allegory to the circumstances of Thurlow's downfall, and Pitt's triumph, that provides the key to the print's satiric operations. Ian Haywood has argued that this caricature's appropriation of Milton, and its concomitant revitalization of an iconography immersed in the iconoclast debates of the seventeenth century, needs to be seen as a response to and an embodiment of the revolutionary moment of the early 1790s.[72] Yet to regard *Sin, Death, and the Devil* as animated by this radical context is seriously to misread it. What's remarkable about the print is Gillray's eschewal of this political exegesis—remarkable because it was so regularly articulated in other quarters. Speaking in the House of Commons in May 1791, Burke decried the revolutionary regime in France as that which defied description and proceeded to quote the very depiction of Death that his *Philosophical Enquiry* had lauded for its sublimity. Traducing France as "a shapeless monster, born of hell and chaos," Burke imagined the Revolution as an instance of the sublime and terrifying uncertainty he had theorized forty years earlier.[73] This trope circulated within Parliament over the next few years, with speakers employing Death or Satan to figure events in France on at least four further occasions, while a broadside of late 1792, *Pain, Sin, and the Devil* (BMC 8152), transformed Milton's trio into the three-headed monster of English radicalism (Thomas Paine, Thomas Erskine, and Satan).[74] Although this anti-Paineite satire almost certainly took its cue from Gillray's print, *Sin, Death, and the Devil* rather resists the prevailing, anti-Jacobin reading of *Paradise Lost* at the very historical moment when it appeared most compelling. To equate the Revolution with Milton's Death, as did Burke, was still to regard the Satan-Sin-Death episode in terms of its dynamic play of abstract ideas and images, what Lucy Newlyn calls "the aesthetics of indeterminacy."[75] Conversely, Gillray's print insists that the scene is—inescapably—an allegory and finds its political resonance precisely in its awkward collision of real and metaphorical bodies. Again, the caricaturist's claim that his figures are "drawn from the life" forestalls a Burkean flight into (ideological) abstraction.

Of course, Satan, Sin, and Death are also, as John N. King has observed, "a ludicrous travesty of the Trinity." Gillray's complex play with form and meaning in this print suggests the self-awareness with which he parodies a parody. His rendering of the scene registers its original satirical and polemical charge, as well as its use of "coarse body language" and unabashed mixing of cultural modes.[76] This view of *Paradise Lost* as the text that initiates the tradition of mock-heroism more than it ends that of epic proper is

now familiar to us; in the middle of the last century both Stanley Fish and
Dennis Burden claimed the poem to be anti-epic.[77] But, as John Leonard
notes, eighteenth-century critics "saw it as essentially the same kind of poem
as the *Iliad* and the *Aeneid*," even if "they had difficulty in making it conform
to their expectations," and Gillray's caricatures thus recover exactly that
aspect of the *Paradise Lost* that Addison, Burke, and Fuseli sought to suppress
in their various formulations of the Miltonic "sublime."[78]

Gillray's interest in passages of *Paradise Lost* that not merely break
with the epic but show the poem's engagement with, as King puts it, "invective, mockery, surly insult, parody, and satire" emerges most fully in the last
of his major *Paradise Lost* prints, *The End of the Irish Farce of Catholic Emancipation* (fig. 5.15).[79] Where *Sin, Death, and the Devil* appropriates one of
the poem's most illustrated sequences, this caricature takes up a scene that
had never before been depicted: the Paradise of Fools, or Limbo of Vanity,
that is described as Satan journeys to Earth, and which is populated by
"Embryo's and Idiots, Eremites, and Friars / White, black, and gray, with all
thir trumperie" (3.474–75). The Irish petition for Catholic Emancipation,
introduced by Fox and Lord Grenville into the Commons and Lords, respectively, had been voted down in May 1805, a week before the publication of
this print. Adapting the moment at which Milton's procession of fools is
scattered by "a violent cross wind" just as it approaches the steps to Heaven
(3.484–89), Gillray shows the lead petitioners beginning the ascent to
"Heav'n's Wicket," here marked "Popish Supremacy," but being thrown
back by the force of a ministerial gale blown by Pitt and Lords Hawkesbury
and Sidmouth, whose heads emerge from dark cloud on the far left. The petition is torn from the hands of Grenville, who heads the group and is dressed
in episcopal robes, while Fox, shown as a cardinal, is hurled from the Irish
bull he is riding and Mrs. Fitzherbert, the secret Catholic wife of the Prince
of Wales and here cast as an abbess, is sent sprawling to the ground. Importantly, Fox carries (or rather loses hold of) a tricolor banner, and his Irish bull
wears a tricolor ribbon from which hangs a medal of Napoleon. The Emancipation campaign, Gillray intimates, is a cover for dangerous Francophile
politics.

We have already encountered *The End of the Irish Farce* as the print held
and studied by the two clerics stood within Hannah Humphrey's shop in
Gillray's *Very Slippy-Weather* (see fig. 2.10). As the contact and close gaze
of these fictional consumers indicates, *The End of the Irish Farce* is a

Fig. 5.15. James Gillray, *End of the Irish Farce of Catholic Emancipation* (Hannah Humphrey, 17 May 1805). BMC 10404. Courtesy of The Lewis Walpole Library, Yale University.

tremendously detailed print, the satirical intricacies of which come into focus only through reading of the most careful kind. More than this, the laughter of the clerics is a knowing one. They are—like the Reverend John Sneyd, who designed *Very Slippy-Weather*—the intended audience of *The End of the Irish Farce:* wealthy, well-educated Protestants who would have both enjoyed its anti-Catholic jest and possessed the cultural expertise to register Gillray's complex engagement not just with *Paradise Lost* but also with its major critical interlocutors. For the Paradise of Fools discomfited eighteenth-century critics more than any other scene in the poem, precisely because its satirical imperatives were too bald for even the most ingenious of glosses to massage. Commentators almost unanimously censured Milton's interruption of his odyssey narrative with a passage that consciously reworks canto 34 of Ariosto's *Orlando Furioso,* where Astolfo visits the moon and discovers a lunar valley strewn with misplaced earthly possessions and trinkets.[80] Again, the eruption of allegory into epic was the key irritant. Addison placed the scene, along with that of Sin and Death, among those "passages [that] are aston-ishing, but not credible"; Voltaire wrote that even "the most passionate Admirers of *Milton* could not vindicate those low comical Imaginations, which belong by Right to *Ariosto*"; and James Beattie noted that "however just as an allegory, however poignant as a satire, [it] ought not to have obtained a place in *Paradise Lost*. Such a thing might suit the volatile genius of Ariosto and his followers; but is quite unworthy of the sober and well-principled disciple of Homer and Virgil." Johnson, characteristically, went the furthest in his condemnation. Milton's "desire of imitating Ariosto's levity," he wrote, "has disgraced his work with the *Paradise of Fools;* a fiction not in itself ill-imagined, but too ludicrous for its place."[81]

It is exactly such "levity," such low comedy, that Gillray harnesses in *The End of the Irish Farce*. The "farce" of the print's title is at once the futile political maneuverings of the petitionists and the generic character of the Miltonic scene being borrowed. In turning to the poem, Gillray again aligns a particular literary mode with a particular political moment, specifically appropriating Milton's set piece of anti-Catholic satire, which excoriates the orders of mendicant friars—the white (Carmelite), black (Dominican), and gray (Franciscan)—and redirecting it toward Fox, Grenville, and the other emancipationists. References to the Paradise of Fools are far from frequent in the eighteenth century, but all such allusions look to the scene for its reli-gious satire. An anti-Methodist pamphlet of 1751, for instance, suggested that "*modern Prophecies and Inspiration*" might be added to Milton's limbo, and in the early 1790s two writers quoted from the passage in their applause of the French for having "cast off the bonds of Rome" and "*annihilated the power of the pope.*"[82] Gillray, likewise, renews Milton's anti-Catholic invective; he gives it contemporary resonance but does not substantively revise it. If "*Angel, gliding*" elicits at the latent absurdity of Miltonic description and *Sin, Death, and the Devil* exploits the formal friction between allegory and epic, what Balachandra Rajan calls the poem's "deep generic uncertainty," then *The End of the Irish Farce* consciously works with *Paradise Lost* as a poem that is, in part, already satirical.[83] For one, the Weimar journal *London und Paris*, which devoted a thirty-eight-page essay to the print, recoiled from its unabashed bigotry. Writing that the piece "drips with poisonous mockery," its reviewer applauded Gillray's invention but protested that "no reasonable Protestant would ever condone" its "sarcasm."[84] Gillray here excavates *Para-dise Lost* not for epic material that can repurposed to mock-heroic effect but rather for religious satire that is in need of very little adjustment. We might well ask how far *The End of the Irish Farce* represents anything we could call Miltonic parody.

This is not to say, however, that the caricature is something other than parody. Rather it is to recognize that it faithfully adopts the parodic and, more generally, comic schema of its source material. First, both Milton and Gillray travesty a particular institutional iconography. Roland Frye has argued that in the Paradise of Fools Milton offers a "*reductio ad absurdum* of the apotheosis ceiling" popular at seventeenth-century courts, an "uproarious parody" of works such as Peter Paul Rubens's *Apotheosis of Buckingham*, at York House, and *The Apotheosis of James I*, at Whitehall, that Milton likely saw as blasphemous.[85] Equally, *The End of the Irish Farce*—like other Gillray prints, such as *Light Expelling Darkness* (30 April 1795; BMC 8644)—upends the grand vocabulary of history painting in its rendition of this scene. Noting that the caricature's "splendidly conceived composition . . . would be worthy a nobler subject," and so failing to register Gillray's remarkable fidelity to Milton, *London und Paris* even commented that the design bore striking similarities to Raphael's Vatican fresco *The Repulse of Attila* (c. 1512–14).[86]

Second, like the Paradise of Fools, Gillray's print offers a comedy of enumeration:

> Cowles, Hoods and Habits, with thir wearers tost
> And fluttered into Raggs, then Reliques, Beads,
> Indulgences, Dispenses, Pardons, Bulls,
> The sport of Winds: all these upwhirld aloft
> Fly o're the backside of the World (3.490–94)

Gillray not only quotes this satirical list at the foot of *The End of the Irish Farce* but also visually transposes its syntax within his design, which features tight clusters of figures and, top right, a concatenation of objects, a "colourful mass of sacred bric-a-brac" as *London und Paris* described it.[87] In the mock apotheoses of Milton and Gillray, there is no ascent of the spirit, merely the worthless accretion of inanimate things. Before Gillray, Alexander Pope was a lone voice in the century in his praise of Milton's architecture of "the ludicrous" in the Paradise of Fools, and the poet offers his own tribute to the scene in his speculation, toward the close of *The Rape of the Lock*, that Belinda's missing lock of hair may have "mounted to the Lunar Sphere," where "all things lost on Earth" are deposited, including "Heroe's Wits . . . The Smiles of Harlots, and the Tears of Heirs."[88] Pope's poem reminds us that the Ariostan and Miltonic joke is one of reification. Abstractions take on the tangibility and obsolescence of things; emotions, memories, and expressive gestures become a kind of detritus.[89] So, in *The End of the Irish Farce,* statesmen are shown to be idolaters and their cherished principles are reduced to—or exposed as—a litany of polished but disposable objects. Like Ariosto, Pope, and, most crucially, Milton before him, Gillray offers as a parody of (trans)substantiation. Once again the caricaturist reads *Paradise Lost* against the Burkean grain. There is no drama of abstraction in this political world. It is the hard facts and defined contours of bodies and objects that, abundant as they are awkward, constitute a kind of comic sublimity in Gillray's Miltonic prints.

This, then, is what Gillray called "Caricatura-Sublime," the term he coined in his 1791 print *Wierd-Sisters* (see fig. 4.8). On the one hand, it gives a name to Gillray's ironic inversion of the aesthetic cultivated by fine art establishments such as the Royal Academy and Boydell's Shakespeare Gallery. On the other, though, and in light of the images we've been considering, the term seems to signal an approach that is about far more than the turning inside out of prevailing conceptions of the sublime, the positing of a mock or antisublime, for the phrase "Caricatura-Sublime" also conjoins two discursive modes, two categories of perception if you will, that are customarily polarized, then and now. Looking across the three caricatures I've just discussed, what emerges is Gillray's attempt, to quote a critic writing in the *London and Westminster Review* in 1837, to show us "that the ludicrous is not divided by a step from the sublime, but blended with it and twined round it."[90]

At the end of the first part of this chapter we saw graphic satirists paradoxically grappling with the difficulty of divesting *Paradise Lost,* and its antihero in particular, of the very sublimity that gave it such cultural cachet at that same moment. The danger inherent to the rhetorical gambit in which such parodists engage is always that mock-epic might rebound into something much closer to epic, and that the satirical target might thus emerge with precisely the charisma and oratorical power that is, by design, to be neutralized. Here, as in the preceding chapters, we can perceive the constitutive tensions of a form that habitually negotiates between the banality of the topical and the prestige of high literary culture. Caricaturists attempted to bring down the full weight of a monument of English literature upon Fox, not only to vilify him but also to belittle his pretentions to political heroism. Yet such an exercise underestimated the cultural power of the very text it appropriated, with the result that Fox seems often to be flattered by the comparison—to be located within a discursive space of enduring myth and cultural canonicity. Gillray's unique negotiation of *Paradise Lost* brings with it no such risk because it draws out of Milton's poem, and then actively fosters, a sublime of an altogether different kind. Gillray's comedy, to take up Raimonda Modiano's extrapolation of Friedrich Theodor Vischer's *On the Sublime and the Comic* (1836), "thrives on . . . incidents in which the high and the low, the serious event and the trivial circumstance crash into one another in the most surprising fashion."[91] Gillray's readings of *Paradise Lost* repeatedly identify the poem as a foundational exercise in mock-epic and generic hybridity, a text in which the registers of polemic, topical satire, and epic coexist. In prints that use formal dissonances to codify political events we find rescued a counterhistory, a counterpolitics, of the sublime far removed from Burke's anatomy of terror—a sublime which subsists, to adapt Coleridge's words, in a vocabulary of "defined things." Grounded in Miltonic precedent, Gillray's caricatura sublime insists that the satiric and the ridiculous are not the antitheses of the sublime but rather its very foundation.

6. Gulliver Goes to War

We are almost too familiar with James Gillray's *King of Brobdingnag, and Gulliver* (fig. 6.1). In a parodic reimagining of part 2, chapter 7 of *Gulliver's Travels*, George III, dressed in military uniform, scrutinizes with his spyglass the diminutive, swaggering Napoleon stood on the palm of his outstretched right hand. It is one of the most reproduced and instantly recognizable political caricatures in British history, and it has come increasingly to be entwined in the cultural memory with the very text it adapts (indeed, at the time of writing, the image even adorns the Oxford World's Classics edition of the book). Of course, the efficacy of this 1803 caricature lies in its striking simplicity—the juxtaposition of two profile figures, one small one large, against a plain background—but the question of how it orients itself in relation both to *Gulliver's Travels* and to the longer history of that text's adaptation and political appropriation is more complex. In contrast to the other case studies in this book, then, this chapter centers on just one print. This does not mean that I'm laying aside my interest in broader historical patterns of political parody but rather that I hope to register the way in which we can find such patterns at once distilled in and refracted through a single image, especially an image as noteworthy as this one.

Here, my concerns are twofold. First, by reading this print reading Swift I seek to understand both the significant ways in which it departs from preceding graphic satirical uses of *Gulliver's Travels* and also the immediate and readily traceable cultural ripple effect of its conscription of Swift's book in the services of anti-Bonaparte propaganda. Such propaganda was urgently and energetically produced following the collapse in May 1803 of the Treaty

Fig. 6.1. James Gillray, after Thomas Braddyll, *The King of Brobdingnag, and Gulliver* (Hannah Humphrey, 26 June 1803). BMC 10019. Yale Center for British Art; Yale University Art Gallery Collection.

of Amiens, which had secured a fifteen-month peace between France and Britain. With the resumption of hostilities and widespread reports that Napoleon was mobilizing a huge fleet to cross the Channel, the country was gripped by fear of imminent invasion, throughout the summer months especially. Along with broadsides, caricatures became an important print medium for the expression and consolidation of patriotism in response to this alarm, and it's no coincidence that this year represents perhaps a high-water mark in the production and dissemination of single-sheet visual satires; as Alexandra Franklin notes, more caricatures "were published in 1803 . . . than in any other year before 1815."[1] Taken as a concentrated body of satire, these political prints are markedly different from those we have considered up to now, in that they almost entirely eschew the partisan concerns by which the form is otherwise animated; the fractious business and personalities of Westminster are held in abeyance as caricatures during the invasion scare instead direct their efforts to projecting reassuring and often bellicose fantasies of British consensus and indomitability—and, concomitantly, of French weakness and Napoleonic delusion. This specific political climate of pervasive fear and (at least seeming) unanimity is not just the context for but also the content of *The King of Brobdingnag*, which was published by Hannah Humphrey on 26 June 1803, just over a month after the breakdown of the peace. We tend to read Gillray's output in terms of its insistent ideological evasiveness, but part of my argument here is that, for all its playfulness, this particular print is remarkably unequivocal in its political message.[2] As we shall see, what's especially interesting about this caricature as an instance of Swiftian appropriation is the success with which it fashions a comedic but stridently patriotic text—and by now I hope we're comfortable broaching graphic satires as texts—out of a complex and always-shifting work of satirical fiction that is well noted for undertaking to "vex" its readers.[3]

This propagandistic refashioning of *Gulliver's Travels* makes far more sense once we recognize that Gillray was etching an original design by Captain Thomas Braddyll of the Coldstream Guards. In June 1803 Braddyll was stationed in London along with the rest of his regiment, and the days immediately surrounding the publication of *The King of Brobdingnag* show him to be immersed in the war effort. On 22 June, four days before the print appeared, the guards were reviewed by the Duke of York in Hyde Park as part of an ostentatious exhibition of military maneuvers that sought to reassure the capital that the nation was on a war footing; and early in the morning of 27 June, within hours of the caricature's posting in Humphrey's shopwindow, Braddyll marched with the rest of his battalion to Chelmsford, where they were better positioned to defend southeast England against possible invasion.[4] This involvement of a senior officer in one of the army's most prestigious regiments takes me to the second of my concerns in this chapter, namely the kinds of collaborative satirical practice that this particular caricature allows us to

trace. *The King of Brobdingnag* testifies to the vital interaction between professional caricaturists and dilettante amateurs in this period, an interaction too
often occluded by our enthrallment to the myth of the satirist as a figure who
stands apart from and unflinchingly speaks truth to power. This print compels
us to think of satire less as a singular vocation and more as a commercial, and
communal, enterprise.

As we saw in Chapter 2, in the early 1770s the ever-entrepreneurial
Darlys pioneered a business model that actively tapped into the revenue potential of the amateur culture of caricature that thrived in the homes of the elite.
"*Ladies and Gentlemen sending their Designs* may have them neatly etch'd and
printed for their own private Amusement at the most reasonable rates," reads
one of their advertisements.[5] Such commissions were a steady source of
income for graphic satirists. According to his biographer, George Cruikshank
"asserted that the most profitable jobs Gillray, Rowlandson, and he himself
had met with in their working careers, were what he termed, the 'washing of
other people's dirty linen,'—by which he meant the putting on to copper [of]
the crude designs of fashionable amateurs."[6] Certainly, Gillray was paid hand-
somely by many amateurs who simply wished to have ideas or sketches of
little public interest etched by his expert hand for circulation among family
and friends. In a letter of 1799, for instance, Francis Hawkesworth of Hick-
leton Hall, Derbyshire, first asks Gillray to send him "a couple of needles and
some wax, the *same* that you etch with yourself," and then goes on to entreat
the caricaturist to touch up a copper plate "that has a very bad etching on it,"
promising considerable remuneration in return for such a favor.

Other amateurs, however, were anxious to have their flair for political
satire more widely acknowledged and freely sent hints and drawings to
Gillray in the hope that he would judge them worthy of taking up. "A good
subject for your pencil," opens one such missive of 1796, sent from Lloyds
Coffee House, which briefly describes a possible scene before noting that
Gillray will "know well how to fill up & improve these outlines." Similarly,
a correspondent of 1803 notes: "You have done me the honor sometimes to
illustrate my ideas, and I am tempted to see them in the vivid portraying of
your pencil once again."[7] In truth, Gillray depended upon and readily used
such hints and sketches—many of which were parodic—and Draper Hill
estimates that more than three-quarters of the caricaturist's output in 1795–96
was based on ideas submitted to him by such amateurs. For this very reason,
from late 1797 onward Gillray consistently used different formulations of his

signature in order to distinguish those prints that were entirely his own invention, which he marked "inv: et fect" (invented and made), from those that worked up the hints or drawings of others, which he respectively inscribed "des: et fect" (designed and made) and simply "fect."[8] In this way, the creative relays between the professional satirist and his public came to be incorporated into the very fabric of Gillray's caricatures.

We've already glimpsed collaboration of this kind in *Very Slippy-Weather*, which Gillray etched to a design by the Reverend John Sneyd, and Braddyll's involvement in *The King of Brobdingnag* once more evinces the extent to which the upper classes participated almost as much in caricature's production as they did in its consumption. The eldest son of the sometime MP Wilson Gale Braddyll and the heir to the family estates at Conishead Priory and High Head Castle, Cumbria, Thomas Braddyll was very much of the gentry. Schooled at Eton and Cambridge, by the first years of the nineteenth century, in his late twenties and evidently not lacking in confidence, he was both a commissioned officer and an active and successful amateur actor. In early 1802, for instance, he twice took to the stage at the Rochester Theatre as part of a company of military thespians. On the first evening, he played Falstaff in *1 Henry IV* and the title character in Arthur Murphy's farce *The Apprentice;* on the second, before an "audience consisting of persons of the first rank and fashion, who were admitted by tickets of invitation," he showcased his versatility by acting the lead role in Shakespeare's *King John* and then tackling two parts in Samuel Foote's comedy *The Minor.*[9] If acting was one of Braddyll's passions, then caricature was a second. Writing home from Portugal during the middle of the Peninsular Campaign in late 1811, a fellow officer of the Coldstream Guards described Braddyll, by then a lieutenant-colonel, as "remarkably entertaining and clever," adding that "the caricature of the King holding Bonaparte in his hands" was one of his "productions."[10] Indeed, the handful of surviving watercolor sketches that Braddyll sent to Gillray show him to be an accomplished caricaturist in his own right, and between 1803 and 1809 Gillray etched at least five of his designs, including *St. George and the Dragon* (2 August 1805, BMC 10424), another stridently nationalistic jab at Bonaparte.[11] *The King of Brobdingnag* is, then, the invention of an urbane, culturally engaged gentleman soldier who well embodied the ideals and charismatic cultural authority of upper-class dilettantism in this period. The print reminds us that the intertextual structures of Gillray's works bespeak not only the caricaturist's erudition but also the expertise, the cultural capital, of the privileged community of amateurs in his orbit and with whom he frequently collaborated, a community that included not only Braddyll and Sneyd but also George Canning and George Steevens, the editor of Shakespeare who likely supplied the Latin tags for Gillray's caricatures.[12] Put differently, the *difficulty* of satirical prints not only aims at but in some sense emerges from a highly educated elite.

Yet, paradoxically, if *The King of Brobdingnag* discloses the upper-class inflection of caricature more directly than any other print we've considered, it also seems to eschew such difficulty and to offer satire that consciously strives to reach beyond the aristocracy of culture. This is a print that rewards but does not finally demand a detailed knowledge of *Gulliver's Travels;* it is an image that arguably seeks to speak to—and perhaps did speak to—a larger audience than most of the parodies we have hitherto looked at. Nor does Swift's text carry with it, then or now, the same carefully shielded sense of cultural prestige as Shakespeare's plays or Milton's poem. As a work that is already topically satirical, already scatological, and that was already circulating fairly widely at this time, a caricaturist could parody it, and could apply it to Napoleon, without in any way jeopardizing the integrity of the national canon or the separation of high and low cultures. Indeed, in this print high and low seem to be differently aligned. *The King of Brobdingnag* presents us with an image in which the "literary" and the aristocratic converge with something approaching the "popular," an image that reveals the role that an elite culture of parody played in the construction of an ostensibly more inclusive patriotism.

The Travels of Gulliver's Travels

The appeal of *Gulliver's Travels* to the graphic satirist most obviously resides in its rich, detailed, and extraordinary tapestry of situations and characters. Yet Jeanne K. Welcher rightly points out that "for eighteenth-century imitators of Swift, the cartoon was a far more appropriate medium than was illustration," for *Gulliver's Travels* also shares with caricature a number of thematic concerns and representational strategies.[13] Both offer parody that, in Claude Rawson's words, "transcends its immediate object"; both deploy a highly descriptive language that delights in hyperbole; both pivot their satire upon the elaboration of physiognomic peculiarity and juxtaposition; and, as we'll see shortly, both are concerned with issues of visual perspective and perception.[14]

The Punishment inflicted on Lemuel Gulliver by applying a Lilliputian fire Engine to his Posteriors for his Urinal Profanation of the Royal Pallace at Mildendo which was intended as a Frontispiece to his first Volume but Omitted.

Fig. 6.2. William Hogarth, *The Punishment inflicted on Lemuel Gulliver* (1726). BMC 1797. Metropolitan Museum of Art, New York, www.metmuseum.org.

William Hogarth, for one, was quick to recognize these confluences. His print *The Punishment inflicted on Lemuel Gulliver* (fig. 6.2)—which shows an assembly of Lilliputians forcibly administering an enema to the protagonist as a reprimand for his urination on the royal palace (pt. 1, ch. 5)—was published in late December 1726, less than two months after Swift's book. Hogarth's imagined scene (it does not take place in the text) is a deft riff on the scatological humor and ironic inversion of its source. Just as Gulliver extinguishes the palace conflagration with his own bodily fluids, so the Lilliputians now exact homeopathic revenge by pumping water into his body using, appropriately, a fire engine. Equally, in its plays with differences of size—at the top right a mouse carries away an infant—and depiction of a prostrate Gulliver much larger than his captors, the print offers a variation on what would quickly become the most illustrated scene from *Gulliver's Travels,* where the washed-up Gulliver awakes to find himself bound and swarmed upon by a throng of alarmed but inquisitive Lilliputians.[15] Like *Gulliver's Travels,* this satire lashes Robert Walpole's administration. "Hogarth interprets Gulliver," suggests Ronald Paulson, "as an image of the honest Englishman—a huge version of Arbuthnot's John Bull—who stupidly gives up his 'liberty' to these pygmy politicians and clergyman." For all that Hogarth conjures an episode entirely of his own invention, then, this print is discernably Swiftian in its tenor and targets. Troubling ideas of authenticity in a manner akin to the disorienting prefatory material of Swift's book—the portrait of Gulliver, Richard Sympson's note to the reader—the print even tells us that it was "intended as a Frontispiece to his first Volume but omitted."

Yet in the history of appropriations of *Gulliver's Travels* Hogarth's *Punishment inflicted on Lemuel Gulliver* represents a false start; sixty years would pass before the next graphic satirical parody of Swift's text appeared. During this intervening period, the print seller John Bowles produced several engraved "Lilliputian" sequences that show capering and often ornately dressed pygmy figures, but these satires are neither political nor parodic; they rather anglicize an older Flemish grotesque tradition and testify in particular to the rapid cultural uncoupling of the term *Lilliputian* from its original Swiftian context.[16] And in 1757, Robert Sayer reissued *The Punishment of Lemuel Gulliver* as *The Political Clyster* (BMC 1797), recalibrating Hogarth's satire to imply that the incumbent government ought to be "purged" of those ministers responsible for the country's stuttering start to the Seven Years' War.[17] Otherwise, though, no political prints make noteworthy—that is, parodic—use of *Gulliver's Travels* until James Sayers's *Gulliver Casting a Damper upon the Royal Fireworks at Lilliput* of 1786 (fig. 6.3), a satire that once more takes inspiration from Swift's scatological imagination.[18] Responding to a debate in the Commons concerning the need to reinforce fortifications at Plymouth and Portsmouth in which the Speaker Charles Wolfran Cornwall had cast the decisive negative vote, Sayers depicts a gigantic Cornwall laying waste to the dockyard ramparts by discharging upon them a forceful stream of urine, labeled "Casting Vote," in a parliamentary parody of Gulliver's urinary extinction of the fire in the Lilliputian palace. It is this print, rather than Hogarth's, that marks the beginning of an era of regular graphic satirical engagement with *Gulliver's Travels*. Across the next forty years, whether through brief quotation or more elaborate parody, above thirty political caricatures take up Swift's text in some way.

It's not my intention here exhaustively to survey all of these Gulliverian political caricatures. Such an exercise would little illuminate the questions with which I am concerned, and in any case Welcher's catalog of visual imitations of *Gulliver's Travels* already provides a resource of this kind. Rather, through a close reading of the parodic structure of the

Fig. 6.3. James Sayers, *Gulliver casting a Damper upon the royal Fireworks at Lilliput* (Thomas Cornell, 1 March 1786). BMC 6919. Courtesy of The Lewis Walpole Library, Yale University.

Braddyll-Gillray *King of Brobdingnag,* I want to consider what it means to put Swift's book to specific political use at a particular and unusually charged moment of cultural crisis, and what strategies of (mis)reading and ideological contortion are involved in pressing into patriotic service a fiction that we are accustomed to thinking of resisting as allegory and denying readers the comfort of stable meaning.[19] Before I do so, however, it is necessary to give a brief account of the status and mediation of *Gulliver's Travels* within the overlapping cultural economies of print, political discourse, and, of course, graphic satire at the close of the eighteenth century.

The bibliographical history of *Gulliver's Travels,* at least in Britain, has been thoroughly charted. The text was rapidly and repeatedly embellished with illustrations, usually one design for each part. Benjamin Motte published the first English illustrated edition in 1728, and by the turn of the century the best-known such edition was that which appeared in 1782, with designs by Thomas Stothard, as part of the series *The Novelist's Magazine.*[20] Equally, *Gulliver's Travels* was subject to abridgment as early as 1726–27, but abbreviated versions that entirely omitted parts 3 and 4 began to appear in the 1770s.[21]

In particular, Francis Newbery's *Adventures of Captain Gulliver* (1772), which was regularly reprinted across the next thirty years, offered a truncated account of the voyages to Lilliput and Brobdingnag that was written in the third person and supplemented with nineteen woodcut illustrations. Marketed as one of Newbery's books "for the Instruction and Amusement of Children" and sold for just sixpence, this edition helped to broaden the readership for Swift's text.[22] This is not to suggest that Newbery brought *Gulliver's Travels* to a genuinely popular culture; David Vincent and Sheila O'Connell rightly caution us that the price of his books, which was well above the penny for which most chapbooks sold, put them "largely out of reach of working-class families."[23] But it is to note, first, that *The Adventures of Captain Gulliver* significantly extended the appeal of Swift's book, if not across the classes then at least across the generations—generically recoding it to achieve this aim—and, second, that the years in which political caricaturists began to appropriate *Gulliver's Travels* with some frequency coincide with a period in which the book was undergoing a fundamental transformation in terms of its audience, textual constitution, and visual proliferation. Tellingly, not a single political print from this period makes reference to the voyages to Lagado or the land of the Houyhnhnms, thus at once reflecting and reinforcing the cultural excision of the second and more discernably misanthropic portion of Swift's satire.

Yet alongside this refashioning of *Gulliver's Travels* as a highly illustrated children's classic, a process usually understood as involving the text's political and satirical sanitization, we need to set a second, citational history, which sees pamphleteers and polemicists of the 1790s marshaling the tropes and characters of Swift's book with uncommon frequency. Lobbying for peace in 1797, Robert Heron asserted that to review the horrors of the war against revolutionary France was to encounter a procession more "terrifying" and "afflicting" than "the ghostly train exhibited to the wondering Gulliver, in the magic palace of the governor Glubdubdrib" (pt. 3, ch. 7).[24] Likewise, two pamphlet attacks on the Act of Union of 1800, which united the parliaments of Dublin and Westminster, referenced *Gulliver's Travels* as a means of pouring scorn on the British government's suggestion that union would commercialize the Irish economy: the first, by Robert Orr, caustically compared the ministry's vision of a suddenly prosperous Ireland to "the ingenious architect in Gulliver's voyage to Laputa, who contrived a new method of building houses by beginning at the roof" (pt. 3, ch. 5), while the second, by Matthew Weld, ridiculed Pitt the Younger's plan, "like another Gulliver . . . to drag the commerce, shipping *and all* of even our enemies to our shores" (alluding to pt. 1, ch. 5).[25] Implicitly invoking Swift as a defender of Irish interests, these two writers draw upon *Gulliver's Travels* as a repository of fantastical motifs that, by sardonic analogy, expose the perilous absurdity of the Pitt government's policies and rhetoric.

Others commentators looked to Swift's book more precisely as a prescient sequence of political parables. In an essay concerned with British cultural decline, George Edwards praised *Gulliver's Travels* for its useful elaboration of "ideas of civilization" and "national perfection"; in the second edition of his *Enquiry Concerning Political Justice* William Godwin applauded Swift's book for its "profound insight into the true principles of political justice" and lamented that "a work of such inestimable wisdom failed, at the period of its publication, from the mere playfulness of its form, in communicating adequate instruction to mankind"; and in *Reflections on the Revolution with France* Burke compared the revolutionary regime to the flying island of Laputa, recommending that his readers "see Gulliver's Travels for the idea of countries governed by philosophers."[26] For Burke, reading Swift's book almost as dystopian fiction, the Laputians exposed the violence and oppression that attend any system of governance prepared to privilege abstract speculation above social reality; entirely lost in their thoughts, the Laputians nonetheless maintain their dominion over the lands below them by threatening to drop their island upon any town that shows resistance (pt. 3, ch. 3).

That political thinkers as diametrically opposed as Burke and Godwin could accommodate *Gulliver's Travels* to their agendas suggests at once the political resonance and ideological pliability of Swift's book at the close of the eighteenth century. But these varied citations do share an understanding of *Gulliver's Travels*—one quite alien from our own critical concern with its strategies of ambiguity, evasion, and entrapment—as a pedagogical fiction that presents its readers with a series of alternately cautionary and exemplary fictional landscapes. And in at least one respect Swift's book was invoked with discernable political consistency. Responding to and inveighing against the outbreak of war between Britain and revolutionary France in 1793, both Godwin's *Enquiry* and Henry Redhead Yorke's *Reasons urged against Precedent* quote at length from the description of human conflict and its causes that Gulliver offers the Master Houyhnhnm in part 4, chapter 5, while another pamphlet of the same year even republished this excerpt as a discrete broadside entitled "Thoughts on War, by Dr. Jonathan Swift."[27] In radical discourse of the 1790s *Gulliver's Travels* emerges as a cogent work of antiwar literature.

Given that polemicists of the final decade of the eighteenth century cite episodes that span all four parts of Swift's text, it's striking that Gulliverian political caricatures of the same period attend exclusively to the scenes in Lilliput. With the exception of a brief allusion in a print of 1790 by William Dent—where John Frith, who had thrown a stone at the king's coach, is compared to "Gulliver the little in Brob-dignag" as a means of pointing to his insignificance, and possibly his delusion, in the face of state prosecution—graphic satirists parody part 1 alone.[28] Two prints by Isaac Cruikshank, for instance, depict Pitt the Younger as a colossal Gulliver. In *The Royal Extinguisher or Gulliver Putting out the Patriots of Lilliput!!!* (fig. 6.4), a response to the Seditious Meetings and Treasonable Practices Acts of 1795 (the so-called Gagging Acts), Cruikshank depicts the prime minister as a watchman suppressing or, rather, playing with the scene that inspired Sayers in 1786, "extinguishing" a Lilliputian crowd of opposition Whigs and radicals; while in *The Modern Gulliver Removing the P——rl——t of Lilliput* (fig. 6.5) the satirist looks, as would Matthew Weld, to Gulliver's one-man rout of the Blefuscan fleet to imagine and ironize the effects of the Act of Union, with Pitt shown striding across the Irish Sea and straining under the weight of the Dublin parliament that he carries back to Westminster with him. In these caricatures, Gulliver the "man-mountain" figures both the considerable personal authority wielded by the prime minister and the ungainly size and seemingly insuperable power of the British state. The earlier print, in particular, gives the character of Gulliver a distinctly menacing inflection; wearing a hunting cap, he gleefully declares, "Aye! Aye! My Seditious Lads I'm down upon You I'll Darken your Day lights I'll stop your Throats." Like the Ariel-Pitt who unleashes the hounds against his political adversaries in *Shakespeare's Prophecy* (see fig. 3.4), another of Cruikshank's 1795 caricatures, the prime ministerial Gulliver of *The Royal Extinguisher* is shown to take perverse pleasure in acts of coercion. Ultimately, what remains implicit to the satiric work performed by both of Cruikshank's Gulliverian prints is the recognition that to appropriate Swift's Lilliput is not only to make use of a fictional scenario but to adopt the specific, ironic perspective on contemporary politics deployed in part 1 of *Gulliver's Travels*. In the 1790s, as in the 1720s, Lilliput serves as a distorted reflection of the incumbent government's machinations.

Fig. 6.4. Isaac Cruikshank, *The Royal Extinguisher or Gulliver Putting out the Patriots of Lilliput!!!* (S. W. Fores, 1 December 1795). BMC 8701. Courtesy of The Lewis Walpole Library, Yale University.

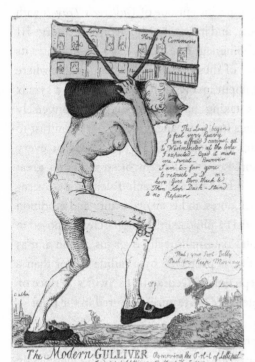

Fig. 6.5. Isaac Cruikshank, *The Modern Gulliver Removing the P—rl——t of Lilliput* (James Aitkin, January 1800). BMC 9507. Courtesy of The Lewis Walpole Library, Yale University.

With these contexts in place we are now in a better position to understand more precisely the parodic strategy of *The King of Brobdingnag, and Gulliver*. In drawing upon *Gulliver's Travels*, Thomas Braddyll and Gillray are appropriating a work of fiction that—thanks especially to the Newbery abridgment—was reaching a new readership; they are constructing a patriotic image out of a text that had begun to acquire the status of an antiwar satire; and by adapting material from the voyage to Brobdingnag they are manifestly breaking with the graphic satirical tradition of mining the first part of *Gulliver's Travels* alone, an innovation which they signal, as Welcher observes, in the note under the print's title: "Vide Swift's Gulliver: Voyage to Brobdingnag."[29] In the remainder of this chapter I want to tease out the implications of each of these points, but I begin with the last and most significant of them, the turn from Lilliput to Brobdingnag, for attention to this shift necessarily illuminates aspects of the caricature's audience and ideological disposition.

Napoleon in Brobdingnag

Thomas Braddyll's design adapts a specific episode of *Gulliver's Travels* with greater care than may at first appear, and in casting Napoleon and George III as Gulliver and the King of Brobdingnag, respectively, the print invites its reader to register the depth and wit of these parallels. Most especially, where Cruikshank's appropriation of Lilliput involved the harnessing of a syntax of political critique, Braddyll's taking up of Brobdingnag conversely marshals a fiction that readily lends itself to panegyric. In stark contrast to the Emperor of Lilliput, the King of Brobdingnag is "possessed of every Quality which procures Veneration, Love and Esteem; of strong Parts, great Wisdom and profound Learning, endued with admirable Talents for Government" (*Travels*, 193). As F. P. Lock notes, in his mental acuity and erudition the king vividly embodies the model of philosophical monarchy proposed in Plato's *Republic*.[30] Equally, he rules paternalistically over his nation and as part of a balanced constitution that is protected by a militia rather than a standing army. Put simply, the depiction of George III as Swift's "Prince of much Gravity, and austere Countenance"—features captured in the print— is stridently positive.

I recognize the potential contentiousness of this statement, but I make it in the full awareness that Gillray elsewhere excoriates the king mercilessly and, equally, that much of his work is consciously polyvalent and prone to a degree of political ambivalence that at moments seems almost to give to way to a kind of nihilism; as we've seen in previous chapters, he repeatedly operates in the interstices of opposed meanings and registers. But it is important to distinguish *The King of Brobdingnag*, a satire conceived by a young officer of the Coldstream Guards and which Gillray did not sign, from a print such as *Buonaparte, 48 Hours after Landing* (26 July 1803; BMC 10041). In that caricature, which *is* signed "Js Gillray. des. & fect.," a triumphant John Bull, dressed as a volunteer, parades the severed head of Napoleon atop a pitchfork in a scene that William Cobbett found to be repellent and that certainly troubles its own evocation of patriotism.[31] As so many of my own readings in this book testify, ambiguity has an inherent appeal for the literary critic or cultural historian, but here I want to resist this impulse and to suggest that in the specific case of *The King of Brobdingnag* what is worthy of analysis, from a critical perspective, is exactly the image's coherence and univocality.

Analogy is, then, a form of flattery in this print. But the efficacy of Braddyll's conceit lies less in its depiction of George III and more in its imagining of Napoleon. The king, after all, had been celebrated and castigated in hundreds of prints published across a period of almost forty years, and caricaturists had a repertoire of familiar and easily adaptable tropes at their disposal in treating the monarch. Representing Napoleon was, however, another matter. As Stuart Semmel has shown, he disrupted the well-worn stereotypes through which the British understood France in the eighteenth century; graphic satirists now had to grapple with a figure whose "political, religious, even . . . ethnic identity did not seem clearly defined" and in whom "elements of the old and new orders coalesced."[32] Six months before the publication of *The King of Brobdingnag*, Gillray made something of an iconographical breakthrough with his *German-Nonchalance; or, the Vexation of Little Boney* (1 January 1803, BMC 9961), a print that established the satirical commonplace of deriding Napoleon for his stature, and in "Little Boney" he created one of the most immediately recognizable and enduring figures of early nineteenth-century caricature. Braddyll's notion of showing the first consul, not as the "man-mountain" of Lilliput, but rather as Grildrig, the tiny "*Mannikin*" of Brobdingnag (135), responds to this new and more stable satirical representation of Napoleon.

Yet the parody of *Gulliver's Travels* in *The King of Brobdingnag* does more than just, quite literally, belittle Napoleon. The sustaining irony of part

2 of *Gulliver's Travels* arises from the incongruity of Gulliver's brazen pride in his own and his country's accomplishments in the face of circumstances that emphatically underline his marked inferiority, as much culturally as physiognomically. The Napoleon-Gulliver of Braddyll's and Gillray's satire is a figure of absurd hubris, a point pressed home in the monologue given in a speech balloon to George III, which reproduces and only slightly revises text from *Gulliver's Travels:* "My little Friend Grildrig, you have made a most admirable panegyric upon yourself and Country, but from what I can gather from your own Relation & the answers I have with much pains wringed & extorted from you, I cannot but conclude you to be one of the most perni- cious, little odious reptiles that nature ever suffer'd to crawl upon the surface of the Earth" (adapting 188–89). Swift's king compares Gulliver to "vermin," and the print's substitution of this insult for "reptile" at once marks Napo- leon's contemptibility and revives the association between Napoleon and Egypt, thereby calling to mind the British victory at the Battle of the Nile in 1798, in the aftermath of which caricaturists cast Bonaparte as a crocodile.[33] More significantly, this speech—itself an innovation, for no earlier Gullive- rian caricature quotes at any length from the source text—locates the print's readers at a specific moment in Swift's book. Gulliver has just delivered a long and unashamedly laudatory description "of the Government of *England,*" and having "heard the whole with great Attention" (179, 182), the king responds in a point-by-point critique that exposes the unsavory political realities so transparently varnished in Gulliver's account. It is a scene of Swiftian ventriloquism: through the voice of the outsider the satirist denatu- ralizes and censures the systemic corruptions of the British political order.

Of course, and as James Baker has argued in relation to the print's 1804 sequel, the problem intrinsic to Braddyll's appropriation of this episode is that it applies to France and Napoleon a satirical scenario that in the original text scolds contemporary England.[34] Yet, once again, we need to be wary of reading the intertextual operations of an image such as *The King of Brob- dingnag*—which was produced under conditions of acute cultural alarm and conceived by a man at the center of efforts to resist Napoleon—as obviously or inevitably polysemous. As is demonstrated by the examples of polemical citation I offered earlier, writers of the period confidently applied the fictional landscapes of *Gulliver's Travels* to a range of political issues and events with considerable regard for the positive or negative complexion of specific voyages but with little or no concern for the original targets of Swift's satire.

In any case, if Gulliver represents the England that is, then in Brobdingnag, or at least its court, Swift imagines an England that might be; eighty years after the book had been published, George III, so often described as the "father of his people," might easily be seen to have realized the image of benevolent monarchy outlined in part 2. Nonetheless, in its harnessing of this scene from *Gulliver's Travels* the print treads with notable caution. The text spoken by George III in *The King of Brobdingnag* tellingly omits the lines in which Swift's king details the problems of the English polity that has been described to him: "You have clearly proved that Ignorance, Idleness and Vice are the proper Ingredients for qualifying a Legislator" (188). In further revisions the phrase "a most admirable Panegyric upon your Country" becomes "a most admirable panegyric upon *yourself* and Country" (emphasis mine), and the king's closing censure of Gulliver's "pernicious Race" is rewritten as criticism of Gulliver alone. That is, the print's reworking of the quoted text transforms cultural critique into personal attack, almost as if to shut down the possibility of counterproductive inference.

In part 2, chapter 6 of *Gulliver's Travels,* Gulliver's puffed-up vision of his own nation—a picture of cultural superiority that is finally inseparable from his egotism—is shown to be to be a farcical delusion, and in their adaptation of this scene Braddyll and Gillray take up a fictional scenario perfectly suited to the ridicule of Napoleon's bravado and ambition. *The King of Brobdingnag, and Gulliver* is propaganda about propaganda, British patriotic sentiment about French patriotic sentiment; through a parody of *Gulliver's Travels* it constructs an image of British indomitability that encourages its viewer to laugh at the hollow fiction of Napoleonic indomitability. In this way, it's also a caricature about seeing or failing to see. As the many evocations of the printshop window as well as caricatures such as Gillray's *Phantasmagoria* (see fig. 4.7) have shown us, vision is one of the perennial tropes of eighteenth-century graphic satire, and countless prints from the 1760s to the 1790s show George III peering through a spy- or quizzing glass, or sometimes simply squinting, as a means of deriding his political myopia.[35] *The King of Brobdingnag* compositionally repeats and updates one of the most mordant of Gillray's satires on George's shortsightedness, *A Connoisseur examining a Cooper* of 1792 (fig. 6.6). This print also depicts the king in profile from the waist upward and carefully studying an opponent in his right hand, in this case a miniature of Cromwell by Samuel Cooper; here his eyes are barely open and his sight is so poor that he holds the image and the "save-all" candle

A CONNOISSEUR examining a COOPER.

Fig. 6.6. James Gillray, *A Connoisseur examining a Cooper* (Hannah Humphrey, 18 June 1792). BMC 8107. Courtesy of The Lewis Walpole Library, Yale University.

that illuminates it—a signal of his frugality—exceptionally close to his face. The king, Gillray intimates, is equally blind to the virtues of art and the perilous nature of the political moment, with Cromwell serving as a motif of the regicide and republicanism that was threateningly resurgent in the wake of the French Revolution. For Welcher, *The King of Brobdingnag*'s visual replaying of this earlier caricature implies a critique of George III, but such an interpretation misses one crucial difference between the two prints: in 1803 the king's eyes are wide open.[36]

In the later 1790s, as Vincent Carretta has argued, "George III's satiric character became a tactic rather than a target," with the king transformed by caricaturists into "a comically positive figure." Importantly, this representational shift recoded rather than discarded the satirical tropes that had gradually developed around the monarch across preceding decades. Not least, George III continued to be shown using a spyglass or similar optical instrument, but Carretta contends, citing *The King of Brobdingnag*, "George no longer needs visual aids because of his own weakness: the insignificance of his opponents demand them."[37] *The King of Brobdingnag* achieves this revaluation of the royal gaze by rechanneling the terms of *A Connoisseur examining a Cooper* through a specific parody of *Gulliver's Travels*. Swift's narrative is punctuated by acts of looking, of failing to look properly, and of looking where or at what one should not. In this "drama of perception," as Pat Rogers aptly describes it, observation rarely attends or facilitates knowledge and understanding.[38] After his conversation with the king in part 2, Gulliver apologizes to the reader for the monarch's "*narrow Principles* and *short Views*" (193), but the ringing irony of these words is that the scene has shown Gulliver to be the one whose vision is blinkered and whose judgment is warped by prejudice. The king of Brobdingnag, by contrast, is a model of clear-sightedness and attentive scrutiny, and he immediately sees through Gulliver's all-too-convenient and self-serving fantasy. In the Braddyll-Gillray print George III is therefore as much the ideal spectator as the ideal sovereign (for Swift, of course, these two roles are very much entwined). In its parody of *Gulliver's Travels*, the caricature stages a comically mismatched encounter between a critically perceptive head of state and an imposter blinded by his own arrogance.

   And there is one further political dimension to the print's appropriation of this specific encounter in Swift's book, for it also serves respectively to cast Napoleon and George III as the warmonger and the peace-loving patriarch. To corroborate his opinion of the king of Brobdingnag's "*confined Education*" (191), Gulliver recalls offering to disclose to him the secrets of gunpowder and modern artillery. The king is, however, horrified at Gulliver's detailed and gleeful description of the devastating effects of such combat technology—"which would rip up the Pavements, tear the Houses to Pieces, burst and throw Splinters on every side, dashing out the Brains of all who came near" (191–92)—and he refuses the offer, much to Gulliver's dismay. In *The King of Brobdingnag* George III is dressed in military uniform, but it is Bonaparte-Gulliver who wields a weapon and adopts the aggressive posture. Six weeks after the breakdown of the Treaty of Amiens, the caricature posits Napoleon as the antagonist and Britain, embodied by its king, as a powerful nation more than capable of defending itself but nonetheless unmistakably pacific in intent. In what can fairly be regarded as an audacious political move, Braddyll and Gillray actively harness the antiwar satire of *Gulliver's Travels* so readily deployed by radical writers of the 1790s; the caricature quietly bends Swift's denunciation of warfare to its own propagandistic and, ultimately, bellicose ends. This juxtaposition carries with it an ideological charge: Gulliver openly recommends guns and gunpowder to the king as a means by which he can subdue any city that "should pretend to dispute his absolute Commands" (192). At this moment in the text, Gulliver is the advocate of tyranny; for Swift, modern weaponry and standing armies were the unwelcome props of arbitrary rule. By contrast, the King of Brobdingnag is shown to be a just and enlightened sovereign who "would rather lose Half his Kingdom" than countenance the use of such brutal force against his subjects (193).[39]

I've elaborated in some detail the way in which *The King of Brobdingnag, and Gulliver* responds to the invasion scare through a highly targeted parody, a political reading or reshaping, of Swift's text. Braddyll and Gillray take up the ironies and cultural binaries staged in the conversation between Gulliver and the king in part 2, chapters 6 and 7, and apply them with great care to the contest between France and Britain. But the power of the image's use of *Gulliver's Travels* lies in its equal appeal to the informed reader, who is equipped to draw the rich intertextual connections I've just unraveled, and also to the viewer who possesses little or no familiarity with Swift's book. That is, and arguably in marked contrast to the Shakespearean and Miltonic parodies we've looked at, the print works at the levels of both sustained attention and immediate impression, and is accessible to spectators across the broadest range of cultural literacies. As one of Gillray's early commentators put it in a description we've encountered before: "This playful effort of our caricaturist had a wondrous effect upon the opinions of the common people of England. Bonaparte had been painted to their imagination, by his admirers in this country, clothed in terror. . . . John Bull laughed at his pigmy effigy strutting in the hand of the good King George."[40] As I noted in Chapter 2, we need to be alert to the nostalgia and class condescension that striate these words, but they do nonetheless suggest that this caricature was at least regarded by its contemporaries as both popular and widely enjoyed. Certainly, *The King of Brobdingnag* adapts a text that was more than usually accessible for an early nineteenth-century audience; a text that by 1803 had long been available in reasonably priced, well-illustrated, abridged forms that might have been bought and read by literate consumers from a diverse range of backgrounds. So Thomas Holcroft, a shoemaker's son who learned to read by working his way through the Old Testament eleven chapters at a time, first encountered *Gulliver's Travels* at the age of twelve. Holcroft's recollection of this experience in his *Memoirs*, where he describes his delight with the book's depictions of "the marvellous" but concedes that he did not properly understand it, both affirms the circulation of *Gulliver's Travels* among the literate metropolitan working class and also reminds us that its appeal often lay in its fantastical narrative architecture, which could be appreciated on its own merits without the need for engagement with Swift's satirical agenda, as the likes of Newbery recognized.[41] In the sense, *The King of Brobdingnag* ridicules Napoleon by recourse to a Swiftian joke— "nothing is great or little otherwise than by Comparison" (124)—that could be enjoyed by the quasi-literate and, at the level of basic visual juxtaposition, by the illiterate too; as Ernst Gombrich once observed, "the contrast of scales" is an "universally intelligible metaphor."[42] For all its submerged complexity and parodic precision, when we look at Braddyll's and Gillray's caricature we might well feel that Samuel Johnson's quip about *Gulliver's Travels*, "When once you have thought of big men and little men, it is very easy to do all the rest," rings true.[43]

To grasp the broad cultural reach of this caricature we need only look at other prints that respond to the invasion scare. It is little exaggeration to suggest that *The King of Brobdingnag* generated a level of imitation from other graphic satirists that was unprecedented in its scale and immediacy. Versions of it rapidly appeared in Spain and Germany, and in Britain it directly inspired at least seven caricatures published in the second half of 1803, all of which now look to Brobdingnag rather than Lilliput for satirical material; as John Ashton, the Victorian historian of anti-Bonaparte satire, put it: "Dean Swift's immortal book did yeoman's service to the caricaturists."[44] In *The Brodignag Watchman preventing Gullivers Landing* (fig. 6.7), likely by Temple West, Napoleon and his diminutive fleet reach the English coast only to find their way blocked by the towering presence of George III, who greets them with the exclamation, "Stand, ho!—What little Reptile's that?"; while William Charles's *Gulliver and his Guide. or a Check string to the Corsican* (fig. 6.8) directly plagiarizes the scrutinizing figure of George III from the Braddyll-Gillray print but redirects attention to the power of the British navy: the king inspects a tiny Napoleon as he climbs the steps toward the royal balcony, but the consul is kept on a leash by a sailor and George happily acknowledges that his crown is "protected—Hearts of Oak are our Ships Jolly tars are our men."

Where these caricatures are largely, indeed contentedly, derivative, two Brobdingnagian prints by Charles Williams engage with *Gulliver's Travels* in a more elaborate manner and politically parody moments from part 2, chapter 3, at which Gulliver is repeatedly tormented by the Queen's Dwarf. The first, *The King's Dwarf plays Gulliver a Trick* (fig. 6.9), reworks the scene in which the Dwarf mischievously wedges Gulliver into a hollowed-out bone at the royal dining table (152); here Williams shows Sholto Henry Maclellan,

THE BRODIGNAG WATCHMAN preventing GULLIVERS LANDING.

Fig. 6.7. (left) Temple West (?), *The Brodignag Watchman preventing Gullivers Landing* (William Holland, December 1803). BMC 10130. © The Trustees of the British Museum.

Fig. 6.8. (below) William Charles, *Gulliver and his Guide. or a Check String to the Corsican* (August 1803). BMC 10051. © The Trustees of the British Museum.

GULLIVER and his GUIDE. or a CHECK string to the CORSICAN.

Lord Kirkcudbright, a man known for being "short in stature and deformed in person," stuffing Napoleon into a bone and punningly exclaiming, "There you little insignificant Pigmy, I've Bone'd you."[45] Published three days later, the second of Williams's prints, *The Little Princess and Gulliver* (fig. 6.10), reimagines the Dwarf's dropping of Gulliver into a bowl of cream (151–52), with the role of Gulliver-Napoleon's persecutor now taken by the Prince of Wales's seven-year old daughter, Charlotte. Though clearly inspired by *The King of Brobdingnag,* Williams's satirical diptych makes discernably different use of part 2 of *Gulliver's Travels.* It patriotically appropriates the narrative less for its idealized image of paternalistic monarchy than for its recurrent staging of the protagonist's shaming and emasculation. Williams's Napoleon is very much Swift's Grildrig, a plaything who finds himself powerless not only in the face of legitimate authority but even against the opportunistic cruelties of children and outsiders.

Fittingly, Braddyll and Gillray have the last word in this brief but intense period of patriotic Gulliveriana, and their sequel *The King of Brobdingnag and Gulliver (Plate 2d)* (fig. 6.11), published in February 1804, is the last caricature to locate Napoleon among the giants of Brobdingnag. Citing, as the subtitle tell us, the scene of "Gulliver maneuvering with his little Boat in the Cistern" (pt. 2, ch. 5), the print shows Napoleon demonstrating his seafaring skills in a large tank of water before a court audience that includes the enthroned George III and Queen Charlotte, four princesses, the Marquess of Salisbury (then lord chamberlain), and attendant pages and beefeaters. This work is considerably more elaborate in compositional terms and parodic conception than Braddyll's and Gillray's original print. In Swift's text, Gulliver informs the reader that "Ladies gave me a Gale with their Fans; and when they were weary, some of the Pages would blow my Sail forward with their Breath" (170), and the print renders these circumstances with care as part of its mockery of Napoleon's prowess as a naval commander and feminization of his persona. As in Williams's prints, Bonaparte is imagined as no more than an innocuous curio with which women and infants toy.

On the one hand, *Plate 2d* is less satirically immediate than both its predecessor and the various caricatures inspired by that print; it yields its meaning only through prolonged engagement and, perhaps, requires a greater degree of cultural literacy on the part of its viewers. On the other hand, the discernable pictorial correspondences between *Plate 2d* and the woodcut illustrating the same episode in Newbery's *Adventures of Captain Gulliver* (fig. 6.12)

There you little insignificant Pigmy,
I've Bone'd you.

THE KING's DWARF plays GULLIVER a TRICK.

Fig. 6.9. Charles Williams, *The King's Dwarf plays Gulliver a Trick* (S. W. Fores, 18 October 1803). BMC 10111. Courtesy of The Lewis Walpole Library, Yale University.

suggest that the caricature's parody was perhaps more accessible to an early nineteenth-century audience than we might at first assume. More significantly, and unlike the 1803 *King of Brobdingnag,* Braddyll's original watercolor sketch of this caricature has survived (fig. 6.13), and we can thus place Gillray's finished etching side by side with the initial design; if you will, we can read Gillray adapting Braddyll adapting Swift. The assiduous fidelity with which Gillray etches Braddyll's sketch is certainly striking, with the compositional arrangement, title, and subtitle retained without obvious alteration. One revision is, however, especially evident, for the final print omits Braddyll's suggested epigraph from *All's Well that Ends Well:* "Who knows himself a braggart, / Let him fear this; for it will come to pass, / That every Braggart shall be found an ass" (4.3.337–39). These lines might simply be taken as an apposite aphorism, but they carry still greater satirical force if we know Shakespeare's play, for there they are spoken by the swaggering military captain

The LITTLE PRINCESS and GULLIVER.

Fig. 6.10. Charles Williams, *The Little Princess and Gulliver*
(S. W. Fores, 21 October 1803). BMC 10112. Courtesy of The
Lewis Walpole Library, Yale University.

Parolles in the immediate aftermath of his exposure as an outright coward and
liar. More than just dismissing Napoleon's bravado, this choice of quotation
prophesies his imminent unmasking as a fool and counterfeit.

But Gillray discards this epigraph and instead includes an extended
passage from *Gulliver's Travels* at the foot of the print:

> I often used to Row for my own diversion, as well as that of the
> Queen & her Ladies, who thought themselves well entertained with
> my skill & agility. Sometimes I would put up my Sail and shew my
> art, by steering starboard & larboard;—However, my attempts
> produced nothing else besides a loud laughter, which all the respect
> due to his Majesty from those about him could not make them
> contain.—This made me reflect, how vain an attempt it is for a man
> to endeavour to do himself honour among those, who are out of all
> degree of equality or comparison with him!!!

The KING of BROBDINGNAG and GULLIVER. (Plate 2d.) — Scene. "Gulliver manœuvring with his little Boat in the Cistern." — Vide Swift's Gulliver

"I often used to Row for my own diversion, as well as that of the Queen & her Ladies, who thought themselves well entertained with my skill & agility. Sometimes I would put up my Sail and then my art by steering starboard & larboard;— However, my attempts produced nothing else besides a loud laughter, which all the respect due to his Majesty from those about him could not make them contain. — This made me reflect, how vain an attempt it is for a man to endeavour to do himself honour among those, who are out of all degree of equality or comparison with him!!" — Sw. Voyage to Brobdingnag

Fig. 6.11. James Gillray, after Thomas Braddyll, *The King of Brobdingnag and Gulliver (Plate 2d)* (Hannah Humphrey, 10 February 1804). BMC 10227. © Victoria and Albert Museum, London.

Fig. 6.12. Woodcut illustration from *The Adventures of Captain Gulliver* (London: E. Newbery, c. 1795), 100. Courtesy of The Osborne Collection of Early Children's Books, Toronto Public Library.

Fig. 6.13. Thomas Braddyll, pen and watercolor sketch for *The King of Brobdingnag and Gulliver (Plate 2d)* (1804). © The Trustees of the British Museum.

Gillray adapts and splices two different excerpts from *Gulliver's Travels* here, adding to Gulliver's description of his sailing (170) further sentences, taken from a slightly later point in the chapter, where, in the wake of his abduction by a monkey, Gulliver's suggestion that he might have fought off the animal is the cause of uncontrollable mirth at court (173–74). Why does Gillray replace Braddyll's Shakespearean quotation with a longer citation from Swift's book? Most obviously, in doing so he lends the caricature a greater sense of parodic and narrative coherence and directs viewers toward the specific episode of *Gulliver's Travels* in question. Equally, we might note that the invocation in this context of Swift, an Irishman, and of *Gulliver's Travels*, a work still on the fringes of the literary canon, brings with it none of the ideological jeopardy that might attend the similar deployment of Shakespeare, with all his culturally totemic value. Gillray keeps the nation's poet, and the nation's cherished heritage, well away from its enemy—a strategy I explore at length in the next chapter.

But the switch of quotations is also a deft revision that at once maintains Braddyll's emphasis on the braggart while also drawing particular attention to the "loud laughter" occasioned by Gulliver-Napoleon's empty bravado. In the 1803 *King of Brobdingnag*, Bonaparte elicits the Englishman's curiosity and censure; in 1804, he evokes general amusement and ridicule. This print not only encourages but is also in some sense *about* laughter. Yet not everyone in the caricature is enjoying the joke, for in a subtle but significant alteration Gillray's king—openly smirking in Braddyll's design, his mouth slightly ajar—looks intently and more solemnly at Napoleon. Taking a cue from the passage it quotes, the king here maintains his composure while those "about him" are unable to "contain" their mirth; George, it seems, is not amused. The structural center of *The King of Brobdingnag and Gulliver (Plate 2d)* thus remains that of the 1803 caricature of the same title: the confrontation between the absurd egoist and the wise, beneficent, ever-alert monarch. What's new is that this encounter is now enveloped by a scene of unbridled hilarity in which laughter works across differences of gender and class: princesses, noblemen, pages, and beefeaters all share the jest and are, perhaps, united by it. Alongside the critically attentive George and the brash but insignificant Napoleon, this second Braddyll-Gillray collaboration now depicts a British audience that responds to Napoleonic threat not with fear or contempt but with laughter; like Piercy Roberts's *Caricature Shop* (see fig. 2.6) it articulates a fantasy of national consensus, of an inclusivity effected by mirth. By replaying the original print's juxtaposition of George III and Napoleon but encircling this face-off with a diverse ensemble of laughing figures, this caricature imagines the kind of public brought into being by its earlier and more famous predecessor. Folded into its anti-Bonaparte satire *Plate 2d* offers a commentary upon the comic and political efficacy of the caricature to which it serves as a direct sequel. In this follow-up print, Braddyll and Gillray not only return to *Gulliver's Travels* but seem also to celebrate their own success in parodically conscripting Swift's book to diminish the specter of Napoleonic invasion.

Of course, this move is freighted by the tension between different and competing senses of the "public," not least because the royal household, where distinctions of rank are written into the very protocols of daily life, makes for a somewhat uneasy microcosm of national togetherness. Such tension is distilled in the print's unusually explicit signature line. Where the first *King of Brobdingnag* remains silent on the question of its authorship, including only the name of Hannah Humphrey, its publisher, *Plate 2d* announces in its bottom right corner that it is "Designed by an Amateur;—Etched by Js. Gillray." By openly signaling its nonprofessional and anonymous origins the caricature might be understood as locating itself within the space of a dutiful public rather than a matrix of commercialized satire in which even propaganda is underwritten by the profit imperative. To this extent, the print not only lays claim to a disinterested patriotism but also offers itself as an image of Napoleon conceived by "the people." Yet through both its signature and the avowed literariness of its satire—a literariness it wears less lightly than the original print—*Plate 2d* could just as easily be regarded as pointing to the determining involvement of the dilettanti within the culture of caricature and, more generally, the political nation. On this reading, "Amateur" does not mean *anyone*. Rather, this term marks the print's emergence from and address to a far less expansive kind of public; the "common people of England" that supposedly gathered round to chuckle at the 1803 *King of Brobdingnag* are suddenly nowhere to be seen. There is, at best, a fractured sense of national consensus, of "popular" politics, in this image.

7. Harlequin Napoleon; or, What Literature Isn't

I want to begin this final chapter with an account of something that did not take place, of an absence in graphic satire's archive where—given the insistent literariness of its parodic and analogic play—one might readily expect to find abundance. Between the late 1790s and 1815 Napoleon was etched and castigated in many hundreds of British caricatures, and among this body of satires are, as we've just seen, a number of prints that mine *Gulliver's Travels* for its tropes and juxtapositions.[1] Yet there are remarkably few that cast the general-turned-consul-turned-emperor as either a Shakespearean or a Miltonic protagonist. In one print (see fig. 1.2) Gillray gives to Napoleon a line of Richard III's as he furiously chases from the room a messenger who brings news of French defeat, while in a further, anonymous caricature Bonaparte is openly compared to Richard by way of a parody of William Hogarth's famous 1745 painting of David Garrick in the character.[2] Equally, two prints depict Napoleon as *Paradise Lost*'s Satan, the best known of which is George Cruikshank's *Boney's Meditations on the Island of St. Helena* of August 1815, an adaptation of Gillray's earlier travesty of Satan's resentful address to the sun (see fig. 5.5) that shows a disheveled and exiled Bonaparte gazing bitterly toward a sun that encircles a portrait of the Prince Regent. But these prints, just four in total, are the only examples of their kind, and in a period in which graphic satirists habitually appropriated the works of Shakespeare and Milton, the paucity of such parodies in relation to Napoleon must be regarded as surprising and telling in equal measure.

This state of affairs becomes more peculiar still when we recognize that caricature's general reluctance to read Napoleon in these terms stands in marked contrast to the representational strategies commonly adopted by adjacent cultural discourses. Coleridge, for instance, compared Napoleon and Macbeth as "tyrants, both indifferent to means, however barbarous to attain their ends," and Simon Bainbridge has shown at length just how often and elaborately romantic writers envisioned Bonaparte in mythic and high literary ways, finding in Milton's Satan an especially compelling analogue.[3] Why, then, such reticence on the part of graphic satirists? What was it that deterred them from venturing correspondences that seemed immediately appealing (if not obvious) for many contemporaries, and from pursuing lines of parody that were otherwise a default ploy for their medium? And if caricature largely rejected the Shakespearean and Miltonic repertoire of personae in its satirical engagements with Bonaparte, to what alternative cultural models did it turn? The Gulliverian Napoleons of the preceding chapter suggest one answer to the last of these questions, of course, but we begin to approach a second—one that will ultimately address each of the questions I've just posed—by listening once more to Coleridge. Writing in the *Morning Post* in January 1800 he scorned Napoleon's decision to grant funerary honors to Pius VI, the pope he had imprisoned only the previous year, as "no more than a handsome patch in the motley coat of a Charlatan—one more trick in the low Harlequinade of Usurpation!"[4] It is this image of Napoleon as Harlequin, of which Coleridge offers perhaps the earliest articulation, that concerns me here, for it was to achieve special currency and propagandistic utility within the parallel media of satirical prints and broadsides during the invasion scare of 1803.

As we'll see, attention to the many depictions of Napoleon as the evasive, shape-shifting protagonist of English pantomime yields particular insight into the cultural status, and discernable political structure, of the harlequinade at the beginning the nineteenth century. There is, however, much more to the ideological work performed by the caricatures and other ephemera I'll be exploring. In appropriating the iconography of pantomime, conscripting it in the service of wartime propaganda, Harlequin-Napoleon prints and broadsides are involved in a complex form of cultural negotiation. They map onto military conflict the vocabulary of a long-standing culture war whereby the highly charged and always renewed binaries of high-low, literature-entertainment, and elite-popular become a means of comprehending the military and political confrontation between Britain and Napoleonic France. That is, in casting Napoleon as a figure of illegitimate theatricality—and think of the acid disdain for "low" theatrics that underlies Coleridge's comment—caricatures take up the syntax not only of pantomime itself but also of the critical discourse that invariably shadowed the form throughout the period and that had its origins in the assault on popular culture mounted by satirists associated with the Scriberlus Club in the first half of the eighteenth century.

Images of Harlequin Napoleon thus implicitly mobilize and affirm particular conceptions of "literature" and "the literary" even as they strenuously avoid visibly naming or referencing them. They do so, moreover, at the very moment in history when, as Paul Keen has shown at length, the definition of literature itself became "the focus of struggles between multiple overlapping social constituencies" who, against the backdrop of new forms of cultural production and commercialized entertainment, variously sought to lay claim "to important forms of symbolic capital, of legitimating or contesting social privileges by writing the myths of a national or regional community."[5] In line with Keen's analysis, and in looking at some of these emergent myths, I'm doing something more here than simply suggesting that graphic satirists invoked the harlequinade in unequivocally pejorative terms. Rather, I want to trace a notable shift in the manner in which pantomime parody was deployed in caricatures of Napoleon between 1803 and 1815, a shift that discloses the ambivalences and interactions that were inherent to and arguably constitutive of the cultural politics of this period.

It is far from coincidental, then, that I close a book about parody of a manifestly literary kind with a consideration of prints which cite a theatrical form that for most commentators was not simply *not* literary but in fact directly antithetical to the values and protocols implied by that term, for this enables us to approach anew the issues of cultural capital and cultural literacy that have animated this study. Caricatures of Harlequin Napoleon, I wish to argue, are significant documents in the modern history of "literature" as a meaningful unitary category, one that claimed a certain version of "Shakespeare" as its exemplary and totemic figure. And they force us to confront once again, and far more directly than in the preceding chapters, graphic satire's negotiation of the vexed relations between literary culture, popular culture, and national identity.

Harlequin, Hybridity, and the History of Violence

At the height of the invasion scare in August 1803, amid widespread fears that Napoleon's fleet was a matter of days away from crossing the Channel, the *Morning Post* anonymously published a long poem by the humorist James Smith entitled "Harlequin's Invasion."[6] Framing itself as a prospectus for "grand new Pantomime," the poem closely reproduces and demands knowledge of the specific formal structure of this mode of theater as it was performed at the beginning of the nineteenth century, which spliced commedia dell'arte with mythological or folkloric material, as well as song, dance, and slapstick forms. As David Mayer has detailed, the panto-mime opened with a cast of characters playing out a recognizable fable (say, from Aesop, Greek myth, popular legend, or nursery rhyme), with this section of the drama abruptly transitioning into the harlequinade with the metamorphosis of the central character—Faustus or Defoe's Friday, for instance—into the disruptive and effervescent figure of Harlequin, a transformation enacted in deus ex machina fashion by some benevolent agency.[7] The remainder of the play would then chart the adventures of Harlequin, who, with his Columbine (changed from the lover), dodged the pursuit of blocking figures such as Pantaloon (usually the father) and Clown (the rival suitor) and guided the audience through a rapid-fire sequence of scenes, each set in a different locale. Along the way, as means of eluding his pursuers, Harlequin would perform a series of evasive maneu-vers, acrobatic tricks, and comic conjurations, transforming the people, objects, and even spaces he encountered with a flick of his magic sword (a slapstick).

Likewise, in the poem "Harlequin's Invasion" we are first taken to the "little Isle" of Corsica, "Where sleeps a peasant boy" named Bonaparte. But this sedate bucolic scene is summarily interrupted by the personification of Anarchy, who wakes Napoleon and transforms him into Harlequin, bequeathing him a sword "whose magic pow'r / Shall sense, and right, and wrong confound." Harlequin then embarks on a series of exploits that include his murder of the pope, now Pantaloon, his courting of the pope's daughter Gallia, now changed to Columbine, and his teasing of the Dutch in the shape of Clown. Finally, though, with the monarchs of Europe prostrate at his "blood-stain'd shrine," Harlequin turns his attention to Britain and fatally overreaches himself:

And now th' Invasion scene comes on;
  The patch'd and pyeball'd renegade
Hurls at Britannia's lofty throne,
  Full many an insolent bravado.

The trembling Clown dissuades in vain,
  And finds too late there's no retreating;
Whatever Harlequin may gain,
  The Clown is sure to get a beating.

They tempt the main, the canvas raise,
  A storm destroys his valiant legions,
And lo! our closing scene displays
  A grand view of th' infernal regions.

The action of Georgian pantomime, as Mayer notes, was "rigidly restricted," and it is precisely its highly formulaic structure that Smith's poem uses to such satiric effect, as it parodies the form's conventions and bipartite shape.[8] In doing so, it gives to its theatrical conceit a far greater level of intricacy and resonance than is suggested by Coleridge's casual comment. Here, the dizzyingly contrapuntal pattern of pantomime's scenographic shifts, the sense of rapid vicarious travel it offered audiences, recasts Napoleon's speedy ascent to power and waging of war across multiple fronts as a comedy of geographic dispersion. As Melynda Nuss writes, pantomime's "sense of constant motion" enabled it "to 'move' its audiences from world to world, creating new perspectives and new audience relations."[9] More than just a rehearsal of the well-worn *theatrum mundi* trope, Smith's poem uses pantomimic space and time to give Bonaparte's frenzied movements across the globe a sense of both the absurd and the inevitable, for each Harlequin must move in the same direction toward the same end. Except that the climax of this parodic pantomime in fact departs from the customary script, which should involve the reappearance of the benevolent agent and the final union of Harlequin and Columbine. Rather, like David Garrick's 1759 pantomime of the same name—to which I turn shortly—it furnishes its readers with the reassuring image of Harlequin's ignominious failure and final damnation.

  Smith's poem caught the print-cultural imagination. It was republished in the *Gentleman's Magazine,* the *Spirit of the Public Journals,* and the patriotic anthology *The Anti-Gallican,* and just a week after its initial appearance in

Fig. 7.1. *Harlequin's Invasion* (William Holland, 12 August 1803). BMC 10060. © The Trustees of the British Museum.

the *Morning Post* the print seller William Holland printed the poem together with an accompanying caricature (fig. 7.1).[10] In this image Napoleon, dressed in motley garb, gestures across the Channel with a wooden sword inscribed "Invincible" and informs the Dutch Clown that since "Pantaloon is no more"—the rigid corpse of Pius VI lies in background—he expects him to help France "invade that little Island." As in the poem, Clown recognizes the futility of Harlequin's enterprise. Puffing on his clay pipe, he gazes with incredulity toward the well-defended English south coast and replies: "D——m me if—if I do Master—for I don't like the look of their little ships." But the caricature is not merely illustrative. Rather than depicting Harlequin Napoleon's demise (an event in the future), it gives particular emphasis to the moment of the reader's present, to the scene just before the poem's conclusion in which Napoleon plots his invasion and, in contrast to the Dutch Clown, is too blinded by his hubris to recognize the danger that lies ahead. Harlequin Napoleon, like Braddyll's Gulliver Napoleon, is a figure of myopic arrogance. Moreover, the print subtly revises the scene it depicts, for where in the poem the Napoleonic armada is destroyed by a storm in the Channel, the caricature rather shows the Kentish coast to be protected by an impressive fleet of warships. In the image's prophecy, it is not Nature but rather the Royal Navy that will finish Napoleon. The print overwrites the implicit fatalism of Smith's poem, which marginalizes the presence and role of Britain's military power, with a more securely patriotic narrative in which Bonaparte's imminent downfall is shown to be a consequence of British indomitability and not simply bad weather.

Two further pieces of anti-Bonaparte propaganda from this period of the war politicize the iconography of the pantomime to similar effect. One of these is a satirical print: Isaac Cruikshank's *Harlequin's last Skip* of August 1804 (fig. 7.2), which portrays a vanquished Napoleon, dressed in Harlequin's motley costume and black mask, pleading for mercy from an imperious John Bull. Where Bonaparte's "Conjuration Sword" lies broken at his feet and has "lost its Power" to convert one thing into another, Bull's simple cudgel threatens transformation of a different and more irrevocable kind. Advising Napoleon that "now you shall carry John Bulls mark about with you as every Swagger should—," Bull prepares to resignify the body of the emperor, inscribing upon it the "marks" (bruises and broken bones) of a supremacy that is British rather than French. But the clearest evidence of both the political efficacy and wide intermedial circulation of the Harlequin-Napoleon trope at this time is a broadside published in 1803 by the bookseller and archjingoist James Asperne (fig. 7.3). This pushes the bellicose appropriation of popular theater to perhaps its logical extreme by adopting the idiom and typographic format of the playbill—a device employed by radicals in the 1790s—and informs the public of a new pantomime "In rehearsal" at the "Theatre Royal of the United Kingdom": "Some dark foggy night about November next, will be ATTEMPTED, by a Strolling Company of French Vagrants, an old Pantomimic Farce, called Harlequin's Invasion or Disappointed Banditti."[11] The lead role of "Harlequin Butcher" is, of course, to be played by "Mr. Buonaparte, / from Corsica, / (Who Murdered that Character in *Egypt, Italy, Swisserland, Holland,* &c.)." Like the *Morning Post*'s poem, this is a description that uses Harlequin to figure Napoleon's restless shuttling from one locale to the next but that adds to this sense of geopolitical kinesis a new emphasis on the tension between the Harlequin role and the reality of the French leader's actions; punning on literal and figurative meanings of *murder*—to kill but also, in the artistic sense, to spoil through a lack of skill—Napoleon is guilty both of slaughter and of failing to perform the role of protagonist adequately. He is not even a good Harlequin.

The rhetorical power of Asperne's broadside resides in the way it carefully harnesses the architecture of the playbill, itself a remediation of the structure of the theatrical occasion, as a means of at once imagining and neutralizing the threat of invasion. It thus reassures the public not only by announcing that the pantomime will show "*Harlequin's Flat-Bottomed Boats* / warmly engaged by the / Wooden Walls of Old England," but also that this harlequinade will be followed by a mainpiece, "the favourite Comic Tragic Uproar of / The Repulse; / Or Britons Triumphant," which will be performed by royal command and feature a large cast of naval commanders and volunteers. And lest there be any lingering doubts about winners and losers, the broadside avers that the evening's entertainment will conclude with a patriotic overture and "a Grand Illumination and a Transparency displaying / Britannia receiving Homage of Gallic Slaves." The chronology

Fig. 7.2. Isaac Cruikshank, *Harlequin's last Skip* (Thomas Williamson, 20 August 1804). BMC 10270. © The Trustees of the British Museum.

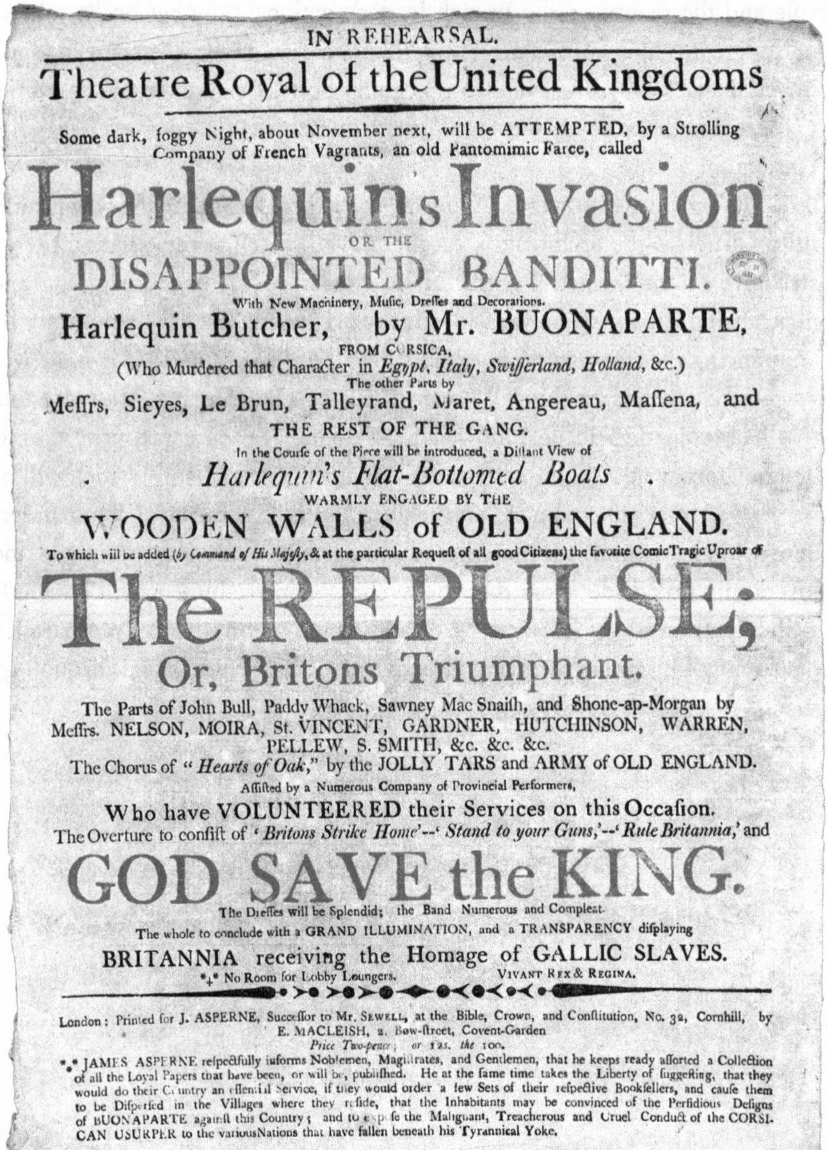

Theatre Royal of the United Kingdoms

Some dark, foggy Night, about November next, will be ATTEMPTED, by a Strolling Company of French Vagrants, an old Pantomimic Farce, called

Harlequins Invasion

OR THE

DISAPPOINTED BANDITTI.

With New Machinery, Music, Dresses and Decorations.

Harlequin Butcher, by Mr. BUONAPARTE,

FROM CORSICA,

(Who Murdered that Character in *Egypt, Italy, Swisserland, Holland*, &c.)

The other Parts by

Messrs, Sieyes, Le Brun, Talleyrand, Maret, Angereau, Massena, and

THE REST OF THE GANG.

In the Course of the Piece will be introduced, a Distant View of

Harlequin's Flat-Bottomed Boats

WARMLY ENGAGED BY THE

WOODEN WALLS of OLD ENGLAND.

To which will be added (*by Command of His Majesty*, & at the particular Request of all good Citizens) the favorite Comic Tragic Uproar of

The REPULSE;

Or, Britons Triumphant.

The Parts of John Bull, Paddy Whack, Sawney Mac Snaith, and Shone-ap-Morgan by Messrs. NELSON, MOIRA, St. VINCENT, GARDNER, HUTCHINSON, WARREN, PELLEW, S. SMITH, &c. &c. &c.

The Chorus of *" Hearts of Oak,"* by the JOLLY TARS and ARMY of OLD ENGLAND.

Assisted by a Numerous Company of Provincial Performers,

Who have VOLUNTEERED their Services on this Occasion.

The Overture to consist of ' *Britons Strike Home*'--' *Stand to your Guns*,'--' *Rule Britannia,*' and

GOD SAVE the KING.

The Dresses will be Splendid; the Band Numerous and Compleat.

The whole to conclude with a GRAND ILLUMINATION, and a TRANSPARENCY displaying

BRITANNIA receiving the Homage of GALLIC SLAVES.

⁎ No Room for Lobby Loungers. VIVANT REX & REGINA.

London : Printed for J. ASPERNE, Successor to Mr. SEWELL, at the Bible, Crown, and Constitution, No. 32, Cornhill, by E. MACLEISH, 2. Bow-street, Covent-Garden

Price Two-pence; or 12s. the 100.

⁎ JAMES ASPERNE respectfully informs Noblemen, Magistrates, and Gentlemen, that he keeps ready assorted a Collection of all the Loyal Papers that have been, or will be, published. He at the same time takes the Liberty of suggesting, that they would do their Country an essential Service, if they would order a few Sets of their respective Booksellers, and cause them to be Dispersed in the Villages where they reside, that the Inhabitants may be convinced of the Perfidious Designs of BUONAPARTE against this Country; and to expose the Malignant, Treacherous and Cruel Conduct of the CORSI-CAN USURPER to the various Nations that have fallen beneath his Tyrannical Yoke,

Fig. 7.3. *Harlequin's Invasion or, The Disappointed Banditti* (James Asperne, 1803). Reproduced by kind permission of the Syndics of Cambridge University Library.

of a night at the playhouse, which routinely closed with a rendition of the national anthem, provides a sequential structure through which the future trajectory of the war can be safely plotted.

Asperne's mock playbill reminds us that the period's theaters were in many ways the most powerful and relentless engines of British nationalism, but it also evinces the propagandistic value of translating war into the comfortingly everyday registers of popular entertainment and of advertising. The broadside specifically works with the peculiar tense of the playbill's language, which gives to the future, to what has yet to happen, the clear and detailed contours of an event that might already have taken place. The "conventional phrases of the playbill," Gillian Russell observes, ". . . were expressions of both the uniqueness of the performance advertised and simultaneously its embeddedness in what was already known."[12] The playbill achieves this effect, of course, because of the inherently recursive nature of theatrical performance itself, and it is important that the broadside describes "Harlequin's Invasion" as "an *old* pantomimic farce," albeit with "New Machinery, Music, Dresses and Decorations" (emphasis mine). Like other stock repertory pieces, the drama of potential invasion is one that the British public has seen before. There is nothing new here, Asperne's broadside insists, nothing to be afraid of. Throughout this book we have seen graphic satirists take up literary narratives in order to project forward from the political present toward a discernable if yet-to-be-arrived-at end. As Asperne's mock playbill suggests, the pantomime parodies of 1803 perform this prophetic operation doubly, first by giving to the war the structure of that most formulaic and predictable of all dramatic genres and second by using the repetitiousness of theatrical performance itself—for performance, as Richard Schechner tell us, means "never for the first time"—as a conceit that envisions the threat of invasion as a recurring and even reassuringly familiar event in the cycle of British history.[13]

Taken together, these patriotic appropriations of pantomime reveal just how heuristically valuable the figure of Harlequin was in enabling the British to negotiate an enemy who was, as Stuart Semmel has shown, disconcertingly resistant to definition and who, in dislodging entrenched stereotypes of the French, seemed even to unsettle the cultural and political distinctions upon which the very category of Britishness itself rested.[14] "There is not a shape, form, figure, or colour, which this Proteus-like consul is not ready to assume, in order to preserve and to increase his power," the well-traveled physician and writer Charles Maclean warned in 1804.[15] Through pantomime's shape-shifting hero, satirists and commentators were able to transform this problem—Napoleon's immunity to categorization— into the solution, for in the motley guise of Harlequin it is exactly the French leader's fluid, kaleidoscopic persona that is given legible shape. "Mr Boney Party you have changed Characters pretty often & famously well," the John Bull of Isaac Cruikshank's print informs his routed adversary. If, as Semmel notes, British discussions of Napoleon habitually turned upon "the trope of *hybridity*," then in the early nineteenth century there was no better, or more instantly recognizable, example of osmotic identity than Harlequin.[16] He is, as Garrick put it, "Mr. Nobody."[17] In the ephemera at which we have been looking, Bonaparte's character is captured in the period's most emphatic embodiment of characterlessness.

This satirical strategy was by no means novel. The harlequinization of Napoleon represents a renewal of a political trope that had long permeated discourses of parliamentary debate and satire in Britain. In readings of William Mountfort's farce *The Life and Death of Doctor Faustus* (1686) and the rival Harlequin Faustus pantomimes of 1723, Judy A. Hayden has shown how playwrights of the late seventeenth and early eighteenth centuries worked to exploit the formal discordances and inherently political configura- tion of commedia dell'arte as a mode of commentary on controversies such as the Catholic question and the South Sea Bubble.[18] In the 1730s and 1740s Robert Walpole, putative "first" prime minister, was cast in the role of Harle- quin in several prints and pamphlets, and John O'Brien persuasively contends that Scriblerian and opposition satirists worked to posit Walpole and Harle- quin as commensurate embodiments of British cultural dissolution.[19] Across the eighteenth century graphic satirists routinely turned to Harlequin to deride public figures such the Methodist preacher George Whitefield, both William Pitts the Elder and Younger, Charles James Fox, Richard Brinsley Sheridan, and Thomas Paine.[20] Nor was this trope exclusive to caricature; Harlequin and harlequinades were regularly invoked in political pamphlets and textual satire. In the polarized political climate of the 1790s, for instance, John Thelwall cautioned the public against the "harlequin tricks" of Edmund Burke's inflammatory, counterrevolutionary rhetoric;[21] Henry Redhead Yorke described events across the Channel as a "political pantomime" and accused the French Directory of indulging in spectacle such as "the most accomplished Harlequin could devise"; radical satirist Charles Pigott derided the Whigs as a "harlequin motley opposition"; and an anonymous pamphleteer accused Paine of showing himself "consistent in inconsistences, and qualified to act the part of Harlequin."[22] Contemporaries, it's clear, understood just how easily pantomime might function as a typology of political characters and motives, and for all their differences of partisan conviction, the many images of Harlequin statesmen similarly look to pantomime's protagonist as an emblem of problematic capriciousness and illegitimacy. In his embodiment of cultural practices that operated beyond and in contradistinction to those of established institution and authorized form, Harlequin offered the interlocutors of eighteenth-century politics a compelling analogue of unconstitutional action and personality. Thus, as I've argued elsewhere, the repeated caricaturing of Sheridan in the role insisted that his principles were a matter of performance rather than ideology, of a costume-deep commitment to the public good that, in its cynical opportunism and insincerity, undermined precisely that which it claimed to espouse.[23]

The case of Sheridan is especially useful in helping us track the constellation of valences that the figure of Harlequin brings to bear upon Napoleon, because Gillray first depicted Sheridan in that character in March 1803, in a print—*Physical Aid,—or—Britannia recover'd from a Trance* (BMC 9972)— that roundly mocks the playwright-politician for his newfound patriotism in response to the invasion threat (Sheridan had vociferously opposed the war in the mid-1790s). Harlequins Sheridan and Napoleon, that is, emerge within the rhetorical field of wartime satire at almost precisely the same moment, and their correspondences and differences are instructive. For example, both Sheridan and Napoleon were regarded as socially suspect; Sheridan was a professional writer, theater manager, and son of an actor whose class status rendered him an outsider even as (or rather, because) he moved within Whig circles that were stridently and self-consciously aristocratic, while Bonaparte was understood to have risen from obscurity—hence his portrayal in Smith's poem as a "peasant boy."[24] And both, too, were seen to be ethnically ambiguous: Sheridan as an Anglo-Irishman, Bonaparte as a Corsican. Harlequin provides a consummate figure for simultaneously imagining and derogating such double alterity. Invariably a servant character who, once transformed and empowered, undertakes to disrupt the elite society he once served, his trajectory is that of the parvenu. He performs this transit from the margins to the center, moreover, in an obligatory black mask, a signifier that is, O'Brien and David Worrall suggest, complicatedly but inextricably racial, as pantomimes such as *Robinson Crusoe; or, Harlequin Friday* (1781) and *Furioso; or, Harlequin Negro* (1807) evidence in their transformation of a blackface character into the black-masked protagonist.[25] If Harlequin is Proteus, then he is also the Other, and in Cruikshank's *Harlequin's last Skip* these two dimensions of the character's political identity, his duplicity and his conspicuous alterity, coalesce in the figure of a Bonaparte who has, John Bull points out, "lied" until he is "black in the face."

Unlike caricatures of Sheridan, however, which marshal the grammar of pantomime in general, the Harlequin-Napoleon satires of 1803–4 cite a specific play: Garrick's *Harlequin's Invasion*. This difference of cultural referents is significant because Garrick's drama was not only generically atypical—not least in introducing a speaking Harlequin—but actively resistant to its own mode of performance. First staged at Drury Lane on 31 December 1759, *Harlequin's Invasion* looks back across a year in which major victories at Ticonderoga, Louisbourg, Quebec, and Quiberon Bay had given Britain a decisive advantage in the Seven Years' War. The play opens with Mercury, speaking at Apollo's behest, warning the citizens of "Dramatica's realm" that "Monsieur Harlequin means to invade ye," and issuing a general rallying cry: "Let the light troops of Comedy march to attack him, / And Tragedy whet all her daggers to hack him . . . King Shakespear for ever" (1.1.38–49). Several adventures later, and following much carefully choreographed confusion, the play reaches its climax with a "*transparency . . . representing the powers of pantomime going to attack Mount Parnassus*" (3.2.109). This armada is destroyed by the sudden onset of a storm, and in a final conceit pilfered from Henry Giffard's 1741 *Harlequin Student*, Harlequin sinks before the rising effigy of Shakespeare, totem of a native English literary canon.[26] "Thrice happy th' nation that Shakespear has charmed, / More happy the bosom his genius has warmed," sings the jubilant chorus (3.2.119–20), amid the entrance of both a litany of Shakespearean characters and also the three graces, who dance to the triumphal hymn with which this Francophobic fantasy closes. In appropriating *Harlequin's Invasion*, then, and I hope that it's clear from this synopsis that such borrowing goes well beyond the title, Smith's poem and the satires that follow it consciously adapt a work in which pantomime's protagonist already stands as a proxy for the French intruder and in which cultural incursion already operates as a means of staging and defusing the threat of military invasion. And these metonymies work all the more cogently in relation to Napoleon, not only because, in contrast to 1759, he gave to Britain's adversaries the face of a particular and exceptional individual but also because his hybrid Italian and French ethnicity made the commedia dell'arte an especially apposite frame of reference.

Garrick's play places repeated emphasis on Harlequin as a figure of menacing difference; it works hard to amplify those unsettling aspects of the character that remained vital but implicit to his presence in other pantomimes. To realize this effect *Harlequin's Invasion* overlays three distinct cultural vocabularies of threat, namely those of race, for Harlequin is twice described as a "blackamoor man" (2.1.24, 3.2.86); of the demonic, for he is recognized as "The Devil" and "Old Nick himself" (1.2.170, 199); and, perhaps most crucially, of bodily mutilation. In one of the central scenes of the play, Harlequin first dupes the veteran soldier Bounce and immigrant Frenchman Gasconade into decapitating their friend Snip the tailor, and then terrifies the same pair by appearing before them in the figure of their victim's headless corpse. Harlequin subsequently brings about Snip's resurrection, but this gesture only reaffirms the character's penchant for slicing and splicing; in "sowing" Snip's head back on (3.2.87), enacting the tailor's given mode of labor upon his own body, Harlequin commits yet one more act of violence. The peril of war—the damage that the French wish to inflict upon British bodies—is barely coded in *Harlequin's Invasion;* its language returns repeatedly (above thirty times across three acts) to images of heads that have been or might be severed. Of course, the staging of physical injury was, in the shape of slapstick humor, a formal prerequisite of the pantomime, but it is nonetheless fundamental to the ideological imperatives not just of Garrick's drama but also of the anti-Bonaparte satires that invoke it in 1803 that this particular Harlequin openly delights in dismemberment as a kind of play. Asperne's mock playbill thus describes Bonaparte as "Harlequin Butcher," an appellation also used by James Smith, whose poem charts the rapid escalation of Harlequin Napoleon's mania for destruction; commuting courage into cruelty with the necromantic powers of his sword, he leaves the "stage ... strew'd with dead and dying." As Garrick's Harlequin—not just any Harlequin—Napoleon has a history of violence.

At the same time, however, this violence is assuredly circumscribed. Garrick's drama articulates and neutralizes perceived threat in the very same theatrical gesture, offering one more manifestation of the prophylactic formulation that we have encountered before in the buffoonish plebeians of John Dryden and William Davenant's *Tempest* and the transvestite witches of *Macbeth*. Garrick's "Monsieur Harlequin" is narratologically *and* politically enclosed within a plot structure that invests him with menace only to deprive him of it, a structure that has been specifically and eccentrically recalibrated to bring about his necessary, and necessarily spectacular, demise. In appropriating this figure in 1803–4, Smith, Holland, Asperne, and Cruikshank thus take up a culturally supercharged version of the Other that conveniently carries within it the antidote to the very peril it poses. Rather than turn, as did the romantic poets, to Milton's Satan in an attempt to make sense of Napoleon's political persona, an analogic move that is freighted with polysemous potential, Harlequin-Napoleon satires find in Garrick's drama a diabolic figure whose threat and appeal might more easily be, indeed already has been, contained. In this regard it's telling that *Boney's Meditations on the Island of St. Helena*—etched by George Cruikshank to a design by his loyalist publisher George Humphrey—is a post-Waterloo image. Only *after* Bonaparte's final defeat and exile, which are the immediate subjects of Cruikshank's print, did it become discursively possible, we might say discursively "safe," for the patriotic satirist to proffer such Miltonic equivalences.

Conscripting the Idea of the "Literary"

In alluding to Garrick's *Harlequin's Invasion*, then, the satirists of the 1803 invasion scare were consciously renewing the central conceit of what John O'Brien rightly calls an "antipantomime."[27] And in doing so, these prints and broadsides, like Garrick's play before them, rehearse a long-standing cultural critique of pantomime as much as, if not more than, the form itself—a critique that dates back to 1720s, the decade in which pantomime properly arrived on the English stage in highly successful pieces staged at Lincoln's Inn Fields and later Covent Garden under the auspices of the impresario and prototypical English Harlequin John Rich. In *The Dunciad*, for instance, Alexander Pope scoffed at the bewilderingly spectacular theatricality of Rich's pantomimes in a concatenation of monosyllables: "Gods, imps, and monsters, music, rage, and mirth, / A fire, a jigg, a battle, and a ball, / 'Till one wide conflagration swallows all."[28] Henry Fielding, writing in *The Champion*, excoriated Rich as the "great Machinist [who] presides over animate and inanimate Machines" and "turns all Things topsy-turvy, subverts the Order of Nature," while in *Tom Jones* he sarcastically suggested that the two parts of the pantomime ought better to be named "*Duller* and *Dullest*" than

"*Serious* and *Comic*."[29] And William Hogarth's 1724 engraving *A Just View of the British Stage* (BMC 1761) imagined a thoroughly debased theatrical culture in which, amid the grotesque clutter of marionette puppets, hanged fiddlers, and scenic dragons, a copy of *Hamlet* serves as toilet paper and the statues of Tragedy and Comedy have playbills for the latest pantomimes nailed to their faces. These satires stridently deride pantomime as a key vector of cultural decline. For Pope, Fielding, Hogarth, and others, Rich's harlequinades were a foreign and effeminate mode of theater that was promulgated with a view to the profit imperative alone, a mode that substituted entertainment for art and spectacle for language, thereby displacing authentic works of the English dramatic tradition. In the frontispiece to the third edition of James Miller's *Harlequin Horace* of 1735 (BMC 1838), Punch and Harlequin drive Apollo from the stage, trampling discarded volumes of Shakespeare, Ben Jonson, and Nicholas Rowe as they do so.

O'Brien traces the vicissitudes of this hostility to pantomime in considerable detail, and the above examples will suffice to give sense of the contours of this discourse as it was deployed in the first half of the eighteenth century. What's significant, in terms of my present discussion, is that this critique was still a live one at the beginning of the nineteenth century. In a print published in the *Satirist* in December 1807 (fig. 7.4), the "monster melo-drama" suckles a host of modern playwrights and, replaying the visual metaphor of *Harlequin Horace,* treads the works of Shakespeare into the dust.[30] This caricature ostensibly denigrates melodrama (another French theatrical import), but it is

Fig. 7.4. Samuel de Wilde, *The Monster Melo-drama* (*Satirist*, 4 December 1804). BMC 10796. © Victoria and Albert Museum, London.

pantomime that provides it with a syntax of cultural degradation, for the imagined theatrical Cerberus is dressed in motley and bears the heads of Harlequin and the clown Joseph Grimaldi, as well as those of Sheridan and John Philip Kemble, the managers of Drury Lane and Covent Garden, respectively. The trope of pantomime overthrowing legitimate drama and its correlates—rationality, sense, taste, form, pedagogy—was commonplace. "*Cart-wheels* and *Candlesticks* full houses draw / Plain sense is *banish'd*, PANTOMIME is *Law!*" lamented one poet in 1797.[31] Writing in *The Histrionade* (1802), Thomas Dermody opined that "Instruction chaste, and Thought Sublime" had been effaced by "the gay Sprite of airy Pantomime," and that "basely exiled from their native shore, / Strong Sense, and pow'ful Shakespeare please no more."[32] In similar terms the satirical poem *The Druriad* (1798) implored the "Genius of Shakespear" to witness this cultural catastrophe from his "heav'nly sphere":

> See pantomimic jargon, ev'ry season
> Usurp the place of common sense and reason.
> Some rising poet, O great Bard! inspire,
> With one bright spark of thy immortal fire,
> Reclaim the taste of this degen'rate age,
> And reign once more triumphant o'er the stage.[33]

What is striking about these turn-of-the-century iterations of the cultural decline narrative is that, like Garrick's play, they hinge rhetorically on the diametric opposition of pantomime and Shakespeare. Though the confidence that pervades the final scene of *Harlequin's Invasion* has been overtaken by escalating fears of degeneration, this binary remains a highly charged shorthand not only for differentiating Britain from its European competitors but also for a stridently bifurcated conception of culture: on the one hand, the low, sensual, senseless, ephemeral, and unabashedly populist domain, as personified and demonized in the alien, always-contingent figure of Harlequin; and on the other, the high, creative, and timeless domain, as represented by an image of Shakespeare that at once embodies these ideals as their ne plus ultra and also stands for an idea of the eternal and transcendent that necessarily resists embodiment.

It was at the very beginning of the nineteenth century, Jacky Bratton argues, that the "British critical assumption . . . that commercialised entertainment is the Other of the art of theatre"—the assumption that underwrites these critiques of pantomime—was fully installed, and it is testament to how quickly this logic was institutionalized that by 1832 it was deemed necessary to establish a parliamentary select committee to inquire into the means by which "literary talent" might be more effectively fostered in the nation's theater.[34] As Bratton recognizes, this polarization was itself symptomatic of a newly emergent and discernably modern conception of "literature" as predicated upon an aesthetic that remained autonomous from the exigencies of the everyday (even as it purported to represent the procedures of the "everyday") and the overlapping matrices of money, marketing, and mass consumption. O'Brien notes of the 1720s to 1740s that "the controversy over pantomime entertainments was in part a public debate about the role and scope of the literary, which found itself doubly threatened by pantomime's success and its shape."[35] The shift in the valency of the terms *literature* and *the literary* that the likes of Raymond Williams, Roger Chartier, and Trevor Ross trace to the late eighteenth century gives this debate new meaning and urgency in the early 1800s.[36] That is, by the Napoleonic Wars antipantomime discourse had come to be inflected less by Scriblerian anxieties regarding unregulated cultural production (though these remain) and more by an ideology of romanticism that hewed to a Kantian notion of aesthetic autonomy and that privileged the imagination as a faculty of and for transcendence. When, in his preface to *Lyrical Ballads,* Wordsworth opines that "the works of Shakespeare and Milton, are driven into neglect" and inveighs against "frantic novels, sickly and stupid German Tragedies, and deluges of idle and extravagant stories in verse," he is only articulating a variation of the formulation deployed by *The Druriad* and *The Histrionade,* where pantomime is "jargon" that comes and goes with each "season" and, conversely, Shakespeare is the "immortal fire."[37]

Of course, pantomime and Shakespeare—or Harlequin and Shakespeare—is not an opposition of equivalents. Shakespeare is an author, *the* author; pantomime, a mode of drama without a text, is conspicuously authorless. In Foucauldian terms, pantomime is the exemplary antithesis of the literary, for it falls outside of the taxonomic work undertaken by the notion of "the author," resisting the heuristic need for an individual through whom coherent meaning can be realized and indeed troubling this ideological operation in its insistence on a namelessness that bespeaks collaborative cultural practice. By the eighteenth century, Foucault contends, " 'literary' discourse was acceptable only if it carried an author's name," with anonymity tolerable "only as a puzzle to be solved," and we might read the climax of *Harlequin's Invasion,* with the rise of Shakespeare and the fall of Harlequin, as allegorizing precisely this need, in the face of generic instability, for an author to serve as the locus for meaning-making, canonicity, and intellectual property.[38] Late-century editors of Shakespeare, and Edmond Malone especially, thus increasingly removed Shakespeare from the communal, profit-oriented practicalities of theater-making, or "entertainment," by engaging in projects grounded upon the philological imperatives of textual authenticity and the integrity and chronology of the corpus; as Malone averred, Shakespeare was to be kept "pure and unpolluted" from "modern sophistication and foreign admixture."[39]

It is hardly surprising, in this regard, that Edmund Burke implicitly rehearses the pantomime-Shakespeare dichotomy in *Letters on a Regicide Peace* (1796) when he compares members of the French Directory to "grinners in the Pantomime . . . the very scum and refuse of the theatre," citing Garrick, "the most acute observer of Nature I ever knew," as his authority for this image of low theatricality.[40] With their structures of dispersion and ensemble action, both the French Revolution and the harlequinade could be seen as a challenge to a unitary model of power (the monarch, the author). "Your admiration of Shakespeare would be ill sorted indeed," Burke wrote to Malone, "if your Taste . . . did not lead you to a perfect abhorrence of the French Revolution, and all its Works."[41] The Harlequin-Napoleon trope thus gains such currency in 1803 in part because Garrick's rendering of an earlier Anglo-French war as a discursive collision between the literary and the popular was all the more resonant for a culture so thoroughly invested in parsing, redefining, and redeploying these terms.

It should be said that Garrick's play certainly has its cake and eats it too; as O'Brien notes, *Harlequin's Invasion* works to "exploit, yet then disavow, pantomime's popularity."[42] Yet critics have sometimes been too quick to emphasize its ambivalence. For Lance Bertelsen, the pantomime "scenically and physically enacts the contradictions in Garrick's dramatic practice," while for Jackson I. Cope—who rightly reads Garrick's Harlequin as an emphatically diabolical figure—the play in fact revives "the spirit of the commedia dell'arte," recovering the irrational and esoteric energies of the form as it was performed in its earliest configuration.[43] Even O'Brien writes of the manner in which "Garrick's attacks on pantomime betray . . . his indebtedness to the form."[44] Though such readings get at the complexity of

Harlequin's Invasion, they miss the underlying unity of the play's design, which coheres around the issues of literacy and cultural capital. In its opening exchanges, several of the lower-class characters around whom the drama spins declare themselves illiterate—"I forgot my reading long ago," "I can't read," "I can do anything but read" (1.1.10–11, 14, 17)—and are therefore unable to understand the "paper" that brings news of imminent invasion. This scenario serves as a kind of ideological overture for the play as a whole, where the susceptibility of these characters to Harlequin's tricks is shown to be a symptom of their plebeian identity. Lacking the requisite cultural skill set to recognize Harlequin for what he is, they repeatedly fall foul of his pranks.

Dolly, the daughter of the decapitated tailor, is initially enthralled by Harlequin's dazzling metamorphoses only to be still more attracted by the suggestion that her father's defeat of the interloper might lead to Snip's family being "qualitified" (2.1.50). And it is through the class-encoded space of the theater auditorium that Dolly maps out this fantasy of social mobility. "I won't be stuffed up twice or thrice a year at holiday time at the top of the playhouse among folks that laugh and cry, just as they feel," she insists; "I shall sit in the side boxes among my equals, laugh, talk loud, mind nothing, stare at the low people in the galleries without ever looking at them" (2.1.101–3, 109–11). Dolly's vision correlates different modes of spectatorship with different viewing positions within the playhouse and thus sites of different class status. Those in the cheapest seats in the upper gallery are defined by their uninhibitedly corporeal responses to "holiday" entertainment (pantomime, then as now, was associated with periods of festivity); in turn, this group provides the diversion for the patrician spectators seated in the boxes, who from their privileged location simultaneously gaze at and studiously ignore their social inferiors. Garrick mocks both strata of his audience here, but within the terms of his play it is the gallery's failure to perform a critical kind of spectatorship that is ultimately meaningful. At the drama's close, Mercury insists that the Snips and their friends leave the stage *before* Shakespeare makes his triumphant entrance—"Hence, you profane, without delay. / This scene is not for you. Away" (3.2.108–9)—and then, as the figure of the bard emerges, follows this injunction with a second: "Ye sons of Taste adore him" (3.2.116). The cultural disenfranchisement of the illiterate plebian community is a precondition of the ascendancy of British literature at the play's climax—an ascendancy inextricably bound with up that of an elite who possess "taste" as an inheritance. It is to these "sons of taste" that *Harlequin's Invasion* directs its final warning: "Ye Britons may fancy ne'er lead you astray, / Nor e'er through your senses your reason betray" (3.2.131–32). Do not be seduced by the sensuality of pantomimic spectacle, Garrick tells his educated patrons; do not behave like those in the galleries, who thoughtlessly succumb to laughter and tears. Remember what it is that distinguishes us (reason, knowledge) from them (bodily instinct).

This maneuver suggests that the apparent contradiction of Garrick's enterprise—a pantomime that rejects its own form—in fact signals the confident appropriation of the low by the high. Garrick's use of pantomime's structure to map distinctions of genre on to those of class and taste needs to be read as an attempt to commute illegitimate theatricality into a valorization of literary culture. To be sure, this reading doesn't entirely remove the shadow of paradox, but it does position Garrick's play within the "recurrent pattern" of cultural negotiations charted by Peter Stallybrass and Allon White, whereby "the low-Other is despised and denied at the level of political organization and social being whilst being instrumentally constitutive of the shared imaginary repertoire of the dominant culture."[45] This process absolutely depends on its productive frictions, but we ought not to underestimate the assuredness with which Garrick arrogates the vitality of pantomime to celebrate and reinforce the boundaries of the elite public and a literary nationhood, for this helps to explain the true appeal of his play for the patriotic satirists of 1803. In looking back to *Harlequin's Invasion* political parodists of the invasion scare are not simply taking up pantomime; rather they are deploying the form as it had already been appropriated by, and converted into a secure sign of, Britain's (and British) cultural hegemony.

It is in exactly these terms that we must understand James Smith's poem in the *Morning Post*. In Smith we encounter a prolific parodist who eschewed the status of professional writer and instead cultivated the persona of a gentleman humorist who sought recognition within the fashionable, upper-class enclaves of Georgian London rather than the public sphere at large. Very much of the bourgeoisie (he would succeed his father as solicitor to the Board of Ordnance in 1832), Smith wished only for "a welcome reception wherever he went, and a distinguished position in society," and he moved comfortably within the circle of the aristocratic Pic Nic Club, playing a key role in organizing that group's amateur theatricals in 1802–3 and also contributing to their journal.[46] His writings are shot through with a deep love of the stage, a self-conscious delight in exhibiting their own classical learning, and a studied insouciance, all of which are manifest in the two works for which he is now best known, *The Rejected Addresses* (1812) and *Horace in London* (1813), a series of parodies of Horace's Odes, both written with his brother Horace. These details are significant because they once again reveal the formative presence of the cultural elite behind a seemingly popular satirical trope. Like Braddyll's *King of Brobdingnag,* the Harlequin-Napoleon analogy draws upon an iconography that would have been legible to the working classes. Without doubt, part of the appeal of pantomime for the satirists of 1803, and the caricaturists especially, is that it offered them a visual syntax capable of reaching exactly the broader audience that propaganda covets. But the figures of Braddyll and Smith nonetheless remind us that we must not make the mistake of presuming that such parodies therefore are populist in origin—or, for that matter, in principal intent, for as we have seen, "Harlequin's Invasion" masks sophisticated cultural play behind an ostensibly straightforward joke. Smith's poems are replete with references to actors, plays, and theatrical occasions; he writes of pantomime in animated and affectionate ways and we know that he contributed a satirical song, "All the World's in Paris," to *Harlequin Whittington,* performed at Covent Garden in 1814.[47] Yet his poems reflexively coopt pantomime as part of their urbane comedy of fashionable metropolitan life, and we need only glance at the titles of Smith's other anti-Bonaparte pieces—"Verses written under the Statue of Apollo at Paris," "Sapphic Ode, Written at Bonaparte's Levee"—to recognize that "Harlequin's Invasion," like its namesake drama, both speaks to pantomime from and reorients it to serve a position of cultural prestige. So, when Smith's brother assures us in a biographical note that the obsessively theatergoing James "was generally to be found . . . in the boxes or the green-room," he casually invokes the same spatial diagram of sociocultural power that structures Dolly Snip's parvenu fantasy.[48]

In this way we might instructively compare Smith to another poet-spectator of the early nineteenth century, for William Wordsworth too found a peculiar pleasure in low theater. Writing just over a year after the publication of Smith's "Harlequin's Invasion," Wordsworth tells of seeing a pantomime amid "the rabblement" at Sadler's Wells, and concedes: "Nor was it mean delight / To watch crude Nature work in untaught minds."[49] In this moment of *The Prelude* the ignorance and sensuality of the illiterate spectatorship, of those who, to quote Dolly, "laugh and cry, just as they feel," becomes the stuff of philosophic verse, of the Miltonic poet's "delight," of the poetics of distinction. It may seem strange to consider Smith and Wordsworth within the same cultural bracket, for their sensibilities and formal repertoires could hardly be further apart. Yet this alignment should be unsurprising within a context in which, as we've seen time and again in this book, satire felt itself to be deeply invested in securing high literary culture against threatening forms of topicality and popular practice. In the works of both Smith and Wordsworth, if in radically different ways, we see the mining of pantomime as raw cultural matter that catalyzes self-consciously literary endeavor; in both, to cite Stallybrass and White once more, we witness the symbolic seizure of the low in the service of the high and "in the very name of exclusion."[50]

Beginning with Smith, then, and always looking back to Garrick, the Harlequin Napoleon satires of 1803–4 pit against the French leader the paradigm of British literary culture; they wield the standard of taste as a kind of weapon that exposes the moral and cultural vacuity masked by Napoleonic bravado. And in deploying the idiom of popular performance as a language that others Britain's opponent or, to invert this statement, in othering popular performance by using it to imagine the enemy, they reinforce the bifurcation of culture into the high and the low, ultimately insisting that a robust British nationhood rests soundly on the products, practices, and values of the former. Let me be clear here. I'm not by any means advocating the bi-polar reading of Georgian culture that remains such a source of historiographical contention;[51] rather, and taking my cue from the work of Morag Shiach, I'm concerned with the contemporary uses to which this *discursive* opposition is put, for in the Harlequin Napoleon satires we see the trope of cultural bifurcation overtly politicized.[52] Insisting that culture is polarized in terms of high and low becomes a central strategy in the satirical fight against Bonaparte.

In contrast to Garrick's play, however—and herein lies the crucial difference—these satires do not depict both sides of this cultural binary. In their express framing of pantomime as a suspiciously alien cultural form and, more especially, in their explicit citation of Garrick's *Harlequin's Invasion,* they perforce mobilize the *idea* of an authorized literary culture, but at no point do they actually name it. To be sure, Asperne's broadside uses the structure of the playbill to juxtapose the illegitimate drama of Napoleonic invasion with the "Comic Tragic" mainpiece of British triumph, but there remains a fundamental asymmetry to Harlequin-Napoleon satires:

Harlequin still falls, but, quite conspicuously, the spirit of Shakespeare, of cultural legitimacy, is nowhere to be seen. These satires manifestly avoid bringing the popular and the literary, the low and the high, into direct contact. And this discursive strategy returns us to the questions I posed at the beginning of this chapter and to the absence within caricature's archive of Shakespearean and Miltonic representations of Bonaparte. What we can now see is that the likes of Smith, Asperne, and Cruikshank were part of a much wider satirical program that worked to sequester British literary culture from the problematically protean and charismatic figure of Napoleon. Satirists seemed alert to the possibility that as cultural signifiers even the most unequivocal villains of canonical texts, of the English classics, as they were becoming known, carried a degree of cultural prestige that might all too easily be bequeathed, at least residually, to the country's enemy. We've already glimpsed the power of this cultural logic in Gillray's omission of the Shakespearean quotation in his working up of Braddyll's *King of Brobdingnag and Gulliver (Plate 2d)* (see fig. 6.11), and we've seen it still more vividly in the anger and incomprehension provoked by Henry James Richter's knowingly provocative caricature of the pope as Prospero (see fig. 3.9). As far as satire was concerned, the integrity of the English literary canon depended on Bonaparte being kept well away it. To imagine him as Swift's Gulliver was one thing; to cast him as Shakespeare's Macbeth or Milton's Satan was quite another.

This is a problem particular to satirical discourse or, more accurately, patriotic-satirical discourse. Where writers such as Coleridge might be seen actively to court polysemy in their comparisons of Napoleon to quasimythic figures, such play of meaning, and with it the possibility of counterproductive association, is fundamentally at odds with the rhetorical matrix of anti-Bonaparte propaganda. Tellingly, Asperne resolutely separated the respective tropes of Harlequin Napoleon and Shakespearean Britain by publishing, the same summer as his mock playbill, a broadside entitled *Shakespeare's Ghost!* (fig. 7.5), in which the spirit of the bard rallies the nation in a speech that splices text from *King John* and *Henry V*. Shakespeare is made to speak to the present here, but in its spectral conceit and deployment of the history plays the broadside stridently renders him in and of the past, thereby emphasizing his ahistorical power as *the* ideal of "an Englishman" and "a Poet." Along with the "emergence of an autonomous literary sphere" in the period, writes Deidre Lynch, came the "relocation into an ever more remote past of real

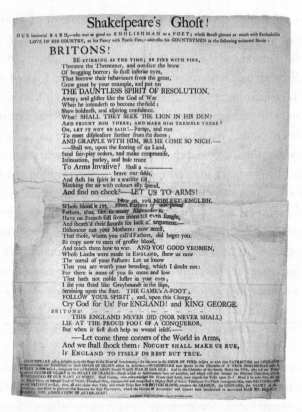

Fig. 7.5. *Shakespeare's Ghost!* (James Asperne, 1803). Courtesy of the Beinecke Rare Book and Manuscript Library, Yale University.

literary value" and thus the "close connection between pastness and canonicity."[53] Asperne's invocation of Shakespeare's spirit indexes exactly this cultural procedure. There is no mention of Bonaparte in this broadside; for Shakespeare to operate properly within this topical context, as a totem of indelible cultural achievement, he needs to be located *outside* of the topical. Just as Asperne's mock playbill for *Harlequin's Invasion* must not name Shakespeare, so *Shakespeare's Ghost!* must not name Napoleon.

That literary culture remains—and must remain—the present absent of the Harlequin-Napoleon satires suggests the extent to which their rhetorical effect is one of litotes, something Semmel gets at when he notes how "Napoleon played a critical (if unintended role) in regulating Britain's national character."[54] To cast Bonaparte as Harlequin was carefully to define the contours of Britishness in the negative; the vocabulary of pantomime functions in these satires, as in Garrick's play, as shorthand for British identity by clearly establishing what that identity is *not*. And just as Britishness was, as Linda Colley tells us, constructed in the eighteenth century in opposition to the Other of Catholic France, so the concept of literature, which intractably resists attempts to prescribe its meaning, could be most effectively understood as the antithesis of low culture.[55] "We know what literature is by knowing what it is not," writes Jonathan Kramnick: "Because, as [Joseph] Warton bemoans, 'the tinsel of a burletta has more admirers than the gold of Shakespeare' we can see the literary value of older texts."[56] It is this logic that images of Harlequin Napoleon advance. Britain is what France isn't; literature is what pantomime isn't.

But, whatever its efficacy, this rhetorical strategy nonetheless is freighted with anxiety. That these patriotic satires prevent Napoleon from inhabiting the same discursive space—or, in material terms, the same printed sheet—as Shakespeare or Milton bespeaks once more the difficulty of delimiting a character as disconcertingly hybrid as Napoleon's. But it also discloses the notion of the "literary" to be all too porous, even in the seemingly impermeable body of Shakespeare. In asking antipantomime discourse to do the work of propaganda, the Harlequin-Napoleon satires expose the fragility of the privileged term in that discourse's structuring binary of Shakespeare-pantomime, a fragility that remains (barely) veiled in those early nineteenth-century complaints that pantomime has "banished" Shakespeare from his "native stage." Such commentaries suggest a tendency, in the years immediately around the invasion scare of 1803, to read Britain's cultural trajectory in a manner that inverted Garrick's winning formula (*"Shakespear rises: Harlequin sinks"*). In their accounts, Harlequin *has* successfully invaded. In their very tense, their plaintive call for Shakespeare to "reign once more," these cultural critiques implicitly throw the value of "the literary" into doubt, undermining exactly what they wish to fortify. If Shakespeare and the native literary tradition possess inherent cultural authority, how could they have been so easily displaced? For the pantomime parodists of the invasion scare, the form's popularity was thus a double-edged sword. On the one hand, it was the very pre-condition of the Harlequin-Napoleon analogy, for it ensured the wide degree of intelligibility that was a pre-requisite of much anti-Bonaparte material; as a symbol, Harlequin was legible across hierarchies of class and education. On the other hand, however, this popularity problematized the very cultural distinctions on which the ideological work of that analogy depended. In 1802–3 *Love and Magic; or, Harlequin's Holiday* was Drury Lane's most successful play, with a total of forty-seven perform- ances, while at Covent Garden *Harlequin's Habeas; or, The Hall of Spectres* played on thirty-six occasions. By comparison, *all* of Shakespeare's works were given just forty-nine and twenty-five stagings at the respective theaters. Pantomime was upstaging the bard. We might contend that in 1803 political parodies of Garrick's play dare not put Shakespeare, and the high cultural ideals he represents, directly to the test against the fluid, deliquescent, fiercely othered figure of Harlequin Napoleon. In the face of such opposition those ideals were better implied than stated. For the category of the literary to operate safely and effectively as a counterpoint to Napoleon's threat it could not be named.

Harlequin Evasions: Embodying Satire

But the story doesn't end here. Though the figure of Harlequin Napoleon seems to have disappeared for a time after 1804, he reemerges in the final two years of the wars. In *The Narrow Escape, or, Boneys Grand Leap. "a la Grimaldi!!—"* (fig. 7.6) of January 1813, George Cruikshank took up the trope employed by his father, Isaac, nine years earlier. Responding to spurious reports that the retreating Napoleon had almost been captured by Russian troops near Ashmyany, the print shows the desperate emperor evading a hoard of Cossacks by launching himself from the upper window of a ramshackle inn. Though not in costume, Cruikshank's Napoleon certainly inhabits the gestural economy of pantomime. Evasive vaults, whether through windows or other openings, were part of the stock reper- toire of Harlequin's balletic movements, and the précis at the foot of the print describes how Napoleon "leapt through the Window, with the nimble- ness of an Harlequin."[57] Then, in 1814, with the seemingly defeated Napo- leon exiled to Elba and the Bourbon monarchy restored in the shape of Louis XVIII, James Asperne once more turned to pantomime and the specific idiom of bills advertising popular entertainments. His gloating broadside *Cruce Dignus. The Grand Menagerie, with an Exact Representation of Napoleon Buonaparte, the little Corsican monkey* (fig. 7.7), features a caricature depicting a half-monkey, half-human Napoleon, dressed in Harlequin's motley doublet, humiliatingly captured and displayed by the showman John Bull. And in 1815 two prints responded to Napoleon's shock return to power by imagining

Fig. 7.6. George Cruikshank, *The Narrow Escape, or, Boneys Grand Leap. "a la Grimaldi!!—"* (S. Knight, January 1813). BMC 12001. © The Trustees of the British Museum.

Fig. 7.7. Detail from the broadside *Cruce Dignus. The Grand Menagerie, with an exact representation of Napoleon Buonaparte, the little Corsican monkey* (James Asperne, 1814). BMC 12267. © The Trustees of the British Museum.

his escape from exile in terms of Harlequin's irrepressibility. In the first, J. Lewis Marks's *European Pantomime* (fig. 7.8), Harlequin Napoleon leaps from Elba to France to confront Louis XVIII as Pantaloon, while in the second, Thomas Rowlandson's *Scene in a New Pantomime to be Performed at the Theatre Royal Paris* (fig. 7.9), Harlequin Napoleon dodges a crowd of incensed European monarchs by diving through the slashed canvas of a portrait of the French king.

While Asperne's *Grand Menagerie* unsurprisingly presents us with a now familiar version of Harlequin as an emblem of suspect hybridity, the other three prints deploy the syntax of pantomime in a manifestly different way to the earlier satires. Here, the figure of Harlequin eludes and frustrates his adversaries at every turn; he is an evasive, unpredictable, and even, in the comic sense, heroic persona. Rather than summoning the threat of cultural incursion, pantomime now seems to cue a celebration of Napoleonic vitality. Even George Cruikshank's *Narrow Escape*—which ridicules Napoleon for displaying archcowardice—willingly invests the French emperor with the energy of pantomime's slapstick physicality. Each of these caricatures places

The European Pantomime

Princeaple Caracters Harlquin Mr Boney Pantaloon Louis xviii Columbine Maria Louiza Clowus &c By Congress

Fig. 7.8. J. Lewis Marks, *The European Pantomime* (c. March 1815). BMC 12515.
© The Trustees of the British Museum.

Fig. 7.9. Thomas Rowlandson, *Scene in a New Pantomime to be Performed at the Theatre Royal Paris* (Thomas Ackermann, 12 April 1815). BMC 12538. Courtesy of the Beinecke Rare Book and Manuscript Library, Yale University.

particular emphasis on movement. Where in the prints of 1803–4, and in *Grand Menagerie* too, Harlequin Napoleon is a figure of curious or enforced stillness, the *in media res* images of George Cruikshank, Marks, and Rowlandson imagine him in and *as* motion. They actively harness the special kinetic quality of pantomime's shifting scenography and, more especially, of Harlequin as a character of unceasing mobility—as what Leigh Hunt called "perpetual motion personified"—in order to fashion caricatured Napoleons that possess undeniable allure and dynamism.[58]

In part, this representational shift is symptomatic of the transformation in British perceptions of Napoleon that took place in 1814–15. "The astonishing, as well as the sublime, approaches the ludicrous," Walter Scott recollected of the public's immediate reaction to Napoleon's escape, "and it is a curious physiological fact, that the first news of an event which threatened the abolition of all their labours, seemed like a trick in a pantomime, that laughter was the first emotion it excited from almost every one."[59] Scott captures both the popular mood and the irresistible appeal of the pantomime conceit at this time, but, rather too defensively, he reads the public as reacting almost in spite of itself; as in Garrick's play, pantomime elicits a response that is disconcertingly pre- and anticognitive. In fact, as Semmel has shown, many liberal Britons met Napoleon's return from Elba with considered enthusiasm, regarding the putatively reformed Bonaparte as a force of liberty who was ready once and for all to end an old order that could no longer claim political legitimacy.[60] The satires of Marks and Rowlandson thus hinge on the juxtaposition of youth and decrepitude; the sprightly Napoleon is opposed by the gouty Louis XVIII, who can at best wield his crutch as an improvised club, or by a cohort of blundering, arthritic monarchs who remain rooted to the ground as Harlequin takes to the air. The generational conflict that drives pantomime's plot, as young lovers outwit a host of older, blocking characters, here comes to stand for the sudden shift in the balance of power across Europe. Marks and Rowlandson find in pantomimic action what Northrup Frye identified as the mythic pattern of comedy itself; in imagining Napoleon's return, their prints depict "the triumph of youth" and the "movement from one kind of society to another."[61] They appropriate pantomime as a structure of political renewal, of regime change.

As this parodic use of pantomime suggests, to compare the Harlequin Napoleons of 1803 and 1815 is therefore also to register a change in pantomime's position within the hierarchies of cultural production by the Regency period, a change that both reflected and contributed to the increased troubling of the cultural binaries harnessed to such effect during the invasion scare. These later prints don't invoke Garrick's play. Rather, they are animated by pantomime very much as it was practiced in the early nineteenth century. As David Mayer and, more recently, Jane Moody have argued, the emergence of Joe Grimaldi's Clown in the early years of the century reinvigorated pantomime, giving the form a new level of popularity and a new kind of cultural centrality and appeal.[62] Performing at both Sadler's Wells and Covent Garden, Grimaldi won unprecedented acclaim as a pantomime actor for his "eloquent gestural and bodily expressiveness," writes Moody, and also catalyzed the form's recalibration as a drama concerned with the rhythms, spaces, and absurdities of metropolitan modernity.[63] Of course, this shift in pantomime's status—the acknowledgment that there might be an art to such theater—only compounded entrenched anxieties about the besieged nature of native and legitimate theatrical forms. We need only recall the many-headed monster of popular drama conjured in the *Satirist* in 1807, which incorporates Grimaldi, to witness the continuing denigration of pantomime at this time. Nonetheless, in the age of Grimaldi pantomime found its first bona fide star and a new degree of cultural ratification, and it is no coincidence that George Cruikshank's *Narrow Escape* equates Napoleon's leap at once with Harlequin and Grimaldi's Clown; the invocation of the Clown in the print's title is crucial in establishing the sense of comic vitality that pervades the design as a whole. Indeed, Cruikshank's ironic suggestion that Napoleon moves "a la Grimaldi" conjoins derision and celebration by reading the French emperor both as a buffoon and as a figure of celebrity and dexterity.

Such parody also knowingly appropriates pantomime as a form of special topicality. Allusion to current affairs was almost a structural imperative of pantomime of this period, and references to Napoleon and the ongoing war effort, made both scenically and in song, were commonplace.[64] Grimaldi's performances were a particular site of patriotic negotiation. In 1803 he appeared as John Bull, embodiment of the commonsense nation, in Charles Dibdin's prelude *New Brooms,* defiantly singing, "None my spirit can tame"; and on the same opening night at Sadler's Wells in 1811 he drew both applause when breaking off from a song to laud "little England, where a man's head is his own freehold property," and also hisses by taking the part of Napoleon in the pantomime *Dulce Donum; or, England, Land of Freedom.*[65] In Cruikshank's triangulation of the figures of Bonaparte, Harlequin, and Grimaldi, and in Rowlandson's imagining of Bonaparte's escape as a "scene in a new pantomime," we see caricaturists looking to pantomime as a form that shares their irreverent commitment to narrating the cultural moment.

Even as it gives free play to a set of equivalences that seem remarkably ambivalent about the persona of Napoleon, the reference to Grimaldi in Cruikshank's print thus mobilizes associations of patriotic theatricality that to some extent anchor the image in the semiotics of loyalism. In the caricatures of Marks and Rowlandson, however, the satire is largely directed away from the figure of Harlequin Napoleon and toward his opponents. In addition to casting a hobbling Louis XVIII as Pantaloon, Marks shows the oblivious members of the Vienna Congress—the conference mandated to arrive at a peace settlement—gleefully casting their eyes over a globe. Meeting in a tent that is topped with a fool's cap and ass's ears, these self-satisfied statesmen are too concerned with mapping the new geopolitical order to notice that Napoleon, the man of action, not talk, once again has overturned it. Likewise, Rowlandson caricatures the physiognomies of the pursuing kings and emperors—their bodies clumsy and grizzled—far more than he does that of a comparatively lithe Napoleon, though such uneven distribution of ridicule is only one dimension of this complex, polysemous image.[66] Here the figure of Harlequin Napoleon allows Rowlandson to broach the politics of mediation, the hierarchy of the arts, and, most important, the cultural function of satire.

As Steven E. Jones notes, early nineteenth-century pantomime thematized its own technology of illusion, staging metamorphoses in metatheatrical ways that worked to foreground issues of perception and representation. Indeed, its bipartite structure, Melynda Nuss contends, gave its audience "the pleasure of illusion" by way of the frame story only to have this conspicuously "puncture[d]" in the harlequinade that followed.[67] It is exactly this metaphorics of representation that Rowlandson's caricature takes up, for it adapts one of the routine visual tropes of pantomime, which sees Harlequin leap through a seemingly solid plane—a mirror, for instance, or a clock-face—thereby transforming a flat object into an opening and revealing, or rather generating, a new space beyond the scenic boundary.[68] Only Rowlandson's Harlequin is not simply jumping through this painting; he is slashing it. Harlequin Napoleon does violence to the royal icon, to the image of the king's body rather than the king's body itself. Cutting through the canvas and slicing through Louis at the waist (so emphasizing the immobility and desuetude of his heavily bandaged legs), he engenders the space of a new political order precisely by exposing royal authority as an easily perforated illusion. The label on the portrait's baroque frame, "Louis / le bien aimé," applies to Louis XVIII the epithet of "beloved" that properly belonged to Louis XV. If this ironic title juxtaposes the Bourbon monarchy's illustrious past with its prosaic and uncertain present, then it also reminds viewers that power lies in the mechanisms of mediation, in the fictions that make it publicly visible and palatable. An effective royal portrait induces the condition of veneration; by interpellating its audience as political subjects, as spectators to Louis's ascendancy, it constitutes state authority in the very act of depicting it. To borrow Marshall McLuhan's famous dictum, the medium is the message.[69] The royal image depends for its impact on the discernable prestige of the aesthetics of portraiture. In Rowlandson's caricature, high and low cultures are once more set in opposition as a means of reading the trajectory of history; only this appropriation now takes place in a manner that seems fully aware of the imbrication of political power and generic status.

Harlequin Napoleon creates the blank, yet-to-be-contoured space of the political future by physically destroying an object that symbolizes and enacts legitimacy both politically and culturally. To strike at a portrait of the *king* is, perforce, to strike at a *portrait* of the king.

We can better understand the satirical import of this imagined act of iconoclasm by placing it alongside two other Rowlandson caricatures that also center on the recalcitrant figure of Harlequin. The first, one of Rowlandson's many erotic prints (fig. 7.10), shows Harlequin and a young woman discovered in a postcoital recline by an aghast Pierrot. The image replays one of the caricaturist's favorite pornographic scenarios, in which a virile younger man gleefully cuckolds a decrepit and impotent husband. The victory of youth over age—the latter invariably depicted as simultaneously prurient and impuissant—is one of the satirical master tropes of Rowlandson's work and is, as I've already suggested, at work in *Scene in a New Pantomime* too.[70] But it is the hypercorporeal presence of Harlequin in the erotic print, his flaccid penis resting on the naked, open thighs of his beautiful lover, that demands our attention, for it suggests, in Bakhtinian

Fig. 7.10. Thomas Rowlandson, untitled (c. 1790—1810). © The Trustees of the British Museum.

terms, Rowlandson's use of Harlequin as a figure of the carnivalesque whose uninhibited joy in the pleasures and processes of his body disrupts the sterile protocols of polite society.[71] Moody observes that in the first decades of the nineteenth century "the decisive emergence of an absolute opposition between authentic and spurious theatrical forms . . . soon begins to be imagined as a nightmarish confrontation between quasi-ethereal textuality and grotesque corporeality," a clash, we might add, that has its origins in Garrick's *Harlequin's Invasion*.[72] In Rowlandson's *Scene in a New Pantomime*, however, this confrontation is not the stuff of nightmares. Rather, in its depiction of a midair Harlequin hacking his way to freedom through the sober portrait of the king, the print imagines and celebrates the victory of the carnivalesque body over its classical counterpart. Garrick's play sets against Harlequin the *effigy* of Shakespeare; as Denise S. Sechelski observes of *Harlequin Student*, from which Garrick borrowed this dichotomy, the popular theater's threatening structures of embodiment and contingency are subdued by a statue that, in its very form, represents culture and its achievements as static, permanent, indissoluble.[73] Rowlandson's caricature turns this collision on its head. In *Scene in a New Pantomime* the finished, never-changing art object—and the canon-dynasty for which it stands—is no match for the dynamic body of Harlequin. The very sensuality that so discomfited pantomime's critics becomes a means of representing revolutionary action. If the ancien régime of the French Bourbon dynasty is given ratifying form in the fixed, sanitized, grandiose aesthetic of official portraiture, then it is pantomime, with its grammar of expressive, ever-mobile bodies, that for Rowlandson provides the image of a new kind of politics.

And if this heroically mischievous Harlequin Napoleon embodies the carnivalesque, then he also personifies the efficacious shape of satire itself, as is suggested by the frontispiece Rowlandson designed early in his career for John Wolcot's *Ode upon Ode* (1787), an irreverent parody of the poet laureate Thomas Warton's New Year's Ode. In this caricature (fig. 7.11) Harlequin startles Pegasus with a flourish of his bat, causing the horse to buck and send its two riders, Warton and George III, tumbling to the ground. This is not an illustration; no such incident occurs in Wolcot's poem. Rather, it is a prosopopaic championing of the intents and effects of satire—as practiced by the likes of Rowlandson and Wolcot—in which the figure of Harlequin embodies the mode's capacity to subvert the artistic pretensions and political sycophancy of institutionalized poetics. A self-consciously literary culture, the

Fig. 7.11. Thomas Rowlandson, frontispiece to Peter Pindar [John Wolcot], *Ode upon Ode* (London: G. Kearlsey, 1787). © The Trustees of the British Museum.

classical ambitions and inheritance of which are aptly signaled by the winged horse, is here brought back down to earth with a bump. In both this print and *Scene in a New Pantomime*, popular theater and classical culture meet in a comic juxtaposition that comments upon the politics of form; in both, Harlequin is cast as the adversary of cultural prestige; and in both, pantomime is posited as a force of satire that works not only to ridicule the political elite but also to disclose and trouble the mutually constitutive alliance between a monarchist regime and the aesthetics of high culture.

Writing in the *Examiner* in 1817, Leigh Hunt not only celebrated the Dionysian rhythms of pantomime but also claimed it to be "at present . . . the best medium of dramatic satire." Harlequin's sword was, Hunt insisted, "excellent at satirical strokes."[74] In Rowlandson's *Scene in a New Pantomime* we see this understanding of the form played out as a means of generating far-reaching parallels between Napoleon's overturning of entrenched structures of political privilege and satire's carnivalesque resistance to the prevailing taxonomy of culture. Indeed, Hunt defined pantomime as "mute caricature," a reading of the form also adumbrated by a reviewer in the *Times* in 1825, who wrote that its "conclave glass" served to "caricature the deformities of the town."[75] Willingly mining this intermedial correspondence, *Scene in a New Pantomime* uses the occasion of Bonaparte's return to Paris as the opportunity to engage in metasatirical reflection: in the figure of Harlequin Napoleon, Rowlandson stages his own art's systematic disregard for the objects and personalities of cultural reverence. Hunt's *Examiner* essay and Rowlandson's pantomime parody share a commitment to problematizing, even collapsing, the established boundaries between the polite and the popular, the high and the low. Both refuse exactly the kind of cultural adjudication performed by Harlequin-Napoleon satires of 1803–4; pantomime is not, by their reckoning, what literature isn't. Where a new comedy or tragedy would more than likely turn out to be "a gross piece of effort from beginning to end," Hunt writes, pantomime "brings out the real abilities of our dramatic writers."[76] Pantomime *is* literature, he seems to say; or rather, he asks whether such a category has any meaningful relation to the realities of cultural praxis. Equally, Rowlandson's Harlequin Napoleon does more than just destroy a painting; he is shown to push through and beyond it, to open up a potentially democratized space in which the hierarchy of the arts has no operative value.

As Vic Gatrell notes, we find in Rowlandson's work "an absence of highs and lows . . . a universal reduction to the comic," and we might regard *Scene in a New Pantomime* as a manifesto for this structuring principle, with the qualification that it shows Rowlandson to be concerned with an *expansion*, not a reduction, to the comic.[77] The print appropriates the syntax of pantomime to map this movement precisely because its theatrics functioned in much the same way; it too, as O'Brien argues, was driven by "a levelling impulse, a desire to undercut pretension by suggesting that high and low share common characteristics."[78] Nowhere is this imperative, and the ambivalences it generated, more evident than in *Harlequin and Fancy; or, The Poet's Last Shilling*, a pantomime performed at Drury Lane on Boxing Day, 1815, six months after Napoleon's final defeat at the Battle of Waterloo. The play opens in a Hogarthian garret, where a poor poet is counseled by the spirit of his final shilling to abandon the pursuit of literature in favor of profit-oriented popular theater: "Thy tragedy scribbling is but a poor trade," the shilling insists; "Write a Pantomime quickly, nay don't be afraid." *Harlequin and Fancy* thus ironically uses the fear of cultural degradation to propel

its own pantomimic plot, a gesture of self-disavowal that is further complicated by the intertextuality of the scene in which it is embedded. Upon the
departure of the spirit, the Poet embarks on a soliloquy that offers extended
travesties of first *Hamlet* and then, prompted by the knocking of his creditors, *Macbeth;* and in turn this speech is followed by a musical parody of the
weird sisters' incantations, in which the creditors sing, "Come away! Come
away!"[79] The play foregrounds the critique against its own form, as that
which literature is not, but does so within a scene that delights in elaborate
Shakespearean parody and that conspicuously displays its own indebtedness
to the literary canon.

In the harlequinade that follows, the Poet, transformed into Harlequin
by the spirit of Fancy, leads the audience through a sequence of scenes that
interweave locations of cultural activity—the State Lottery Office, a
Masquerade house, the exteriors of Drury Lane and Covent Garden Theatres—with those that reference Britain's defeat of Napoleon, including a
village on the Kentish coast where volunteers are being drilled, the interior
of the Waterloo Museum in Pall Mall, and, finally, the farmhouse known as
"La Belle Alliance," where the victorious British and Prussian commanders
met at the close of the battle. This scene, which shows "The Triumph of the
British Lion over the [Napoleonic] Eagle," precipitates a sudden shift in the
pantomime's trajectory, as Fancy returns to conjure "The Court of Shakespeare, in the Temple of Dramatic Genius," a sequence that includes trans-
parencies of Shakespeare in the company of his most famous characters and
a "procession of Apollo, the Graces, and the Muses." *Harlequin and Fancy*
thus reworks the climax of Garrick's *Harlequin's Invasion,* with the preemi-
nence of Shakespeare now symbolically tied to Britain's victory at Waterloo.
Yet, paradoxically, this recuperation of a national literature is overseen by
the very same benevolent spirit that earlier initiates the harlequinade. The
play repeatedly works across and between ostensibly opposed cultural
discourses in an almost dizzying set of maneuvers that reveal deep ambivalence about both pantomime's and Shakespeare's generic status, an ambivalence that is hardly reconciled by Fancy's epilogue, in which, noting that
"Shakespeare and Jonson were willing / To laugh at a Joke," she retroac-
tively dismisses the whole play as a nothing more than a jest.[80]

Such cultural ambivalence is distilled in the at-once-suspect and
irrepressible figure of Harlequin Napoleon. In 1803 satirists depict him in
ways that make precarious use of pantomime as both a helpfully and

problematically ubiquitous form. Pantomime is the Other against which "literature" and "Britain" come into clear view but which also threatens to efface those imbricated terms through its sheer popularity and cultural reach. By the second decade of the nineteenth century, with pantomime's success and innovation offering an increasing challenge to the cultural hierarchy, the contradictions inherent to this project are no longer really concealed. At once a version of Grimaldi and Harlequin, George Cruikshank's Napoleon invites derision and celebration in the same satirical glance; the parodic citation of pantomime works to exorcize *and* valorize. This ambivalence is, of course, symptomatic of cultural anxieties concerning the integrity of the canons of art and literature on which a certain conception of British nationhood rested at this time, as the peculiar climax of *Harlequin and Fancy* reveals. But in *Scene in a New Pantomime* Rowlandson is alert to the culturally constitutive potential of such uncertainty. The permeability and promiscuous intermingling of different, even seemingly opposed, cultural modes is, on his reading, to be embraced rather than feared. In Rowlandson's political harlequinade there is no permanence, only continual interaction and movement.

Yet this image of a dynamic and accommodating—dare we say, democratic—model of cultural production is rare, not least within the field of satire. Indeed, the celebration of Shakespeare, Apollo, and the muses that closes *Harlequin and Fancy* is made possible only by the disciplinary figure of Satire. Played by one Mr. Coveney, Satire appears immediately before the final scene in order to "cleanse" the stage of the "vile crew" of strange and exotic beasts, chide spectators for tolerating drama that does them much "discredit," and reclaim the theater for "Phoebus's glory, and the Poet's lay."[81] Over the course of this book we've become familiar with satire in this guise: as a form that polices rather than effaces the cultural boundaries. For this particular pantomime as for many of the caricatures we've considered, it is part of satire's work—and perhaps of parodic satire's work most especially—to sequester the literary from the popular, the commercial, and the everyday. So, conceding that the play was "no small puzzle," a reviewer for the *Times* assured his readers that *Harlequin and Fancy*'s use of allegory and parody rendered it "too obscure for the genius of the galleries."[82] We are back, of course, in the rigidly coded space of Dolly's playhouse—and, for that matter, of Sneyd's and Gillray's printshop. The need carefully to segregate those who don't understand from those who do, to distinguish the appeal of the body from the appeal of the intellect, remains as strong as ever.

Appendix

Dramatis Personae

Addington, Henry, 1st Viscount Sidmouth (1757–1844). Prime minister, 1801–4. Created Viscount Sidmouth in 1805 and served as home secretary in the Liverpool ministry, 1812–22.

Bonaparte, Napoleon (1769–1821). Elected first consul of France in 1799 and crowned emperor in 1804. Forced to abdicate in 1814 and exiled to Elba, but made a dramatic return to power in 1815. Exiled to St. Helena following defeat at the Battle of Waterloo the same year.

Brougham, Henry Peter, 1st Baron Brougham (1778–1868). A liberal Whig, vocal advocate of reform, and opponent of slavery. Supported Queen Caroline in 1820 and served as lord chancellor, 1830–34.

Burdett, Francis (1770–1844). Reformist politician and, from 1809, MP for Westminster.

Burke, Edmund (1729–1797). Irish MP who led impeachment proceedings against Warren Hastings, former governor-general of the East India Company, in the 1780s. Appalled by the French Revolution, he turned his back on the Foxite Whigs in the early 1790s. Author of *A Philosophical Enquiry into the Sublime and Beautiful* (1757).

Bute, John Stuart, 3rd Earl of (1713–1792). Prime minister, 1762–63. Widely perceived to have risen to this position as a consequence of his sway over the young George III, to whom he had served as tutor.

Canning, George (1770–1827). Foreign secretary, 1807–9 and 1822–27. Briefly prime minister in 1827.

Castlereagh, Robert Stewart, Viscount (1769–1822). Served in the Liverpool ministry as foreign secretary and leader of the House of Commons, 1812–22.

Caroline of Brunswick (1768–1821). Estranged wife of the Prince of Wales, later George IV, whom she married in 1795. George sought to annul the marriage when he became king in 1820, citing serial infidelity on her part.

Charlotte, Queen (1744–1818). Wife of George III.

Cumberland, William Augustus, 1st Duke of (1721–1765). Uncle of George III and captain-general of the British army during the Jacobite Rebellion of 1745.

Devonshire, Georgiana Cavendish, Duchess of (1757–1806). Writer and hostess at the center of Whig society in the 1780s. Campaigned for Charles James Fox at the Westminster election of 1784.

Dundas, Henry, 1st Viscount Melville (1742–1811). Served under Pitt the Younger as home secretary, 1791–94, and secretary of state for war, 1794–1801.

Eldon, John Scott, 1st Earl of (1751–1838). Lord chancellor, 1801–6 and 1807–27.

Fitzherbert, Maria (1756–1837). Secretly married the Prince of Wales in 1785. Her Catholicism would have prevented George from taking the throne.

Fox, Charles James (1749–1806). Leading Whig statesman and vocal opponent of the king's use of the royal prerogative. Served as foreign secretary in Rockingham's brief government of 1782 and then governed in coalition with his former opponent, Lord North, in 1783. The split of the Whigs in the 1790s left him largely alienated in the Commons.

Fox, Henry (1704–1774). Leader of the House of Commons, 1762–63. Great rival of Pitt the Elder.

George III (1738–1820). Crowned in 1760 and played an active role in determining the character of his governments. Suffered a bout of apparent madness in 1788, throwing his reign into crisis, but recovered in spring 1789. Permanently declined into mental incapacity in 1810, leading to the creation of a regency.

George IV (1762–1830). A notorious profligate, both as Prince of Wales and later as regent and king. Secretly married the Catholic Maria Fitzherbert in 1785. Married Caroline of Brunswick in 1795 as a means of alleviating his many debts but soon separated from her. Became regent in 1810 and king in 1820.

Grattan, Henry (1746–1820). Member of the Irish Parliament. A vocal opponent of the Act of Union of 1800.

Grenville, William Wyndham, 1st Lord (1759–1834). Held various cabinet posts in the Pitt ministry, including foreign secretary, 1791–1802. Served as prime minister, 1806–7.

Grey, Charles, 2nd Earl Grey (1764–1845). Prominent reformist MP who stuck with Fox when the Whig Party split in 1794. Pushed the Reform Act through Parliament while prime minister, 1830–34.

Liverpool, Charles Jenkinson, 2nd Earl of (1770–1828). Prime minister during the politically tumultuous years of 1812–27.

North, Frederick, Lord (1732–1792). Oversaw the loss of the American colonies as prime minister, 1770–82. Entered into a short-lived coalition with Charles James Fox in 1783.

Perceval, Spencer (1762–1812). Prime minister, 1809–12. Assassinated in the lobby of the Commons.

O'Connell, Daniel (1775–1847). Irish politician and, by 1815, leader of the campaign for Catholic Emancipation.

Pitt the Elder, William (1708–1778). Secretary of state for the southern department, 1757–61, and spearheaded British military efforts during the Seven Years' War. Prime minister, 1766–68, and took the title of the Earl of Chatham.

Pitt the Younger, William (1759–1806). Became prime minister in 1783, aged twenty-four. Resigned in 1801, having failed to win support for Catholic Emancipation, which the king opposed. Prime minister again, 1804–6.

Portland, William Cavendish-Bentinck, 3rd Duke of (1738–1809). Twice nominal prime minister, 1783 and 1807–9. Led the large group of conservative Whigs who in 1794 joined the Pitt ministry and served as home secretary in this coalition.

Prince of Wales. *See* George IV

Rockingham, Charles Watson-Wentworth, 2nd Marquis of (1732–1782). Whig prime minister, 1765–66, and chief opponent of Lord North during the 1770s. Briefly prime minister again in 1782.

Shelburne, William Petty, 2nd Earl of (1737–1805). Home secretary in the Rockingham ministry of 1782, and fell out with Charles James Fox over peace negotiations with America. Prime minister, 1782–83.

Sheridan, Richard Brinsley (1751–1816). Dramatist, theater manager, and loyal Foxite MP.

Thurlow, Edward, 1st Baron Thurlow (1731–1806). Lord chancellor, 1778–83 and 1784–92.

Wellington, Arthur Wellesley, 1st Duke of (1769–1852). General during the Peninsular War and the Battle of Waterloo. Prime minister, 1828–30, and then a prominent opponent of the Reform Bills of 1831–32.

Wilberforce, William (1759–1833). Leading evangelical, antislavery campaigner, and MP.

Wilkes, John (1725–1797). Notorious rake, radical politician, and relentless opponent of Lord Bute. Charged with seditious libel in 1763 for his criticisms of the king in the *North Briton*.

Notes

1. The Literariness of Graphic Satire

1. On the problematic history implied in the term *cartoon*, see Eirwin Nicholson, "Soggy Prose and Verbiage: English Graphic Political Satire as a Visual/Verbal Construct," *Word and Image* 20, no. 1 (2004): 33.

2. *The Caricatures of James Gillray; with Historical and Political Illustrations, and Compendius Biographical Anecdotes and Notices* (Edinburgh: William Blackwood, 1818), 1.

3. Charles Lamb, *The Works of Charles Lamb*, 2 vols. (London: C. and J. Ollier, 1818), 2:89.

4. Michael Baxandall, *Painting and Experience in Fifteenth-Century Italy: A Primer in the Social History of Pictorial Style*, 2nd ed. (Oxford: Oxford University Press, 1988), 29–108.

5. Shakespeare, *Macbeth*, 2.3.138–40.

6. Colley Cibber, *The Tragical History of Richard III: Altered from Shakspeare by Colley Cibber Esq.* (London: T. and W. Lowndes, 1784), 49, 17, 58.

7. M. Dorothy George, *English Political Caricature: A Study of Opinion and Propaganda*, 2 vols. (Oxford: Clarendon Press, 1959), 1:3; Peter Wagner, *Reading Iconotexts: From Swift to the French Revolution* (London: Reaktion Books, 1995); Nicholson, "Soggy Prose and Verbiage."

8. Roland Barthes, *Image-Music-Text*, trans. Stephen Heath (London: Fontana, 1997), 39–41.

9. David Bindman, "Text as Design in Gillray's Caricatures," in *Icons— Texts—Iconotexts: Essays on Ekphrasis and Intermediality*, ed. Peter Wagner (New York: Walter de Gruyter, 1996), 323. For prints that reify language, see *The Long-Winded Speech, or the oratorical organ harmonized with sublime and beautiful inflation* (4 June 1788; BMC 7330), and *The Wonderful Word Eater, lately arrived from abroad* (29 December 1788; BMC 7390), both by William Dent.

10. See Norman Bryson's discussion of "discursive" and "figurative" images in *Word and Image: French Painting of the Ancien Régime* (Cambridge: Cambridge University Press, 1981).

11. David Solkin, "The British and the Modern," in *Towards a Modern Art World*, ed. Brian Allen (New Haven: Yale University Press, 1995), 3.

12. See Ronald Paulson, *Book and Painting: Shakespeare, Milton, and the Bible: Literary Texts and the Emergence of English Painting* (Knoxville: University of Tennessee Press, 1982), 15–16; and Frédéric Ogée, "From Text to Image: William Hogarth and the Emergence of a Visual Culture in Eighteenth-Century England," in *Hogarth: Representing Nature's Machines*, ed. David Bindman, Frédéric Ogée, and Peter Wagner (Manchester: Manchester University Press, 2001), 3–22.

13. Gary Dyer, *British Satire and the Politics of Style, 1789–1832* (Cambridge: Cambridge University Press, 2007), 10. Vincent Carretta models this approach in *George III and the Satirists from Hogarth to Byron* (Athens: University of Georgia Press, 1990).

14. Gillray takes his quotation from Shakespeare, *Richard III*, 4.4.425. For Gillray's care in creating titles, see Marcus Wood, *Radical Satire and Print Culture, 1790–1822* (Oxford: Clarendon Press, 1994), 169.

15. For the disappearance of graphic satire in the Gillrayan tradition in the 1830s, see Vic Gatrell, *City of Laughter: Sex and Satire in Eighteenth-Century London* (London: Atlantic, 2006), 530–46; and Frank Palmeri, "Cruikshank, Thackeray, and the Victorian Eclipse of Satire," *Studies in English Literature, 1500–1900* 44, no. 4 (2004): 753–77.

16. Mark Hallett, *The Spectacle of Difference: Graphic Satire in the Age of Hogarth* (New Haven: Yale University Press, 1999), 61, 37–55.

17. Helen Pierce, *Unseemly Pictures: Graphic Satire and Politics in Early Modern England* (New Haven: Yale University Press, 2008), 33.

18. *The Three Trials of William Hone*, 3 vols. in 1 (London: William Hone, 1818), 1:39–41.

19. Ibid., 1:18, 3:21.

20. Samuel Johnson, *A Dictionary of the English Language*, 2 vols. (London: W. Strahan, 1755–56), entry for "parody." Alexander Pope distinguished between parody that mocks the text it imitates and parody where "the ridicule falls not on the thing *imitated*, but *imitating*." See Pope, *The Dunciad in Four Books* (London: M. Cooper, 1743), 116.

21. Jonathan Swift, *A Tale of the Tub*, in *A Tale of the Tub and Other Works*, ed. Marcus Walsh, The Cambridge Edition of the Works of Jonathan Swift (Cambridge: Cambridge University Press, 2010), 7.

22. Mark Turner, *The Literary Mind* (Oxford: Oxford University Press, 1998), esp. 4–5.

23. Hayden White, *The Content of Form: Narrative Discourse and Historical Representation* (Baltimore: Johns Hopkins University Press, 1987), 14.

24. See René Girard, *Violence and the Sacred*, trans. Patrick Gregory (Baltimore: Johns Hopkins University Press, 1977).

25. White, *Content of Form*, 21.

26. Margaret A. Rose, *Parody/Metafiction: An Analysis of Parody as a Critical Mirror to the Writing and Reception of Fiction* (London: Croom Helm, 1979), 59.

27. See David V. Erdman, *Blake: Prophet against the Empire*, 3rd ed. (Princeton, NJ: Princeton University Press, 1977), 201–4.

28. Frank Kermode, *The Sense of an Ending: Studies in the Theory of Fiction*, new ed. (Oxford: Oxford University Press, 2000), 46. On this issue of temporality in paintings of literary scenes, see Richard D. Altick, *Paintings from Books: Art and Literature in Britain, 1760–1900* (Columbus: Ohio State University Press, 1985), 130.

29. Fredric Jameson, "Postmodernism, or the Cultural Logic of Late Capitalism," *New Left Review* 146 (1984): 65.

30. Linda Hutcheon, *A Theory of Parody: The Teachings of Twentieth-Century Art Forms* (New York: Methuen, 1985), 7.

31. See Stuart Sillars, *Painting Shakespeare: The Artist as Critic, 1720–1820* (Cambridge: Cambridge University Press, 2006), which contends that the period's Shakespeare paintings operated as critical readings of the plays.

32. Jonathan Bate, *Shakespearean Constitutions: Politics, Theatre, Criticism, 1730–1830* (Oxford: Clarendon Press, 1989). Shakespeare's plays were equally popular with the period's novelists. See Kate Rumbold, *Shakespeare and the Eighteenth-Century Novel: Cultures of Quotation from Samuel Richardson to Jane Austen* (Cambridge: Cambridge University Press, 2016).

33. These numbers are the result of extensive searches of archives at the British Museum, the Lewis Walpole Library, the Huntington Library, and the Library of Congress.

34. M. Dorothy George, *Catalogue of Political and Personal Satires Preserved in the Department of Prints and Drawings in the British Museum*, vol. 5: *1771–1783* (London: British Museum, 1935), xi.

35. Paul Fussell, *The Great War and Modern Memory* (1975; reprint, Oxford: Oxford University Press, 2013), 149–55.

36. Quoted in Robin Simon, "Hogarth and the Popular Theatre," *Renaissance and Modern Studies* 22 no. 1 (1978): 13.

37. Deidre Shauna Lynch, *The Economy of Character: Novels, Market Culture, and the Business of Inner Meaning* (Chicago: University of Chicago Press, 1998), esp. 23–79.

38. Amelia Rauser, *Caricature Unmasked: Irony, Authenticity, and Individualism in Eighteenth-Century Prints* (Newark: University of Delaware Press, 2008), 20. For a critique of this view of emblematism, see Eirwin E. C. Nicholson, "Emblem v. Caricature: A Tenacious Conceptual Framework," in *Emblems and Art History: Nine Essays*, ed. Alison Adams (Glasgow: Glasgow Emblem Studies, 1996), 141–68.

39. Diana Donald, *The Age of Caricature: Satirical Prints in the Reign of George III* (New Haven: Yale University Press, 1996), 67.

40. For the first prints to quote Shakespeare, see George, *English Political Caricature*, 1:86–87.

41. Michel de Certeau, *The Practice of Everyday Life*, trans. Steven F. Rendall (Berkeley: University of California Press, 1984), xviii.

42. Fredric Jameson, *The Political Unconscious: Narrative as a Socially Symbolic Act* (Ithaca, NY: Cornell University Press, 1981), 79.

43. For Cibber's revisions to *Richard III*, see John Jowett's introduction to his edition of *Richard III* (Oxford: Oxford University Press, 2000), 83–86.

44. Paulson, *Book and Painting*, 3. See also Marcia R. Pointon, *Milton and English Art* (Manchester: Manchester University Press, 1970); Altick, *Paintings from Books;* Morris Eaves, *The Counter-Arts Conspiracy: Art and Industry in the Age of Blake* (Ithaca, NY: Cornell University Press, 1992), 33–55; Christopher Rovee, *Imagining the Gallery: The Social Body of British Romanticism* (Stanford, CA: Stanford University Press, 2006); Luisa Calè, *Fuseli's Milton Gallery: "Turning Readers into Spectators"* (Oxford: Oxford University Press, 2006); and Rosie Dias, *Exhibiting Englishness: John Boydell's Shakespeare Gallery and the Formation of the National Aesthetic* (New Haven: Yale University Press, 2013).

45. Clifford Siskin and William Warner, "This Is Enlightenment: An Invitation in the Form of an Argument," in *This Is Enlightenment*, ed. Siskin and Warner (Chicago: Chicago University Press, 2009), 1–33. For an analysis of caricatures as metapictures, see Joseph Monteyne, *From Still Life to the Screen: Print Culture, Display, and the Materiality of the Image in Eighteenth-Century London* (New Haven: Yale University Press, 2013).

46. David Bindman, "Prints," in *An Oxford Companion to the Romantic Age*, ed. Iain McCalman (Oxford: Oxford University Press, 2009), 209–10; Roy Porter, "Seeing the Past," *Past and Present* 118, no. 1 (1988): 190; Timothy

Clayton, "The London Printsellers and the Export of English Graphic Prints," in *Loyal Subversion? Caricatures from the Personal Union between England and Hanover (1714–1837)*, ed. Anorthe Kremers and Elisabeth Reich (Göttingen: Vandenhoeck and Ruprecht, 2014), 154. See also Richard Godfrey, *James Gillray: The Art of Caricature* (London: Tate, 2001), 17; Eirwin E. C. Nicholson, "English Political Prints and Pictorial Political Argument, c.1640—c.1832: A Study in Historiography and Methodology" (PhD diss., University of Edinburgh, 1994), 332–37; and James Baker, "Isaac Cruikshank and the Notion of British Liberty, 1783–1811" (PhD diss., University of Sussex, 2010), 19–20.

47. On Tegg, see Gatrell, *City of Laughter*, 245–51.

48. Ibid., 245. For the pricing of prints, see Timothy Clayton, *The English Print, 1688–1802* (New Haven: Yale University Press, 1997), 232.

49. Numbers taken from Richard D. Altick, *The English Common Reader: A Social History of the Mass Reading Public* (Chicago: University of Chicago Press, 1957), 392.

50. James Gillray to Sir James Dalrymple, 2 March 1798, quoted in Draper Hill, *Mr. Gillray, the Caricaturist: A Biography* (London: Phaidon, 1965), 77; *Morning Post*, 15 March 1798.

51. Robert L. Patten, "Conventions of Georgian Caricature," *Art Journal* 43, no. 4 (1983): 331–32.

52. *Public Advertiser*, 5 June 1765.

53. Bate, *Shakespearean Constitutions*, 2; Ian Haywood, *Romanticism and Caricature* (Cambridge: Cambridge University Press, 2013), 7.

54. Simon Dentith, *Parody* (London: Routledge, 2000), 27; Henry Fielding, *Joseph Andrews*, ed. Thomas Keymer (Oxford: Oxford University Press, 1999), 4. On parody and readerly competence reader, see also Hutcheon, *Theory of Parody*, 94–95; and Rose, *Parody/Metafiction*, 25–28.

55. Maria Edgeworth, with Richard Lovell Edgeworth, *Readings on Poetry*, 2nd ed. (London: R. Hunter, 1816), 206.

56. William Hogarth, *The Analysis of Beauty*, ed. Ronald Paulson (New Haven: Yale University Press, 1997), 41–42.

57. See David Francis Taylor, " 'The Fate of Empires': The American War, Political Parody, and Sheridan's Comedies," *Eighteenth-Century Studies* 42, no. 2 (2009): 379–95.

58. *Middlesex Journal*, 24–26 October 1771; *World*, 26 October 1793–4, January 1794; *Gentleman's Magazine*, December 1798, 1065, and July 1802, 655.

59. *Public Advertiser*, 28 January 1793.

60. Robert L. Mack, *The Genius of Parody: Imitation and Originality in Seventeenth- and Eighteenth-Century English Literature* (Basingstoke: Palgrave Macmillan, 2007), 232.

61. Christiane Banerji and Diana Donald, eds. and trans., *Gillray Observed: The Earliest Accounts of His Caricatures in "London und Paris"* (Cambridge: Cambridge University Press, 1999).

62. See, e.g., *Monthly Magazine*, 1 March 1806, 158, and 1 May 1806, 336.

63. Peter de Bolla, *The Education of the Eye: Painting, Landscape, and Architecture in Eighteenth-Century Britain* (Stanford, CA: Stanford University Press, 2003), 9–10, 17.

64. Godfrey, *James Gillray*, 149.

65. See Hill, *Mr. Gillray*, 57–63.

66. Christopher Reid, *Imprison'd Wranglers: The Rhetorical Culture of the House of Commons, 1760–1800* (Oxford: Oxford University Press, 2012), 218–24; Pierre Bourdieu, *Distinction: A Social Critique of the Judgment of Taste*, trans. Richard Nice (Cambridge, MA: Harvard University Press, 1984), 372–74.

67. R. S. Schofield, "Dimensions of Illiteracy, 1750–1850," *Explorations in Economic History* 10, no. 4 (1973): 446.

68. William St. Clair, *The Reading Nation in the Romantic Period* (Cambridge: Cambridge University Press, 2004); esp. 103–21 (quotation at 109); Trevor Ross, *The Making of the English Literary Canon: From the Middle Ages to the Late Eighteenth Century* (Montreal: McGill-Queen's University Press, 1998), 297.

69. J. E. Elliott, "The Cost of Reading in Eighteenth-Century Britain: Auction Catalogues and the Cheap Literature Hypothesis," *ELH* 77, no. 2 (2010): 353–84 (quotation at 373); Altick, *English Common Reader*, 52.

70. See, e.g., Edward Bysshe's *The British Parnassus: or, A Compleat Common-Place-Book of English Poetry*, 2 vols. (London: J. Nutt, 1714), 1:441; and William Dodd's much-reprinted *The Beauties of Shakespear*, 2 vols. (London: T. Waller, 1752), 2:40–41.

71. Donald connects the iconography of Wilkesite prints to "an authentic popular culture" (*Age of Caricature*, 50).

72. Paul Keen, *The Crisis of Literature in the 1790s: Print Culture and the Public Sphere* (Cambridge: Cambridge University Press, 1999). Keen draws on the arguments made in Isaac Kramnick, *Republicanism and Bourgeois Radicalism: Political Ideology in Late Eighteenth-Century England and America* (Ithaca, NY: Cornell University Press, 1990).

73. James Barry, *A Letter to the Dilettanti Society* (London: J. Walker, 1798), 23.

74. *European Magazine*, June 1784, 441.

75. William Wordsworth, *The Prelude: A Parallel Text*, ed. J. C. Maxwell (London: Penguin, 1986), 7.466–67 (1805 version).

76. Jürgen Habermas, *The Structural Transformation of the Public Sphere: An Inquiry into a Category of Bourgeois Society*, trans. Thomas Burger (Cambridge: Polity, 1989).

77. Bourdieu, *Distinction*, 24, 70.

78. Olivia Smith, *The Politics of Language* (Oxford: Clarendon Press, 1986), 154–201; Wood, *Radical Satire and Print Culture*, 96–154; Kyle Grimes, "Spreading the Radical Word: The Circulation of William Hone's 1817 Liturgical Parodies," in *Radicalism and Revolution in Britain, 1775–1848: Essays in Honour of Malcolm I. Thomis*, ed. Michael T. Davis (London: Macmillan, 2000), 143–56.

79. *Trials of Hone*, 2:6.

80. Haywood, *Romanticism and Caricature*, 4.

81. *Trials of Hone*, 1:41.

82. Mikhail Bakhtin, "From the Prehistory of Novelistic Discourse," in *The Dialogic Imagination: Four Essays*, trans. Caryl Emerson and Michael Holquist (Austin: University of Texas Press, 1981), 61, 71; Mack, *Genius of Parody*, 21.

83. Dyer, *British Satire and the Politics of Style*, 41.

84. Roy Porter, "Georgian Britain: An Ancien Regime?," *Journal of Eighteenth-Century Studies* 15, no. 2 (1992): 141. Porter is responding to historiographical debates surrounding J. C. D. Clark's *English Society, 1688–1832: Ideology, Social Structure and Political Practice during the Ancien Régime* (Cambridge: Cambridge University Press, 1985) and *Revolution and Rebellion: State and Society in England in the Seventeenth and Eighteenth Centuries* (Cambridge: Cambridge University Press, 1986).

85. Ross, *Making of the English Literary Canon*, 3–20.

86. John Guillory, *Cultural Capital: The Problem of Literary Canon Formation* (Chicago: University of Chicago Press, 1993), ix.

2. Looking, Literacy, and the Printshop Window

1. *The Mirror; or, Literature, Amusement, and Instruction* 35 (21 June 1823): 70.

2. So reads the puff on Frederick George Byron, *Contrasted Opinions of Paine's Pamphlet*, 26 May 1791.

3. See Diana Donald, *The Age of Caricature: Satirical Prints in the Reign of George III* (New Haven: Yale University Press, 1996), 19.

4. Grantley Berkeley, *My Life and Recollections,* 4 vols. (London: Hurst and Blackett, 1866), 4:133.

5. See, e.g., British Museum nos. 1948,0214.604, 1948,0214.606, and 1948,0214.640.

6. Fores included the notice "Folios of Caricatures lent for the Evening" on many caricatures. See, e.g., *Johnny in a Flatting Mill* (25 May 1796; BMC 8808).

7. [William Kenrick and Mcnamara Morgan?], *The Scandalizade: A Panegyri-Satiri-Serio-Comi-Dramatic Poem* (London: G. Smith, 1750), 2–3.

8. See Brian Maidment, *Comedy, Caricature, and the Social Order, 1820–50* (Manchester: Manchester University Press, 2013), 113–43.

9. John Trusler, *The London Adviser and Guide* (London: printed for the author, 1786), 115.

10. [Henry Fielding], *Covent-Garden Journal* 12 (11 February 1752): 39.

11. *Stuart's Star and Evening Advertiser,* 12 March 1789; John Corry, *A Satirical View of London,* 3rd ed. (London: R. Ogle, 1804), 156.

12. Barbara Maria Stafford, *Good Looking: Essays on the Virtue of Images* (Cambridge, MA: MIT Press, 1996), 123; W. J. T Mitchell, *What Do Pictures Want? The Lives and Loves of Images* (Chicago: University of Chicago Press, 2005), 47–48.

13. See, e.g., Nicholas Ridley, "A Treatise on the Worship of Images" (1583), in *The Works of Nicholas Ridley,* ed. Henry Christmas (Cambridge: Cambridge University Press, 1841), 81–96.

14. John Shebbeare, *Letters on the English Nation,* 2 vols. (London, 1755), 1:68–69.

15. See Nicholas Rogers, *Crowds, Culture, and Politics in Georgian Britain* (Oxford: Clarendon Press, 1998), 176–77.

16. Edmund Burke, *Reflections on the Revolution in France,* ed. L. G. Mitchell (Oxford: Oxford University Press, 1993), 79. On the period's attitudes toward the crowd, see Mary Fairclough, *The Romantic Crowd: Sympathy, Controversy and Print Culture* (Cambridge: Cambridge University Press, 2013), esp. 59–121.

17. Vicesimus Knox, *Winter Evenings; or, Lucubrations on Life and Letters,* 2 vols. (London: Charles Dilly, 1795), 1:140–41.

18. *The Parliamentary Register,* vol. 33 (London: J. Debrett, 1792), 416.

19. *True Briton,* 19 December 1795.

20. Knox, *Winter Evenings,* 1:141.

21. *Literary Chronicle and Weekly Review* 380 (2 July 1825): 430.

22. William Makepeace Thackeray, *An Essay on the Genius of George Cruikshank* (1840), ed. W. E. Church (London: George Redway, 1884), 23.

23. John Wardroper, *Cruikshank 200: An Exhibition to Celebrate the Bicentenary of George Cruikshank* (London: John Wardroper, 1992), 5.

24. Roy Porter, "Seeing the Past," *Past and Present* 118, no. 1 (1988): 200–201.

25. W. J. T. Mitchell, *Picture Theory: Essays on Verbal and Visual Representation* (Chicago: University of Chicago Press, 1994), 48.

26. Mike Goode, "The Public Age and the Limits of Persuasion in the Age of Caricature," in *The Efflorescence of Caricature, 1759–1838*, ed. Todd Porterfield (Farnham, Surrey: Ashgate, 2011), 124–25; Maidment, *Comedy, Caricature, and Social Order*, 115.

27. This point is also made in Eirwen E. C. Nicholson, "Consumers and Spectators: The Public of the Political Print in Eighteenth-Century England," *History* 81 (1996): 17.

28. C. Suzanne Matheson, "Viewing," in *An Oxford Companion to the Romantic Age*, ed. Iain McCalman (Oxford: Oxford University Press, 2009), 195.

29. Martin Jay, *Downcast Eyes: The Denigration of Vision in Twentieth-Century French Thought* (Berkeley: University of California Press, 1993), 3.

30. See Amelia Rauser, *Caricature Unmasked: Irony, Authenticity, and Individualism in Eighteenth-Century Prints* (Newark: University of Delaware Press, 2008), 58–62.

31. *The Vauxhall Affray; or, The Macaronis Defeated* (London: J. Williams, 1773), 59; John Cooke, *The Macaroni Jester, and Pantheon of Wit* (London: J. Cooke, [1773]), 7; *The Macaroni, Scavoir Vivre and Theatrical Magazine*, March 1774, 241.

32. Shearer West, "The Darly Macaroni Prints and the Politics of 'Private Man,'" *Eighteenth-Century Life* 25, no. 2 (2001): 170–82.

33. Rauser, *Caricature Unmasked*, 56.

34. Samuel Johnson, *A Dictionary of the English Language*, 2nd ed., 2 vols. (London: W. Strahan, 1755), s.v. "enthusiast."

35. See Misty G. Anderson, *Imagining Methodism in Eighteenth-Century Britain: Enthusiasm, Belief, and the Borders of the Self* (Baltimore: Johns Hopkins University Press, 2012).

36. Rauser, *Caricature Unmasked*, 18.

37. Quoted in Richard Godfrey, "Introduction," in *English Caricature, 1620 to the Present: Caricaturists and Satirists, Their Art, Their Purpose and Influence* (London: Victoria and Albert Museum, 1984), 15.

38. Rauser, *Caricature Unmasked*, 64–76.

39. Frederic V. Bogel, *The Difference Satire Makes: Rhetoric and Reading from Jonson to Byron* (Ithaca, NY: Cornell University Press, 2001), 48.

40. Peter de Bolla, *The Education of the Eye: Painting, Landscape, and Architecture in Eighteenth-Century Britain* (Stanford, CA: Stanford University Press, 2003), 57–58, 70.

41. Pierre Bourdieu, *Distinction: A Social Critique of the Judgment of Taste*, trans. Richard Nice (Cambridge, MA: Harvard University Press, 1984), 7.

42. John Barrell, *The Political Theory of Painting from Reynolds to Hazlitt: The Body of the Public* (New Haven: Yale University Press, 1995).

43. John Barrell, *The Dark Side of the Landscape: The Rural Poor in English Painting, 1730–1840* (Cambridge: Cambridge University Press, 1980), 5.

44. David Francis Taylor, "Edgeworth's *Belinda* and the Gendering of Caricature," *Eighteenth-Century Fiction* 26, no. 4 (2014): 608–10.

45. Maidment, *Comedy, Caricature, and Social Order*, 137.

46. Donald, *Age of Caricature*, 129.

47. Besides those already discussed, these prints are John Raphael Smith's *Spectators at a Print-Shop in St. Paul's Church Yard* (25 June 1774; BMC 3758) and *Ecce Homo* (1775; BMC 5318).

48. On humor's importance to British exceptionalism, see Martin Myrone's "What's So Funny about British Art?," in *Rude Britannia: British Comic Art* (London: Tate, 2010), 8–10.

49. J. P. Malcolm, *An Historical Sketch of the Art of Caricaturing* (London: Longman et al., 1813), iv.

50. Donald, *Age of Caricature*, 5.

51. On Gillray's friendship with Sneyd, see Draper Hill, *Mr. Gillray: The Caricaturist* (London: Phaidon, 1965), 56–72. *Very Slippy-Weather* is part of a series of seven satires on the English weather, all designed by Sneyd (BMC 11094–100).

52. Tamara L. Hunt, *Defining John Bull: Political Caricature and National Identity in late Georgian England* (Aldershot: Ashgate, 2003), 11.

53. See Richard Godfrey, *James Gillray: The Art of Caricature* (London: Tate, 2001), 200.

54. *The Caricatures of James Gillray; with Historical and Political Illustrations, and Compendius Biographical Anecdotes and Notices* (London: John Miller, Rodwell and Martin, [1818]), 13.

55. For one such reading, see Steven E. Jones, "Satire," in *A Handbook to Romanticism Studies*, ed. Joel Faflak and Julia M. Wright (Oxford: Blackwell, 2012), 215.

56. John Brewer, *The Common People in Politics, 1750–1790s* (Cambridge: Chadwyck-Healey, 1986), 26.

57. Quoted in Christiane Banerji and Diana Donald, eds. and trans., *Gillray Observed: The Earliest Accounts of His Caricatures in "London und Paris"* (Cambridge: Cambridge University Press, 1999), 246.

58. Maidment, *Comedy, Caricature, and Social Order,* 17, 19.

3. The Tempest; *or, The Disenchanted Island*

1. Jonathan Bate, *Shakespearean Constitutions: Politics, Theatre, Criticism, 1730–1830* (Oxford: Clarendon Press, 1989), 6–7.

2. Michael Dobson provides the best such transmission history in " 'Remember / First to Possess His Books': The Appropriation of *The Tempest,* 1700–1800," in *Shakespeare Survey* 43 (1991): 99–107.

3. See Katharine Eisaman Maus, "Arcadia Lost: Politics and Revision in the Restoration *Tempest,*" *Renaissance Drama,* n.s., 13 (1982): 189–209; and Michael Dobson, *The Making of the National Poet: Shakespeare, Adaptation and Authorship, 1660–1769* (Oxford: Clarendon Press, 1992), 38–59.

4. Bate, *Shakespearean Constitutions,* 73.

5. Kathleen Wilson, *The Island Race: Englishness, Empire and Gender in the Eighteenth Century* (London: Routledge, 2003), 5.

6. Charles Beecher Hogan, *Shakespeare in the Theatre, 1701–1800,* 2 vols. (Oxford: Clarendon Press, 1952–1957), 2:716–19.

7. *London Evening Post,* 2–4 September 1762.

8. See George Winchester Stone Jr., "Shakespeare's *Tempest* at Drury Lane during Garrick's Management," *Shakespeare Quarterly* 7, no. 1 (1956): 1–7.

9. David Garrick, *The Poetical Works of David Garrick,* 2 vols. (London: George Kearsley, 1785), 1:144, 148.

10. *Gisbal, an Hyperborean Tale* (London: J. Pridden, 1762), an Ossian parody.

11. For Wilkes's response to the loss of Newfoundland and the proposed peace, see *North Briton* 9 (31 July 1762) and 15 (11 September 1762).

12. The Dryden-Davenant adaption, with Thomas Shadwell's revisions, was last performed in London on 27 April 1750, at Drury Lane, though John Philip Kemble returned to it in 1789.

13. See Anna Clark, *Scandal: The Sexual Politics of the British Constitution* (Princeton, NJ: Princeton University Press, 2004), 21–29.

14. Marie Peters, *Pitt and Popularity: The Patriot Minister and London Opinion during the Seven Years' War* (Oxford: Clarendon Press, 1980).

15. For example, *Coalition Minuet* (29 March 1783; BMC 6197).

16. See L. G. Mitchell, *Charles James Fox and the Disintegration of the Whig Party, 1782–1794* (Oxford: Oxford University Press, 1971).

17. *The Speeches of the Right Honourable Charles James Fox*, 6 vols. (London: Longman et al., 1815), 1:438.

18. See Mitchell, *Disintegration of the Whig Party*, 47–91.

19. John Dryden and William Davenant, *The Tempest; or, The Enchanted Island: A Comedy* (London: Henry Herringman, 1670), 21–22.

20. See John Brewer, " 'This Monstrous Tragic-Comic Scene': British Reactions to the French Revolution," in David Bindman, *The Shadow of the Guillotine: Britain and the French Revolution* (London: British Museum, 1989), 19.

21. See my *Theatres of Opposition: Empire, Revolution, and Richard Brinsley Sheridan* (Oxford: Oxford University Press, 2012), 157–221.

22. Statistics taken from Hogan, *Shakespeare in the Theatre*, 1:422–37, 2:636–54.

23. [John Philip Kemble], *The Tempest; or, The Enchanted Island. Written by Shakespeare; with Additions from Dryden; as Compiled by J. P. Kemble* (London: J. Debrett, 1789), 56.

24. John Watkins, *The Life and Times of "England's Patriot King," William the Fourth* (London: Fisher, Son, and Jackson, 1831), 198.

25. For Sheridan as a press manager, see Lucyle Werkmeister, *The London Daily Press, 1772–1792* (Lincoln: University of Nebraska Press, 1963).

26. On Bell's illustrated Shakespeare, see Stuart Sillars, *The Illustrated Shakespeare, 1709–1875* (Cambridge: Cambridge University Press, 2009), 111–47. Sillars discusses this illustration at 137–38.

27. See Bell's advertisement in the *Morning Post*, 28 April 1785.

28. *London Chronicle*, 12–14 August 1784.

29. See Frank O'Gorman, *The Whig Party and the French Revolution* (London: Macmillan, 1967).

30. Dryden and Davenant, *Tempest*, 73; Kemble, *Tempest*, 48.

31. Caliban was likely costumed in a suit of goat's hair at this time. See Alden T. Vaughan and Virginia Mason Vaughan, *Shakespeare's Caliban: A Cultural History* (Cambridge: Cambridge University Press, 1991), 100, 180.

32. Edmund Burke, *Reflections on the Revolution in France*, ed. L. G. Mitchell (Oxford: Oxford University Press, 1993), 10, 79, 196.

33. [William Cusack Smith], *The Patriot* (Dublin: H. Watts, 1792), 45–46.

34. Jerome Alley, *Observations on the Government and Constitution of Great Britain* (Dublin: William Sleater, 1792), 65.

35. John Whitaker, *The Real Origin of Government* (London: John Stockdale, Piccadilly, 1795), 48.

36. Dobson, *Making of the National Poet*, 134–36.

37. Dryden and Davenant, *Tempest*, prologue.

38. See *The Tempest, a Comedy, by Shakespeare, as performed at the Theatre Royal, Drury-Lane* (London: J. Rivington et al., 1775), 54.

39. *Morning Post*, 7 January 1777; Kemble, *Tempest*, 54.

40. Joseph Roach, *Cities of the Dead: Circum-Atlantic Performances* (New York: Columbia University Press, 1996), 36.

41. Francis Godolphin Waldron, *The Virgin Queen, a Drama in Five Acts; Attempted as a Sequel to Shakespeare's Tempest* (London: printed for the author, 1797), 23, 51, 99, 104.

42. Henry E. Huntington Library, San Marino, CA, Larpent MS 1418.

43. Daniel Defoe, *Robinson Crusoe*, ed. Thomas Keymer (Oxford: Oxford University Press, 2007), 172.

44. Bate, *Shakespearean Constitutions*, 96.

45. Richard Brinsley Sheridan, *Speeches of the Late Right Honourable Richard Brinsley Sheridan*, 5 vols. (London: Patrick Martin, 1816), 4:9, 23.

46. The online catalog for the Guildhall Art Gallery, London, lists this caricature as a parody of Copley's painting (http://collage.cityoflondon.gov.uk/view-item?i=31939).

47. Reported in the *Standard*, 28 May 1827.

48. Richard Lalor Sheil, *The Speeches of the Right Honourable Richard Lalor Sheil*, 2nd ed. (Dublin: James Duffy, 1865), 67.

49. Maus, "Arcadia Lost," 195–96; Kemble, *Tempest*, 42.

50. Dobson, "Appropriation of *The Tempest*," 106.

51. See Jane Moody, *Illegitimate Theatre in London, 1770–1840* (Cambridge: Cambridge University Press, 2000), 42–45.

52. *Examiner* 699 (27 May 1821): 330.

53. See Kenneth Baker, *George IV: A Life in Caricature* (London: Thames and Hudson, 2005).

54. John Sartain, *The Reminiscences of a Very Old Man, 1808–1897* (New York: D. Appleton, 1900), 122.

55. Ibid., 122–23.

56. Terry Eagleton, *The Function of Criticism* (London: Verso, 1984), 40.

4. Macbeth as *Political Comedy*

1. Edmund Burke, *Reflections on the Revolution in France*, ed. L. G. Mitchell (Oxford: Oxford University Press, 1993), 71; William Wordsworth, *The Prelude: The 1805 Text*, ed. Ernest de Selincourt, corr. Stephen Gill (Oxford: Oxford University Press, 1970), 10.6–77.

2. A search of the British Cartoon Archive, University of Kent (http://www.cartoons.ac.uk), finds *Macbeth* cited in more than seventy political cartoons between 1900 and 2010.

3. See especially Dennis Biggins, "Sexuality, Witchcraft, and Violence in *Macbeth*," *Shakespeare Studies* 8 (1976): 255–77; Gary Wills, *Witches and Jesuits: Shakespeare's Macbeth* (New York: Oxford University Press, 1995); and Diane Purkiss, *The Witch in History: Early Modern and Twentieth-Century Representations* (London: Routledge, 1996), 199–230.

4. Mary Jacobus, " 'That Great Stage Where Senators Perform': *Macbeth* and the Politics of Romantic Theatre," *Studies in Romanticism* 22, no. 3 (1983): 353–87; Jonathan Bate, *Shakespearean Constitutions: Politics, Theatre, Criticism, 1730–1830* (Oxford: Clarendon Press, 1989), 88–94, and *Shakespeare and the English Romantic Imagination* (Oxford: Clarendon Press, 1986), 54, 114; Matthew Buckley, " 'A Dream of Murder': *The Fall of Robespierre* and the Tragic Imagination," *Studies in Romanticism* 44, no. 4 (2005): 515–49.

5. For *Macbeth*-inspired attacks on Bute, see Rebecca Rogers, "How Scottish Was 'the Scottish Play'? *Macbeth*'s National Identity in the Eighteenth Century," in *Shakespeare and Scotland*, ed. Willy Maley and Andrew Murphy (Manchester: Manchester University Press, 2004), 104–23.

6. Peter Seitel, "Theorizing Genres: Interpreting Works," *New Literary History* 34, no. 2 (2003): 277; Fredric Jameson, *The Political Unconscious: Narrative as a Socially Symbolic Act* (Ithaca, NY: Cornell University Press, 1981), 106.

7. Buckley, " 'Dream of Murder,' " 516.

8. Ian Haywood, *Romanticism and Caricature* (Cambridge: Cambridge University Press, 2013), 8.

9. *London Daily Post*, 6 January 1744.

10. Information taken from Charles Beecher Hogan, *Shakespeare in the Theatre, 1701–1800*, 2 vols. (Oxford: Clarendon Press, 1952). The only actress to play one of the witches in eighteenth-century London was Ann Pitt (Covent Garden, 1772–76).

11. The epigraph reassures readers: "The Earth hath bubbles as the Water has" (1.3.77).

12. Thomas Davies, *Memoirs of the Life of David Garrick*, 2 vols. (London: Thomas Davies, 1780), 1:114.

13. Horace Walpole, writing in his manuscript "Book of Materials," in *William Shakespeare: The Critical Heritage*, ed. Brian Vickers, 6 vols. (London: Routledge and Kegan Paul, 1974–81), 5:485; Jacques-Henri Meister, *Letters Written during a Residence in England* (London: T. N. Longman and O. Rees, 1799), 212.

14. Samuel Taylor Coleridge, "Lectures on the Characteristics of Shakespear" (1813), in *The Romantics on Shakespeare,* ed. Jonathan Bate (London: Penguin, 1992), 132; William Hazlitt, *Characters of Shakespear's Plays* (London: C. H. Reynell, 1817), 30.

15. Samuel Johnson, *Miscellaneous Observations on the Tragedy of Macbeth* (1745), in *Johnson on Shakespeare,* ed. Arthur Sherbo, vol. 7 of *The Yale Edition of the Works of Samuel Johnson* (New Haven: Yale University Press, 1968), 6.

16. Maurice Morgan, *Essay on the Dramatic Character of Sir John Falstaff* (1777), in Vickers, *Critical Heritage,* 6:172.

17. Francis Gentleman, *The Dramatic Censor; or, Critical Companion* (1770), in Vickers, *Critical Heritage,* 5:384.

18. For Johnson's interest in the Shakespearean supernatural, see G. F. Parker, *Johnson's Shakespeare* (Oxford: Clarendon Press, 1989), 111–26.

19. Vickers, *Critical Heritage,* 5:395.

20. Jonathan Bate, *Shakespeare and the English Romantic Imagination* (Oxford: Clarendon Press, 1986), 10; Coleridge, "Lectures," 132.

21. Samuel Badock, in *Monthly Review* 62 (January 1780), in Vickers, *Critical Heritage,* 6:217. Joseph W. Donohue surveys eighteenth-century interpretations of Macbeth's character in *Dramatic Character in the English Romantic Age* (Princeton, NJ: Princeton University Press, 1970), 189–215.

22. Elizabeth Montagu, *An Essay on the Writing and Genius of Shakespeare* (1769), in Vickers, *Critical Heritage,* 5:336–37.

23. *St. James's Chronicle,* 14–16 July 1791.

24. Rogers, "*Macbeth*'s National Identity," 117.

25. On the political symbolism of the ring dance, see my " "Coalition Dances: Georgian Caricature's Choreographies of Power," *Music in Art* 36, nos. 1–2 (2011): 121–27.

26. Bate, *Shakespearean Constitutions,* 89.

27. *Star,* 20 February 1792.

28. Charles Pigott, *A Political Dictionary: Explaining the True Meaning of Words* (London: D. I. Eaton, 1795), 69, 84.

29. See, e.g., William Playfair, *The History of Jacobinism, its Crimes, Cruelties and Perfidies* (London: John Stockdale, 1795), 814. Buckley discusses the equation of Robespierre with Macbeth in " 'Dream of Murder,' " 532–49.

30. [Thomas Ford], *Confusion's Master-Piece; or, Paine's Labour's Lost; Being a specimen of some well-known scenes in Shakespeare's Macbeth* (London: J. Nichols, 1794), 5; *The Antigallican; or, Strictures on the Present Form of Government established in France* (London: R. Faulder, 1793), 34.

268 NOTES TO PAGES 116–122

31. *The History and Proceedings of the Lords and the Commons during the First Session of the Seventeenth Parliament of Great Britain* (London: John Stockdale, 1791), 444.

32. Marcus Wood, "William Cobbett, John Thelwall, Radicalism, Racism and Slavery: A Study in Burkean Parodics," *Romanticism on the Net* 15 (1999), http://id.erudit.org/iderudit/005873ar.

33. *Macbeth, a Tragedy; With Alterations, Amendments, Additions, and News Songs; As it's now Acted at the Dukes Theatre* (London: P. Chetwin, 1674), 27.

34. Terry Eagleton, *Walter Benjamin; or, Towards a Revolutionary Criticism* (London: Verso, 1981), 148. See Mikhail Bakhtin, *Rabelais and His World*, trans. Hélène Iswolsky (Bloomington: Indiana University Press, 1984).

35. See *Macbeth, written by Shakspeare; As represented by Their Majesties servants, on opening the Theatre Royal Drury Lane, on Monday, April 21st 1794* (London: C. Lowndes, 1794), 30.

36. John Fenwick, *Letters to the People of Great Britain, respecting the present state of their public affairs* (London: J. Ridgeway et al., [1795]), 4.

37. Horace Walpole, *The Dear Witches: An Interlude; being a Parody on some Scenes of Mackbeth*, published in *Old England; or, The Constitutional Journal*, 18 June 1743. For an elaboration of this parody, see Catherine M. S. Alexander, "*The Dear Witches:* Horace Walpole's *Macbeth*," *Review of English Studies* 49 (1998): 131–44.

38. *The Three Conjurers, a Political Interlude; Stolen from Shakespeare* (London: E. Cabe, [1763]), 10, 15.

39. On Dent's alignment of the radicals with medieval uprisings, see Tamara L. Hunt, *Defining John Bull: Political Caricature and National Identity in Late Georgian England* (Aldershot: Ashgate, 2003), 102.

40. Vickers, *Critical Heritage*, 5:392.

41. Huston Diehl, "Horrid Image, Sorry Sight, Fatal Vision: The Visual Rhetoric of *Macbeth*," *Shakespeare Studies* 16 (1983): 191, 201. See also Karin S. Coddon, " 'Unreal Mockery': Unreason and the Problem of Spectacle in *Macbeth*," *ELH* 56, no. 3 (1989): 485–501; and Stuart Clark, *Vanities of the Eye: Vision in Early Modern European Culture* (Oxford: Oxford University Press, 2007), 236–65.

42. On the phantasmagoria, see Richard D. Altick, *The Shows of London* (Cambridge, MA: Belknap Press of Harvard University Press, 1978), 217–20.

43. Gillen D'Arcy Wood discusses these anxieties in *The Shock of the Real: Romanticism and Visual Culture, 1760–1860* (New York: Palgrave, 2001).

44. *Morning Post*, 29 October 1801.

45. Barbara Maria Stafford, *Artful Science: Enlightenment Entertainment and the Eclipse of Visual Education* (Cambridge, MA: MIT Press, 1994), esp. 73–87. See also Terry Castle, *The Female Thermometer: Eighteenth-Century Culture and the Invention of the Uncanny* (Oxford: Oxford University Press, 1985), 140–67.

46. Stafford, *Artful Science*, 10–16.

47. Joseph Monteyne, *From Still Life to the Screen: Print Culture, Display, and the Materiality of the Image in Eighteenth-Century London* (New Haven: Yale University Press, 2013), 195–96

48. Lord John Townshend, "Prologue to Urania," in *Morning Post*, 26 January 1802.

49. Clark, *Vanities of the Eye*, 254.

50. Bate, *Shakespearean Constitutions*, 94.

51. See Leslie Mitchell, *The Whig World, 1760–1837* (London: Hambledon Continuum, 2005), 55.

52. Martin Myrone, *Bodybuilding: Reforming Masculinities in British Art, 1750–1810* (New Haven: Yale University Press, 2005), 1–14.

53. Madame Anne Louise Germaine de Staël, *De la littérature considérée dans ses rapports avec les institutions sociales* (1800), in Bate, *Romantics on Shakespeare*, 81.

54. *Morning Post*, 29 April 1783.

55. Edmund Burke to the Earl of Charlemont, 10 July 1789, in *Selected Letters of Edmund Burke*, ed. Harvey C. Mansfield (Chicago: University of Chicago Press, 1984), 390.

56. *The Arcana of Polite Literature; or, A Compendious Dictionary of Fabulous History* (Dublin: J. Magee, 1779), s.v. "Hecate."

57. See Marina Warner, *Monuments and Maidens: The Allegory of the Female Form* (London: Weidenfeld and Nicolson, 1985).

58. Squire says: "Sweet mercy is nobility's true badge" (*Titus Andronicus*, 1.1.119).

59. See Amelia F. Rauser, "The Butcher-Kissing Duchess of Devonshire: Between Caricature and Allegory in 1784," *Eighteenth-Century Studies* 36, no. 1 (2002): 23–46.

60. *The True Sentiments of America* (London: I. Almon, 1768), 136.

61. Vickers, *Critical Heritage*, 6:449, 467

62. William Hazlitt, *A View of the English Stage; or, A Series of Dramatic Criticisms* (London: Robert Stodart et al., 1818), 134.

63. See Gay Smith, *Lady Macbeth in America: From the Stage to the White House* (New York: Palgrave, 2010), 10–17.

64. Frans De Bruyn, "William Shakespeare and Edmund Burke: Literary Allusion in Eighteenth-Century British Political Rhetoric," in *Shakespeare and the Eighteenth Century,* ed. Peter Sabor and Paul Yachnin (Aldershot: Ashgate, 2008), 100.

65. For more on Shakespeare's cultural multivalency, see the essays in *The Cambridge Companion to Shakespeare and Popular Culture,* ed. Robert Shaughnessy (Cambridge: Cambridge University Press, 2007).

66. Michael Dobson, *The Making of the National Poet: Shakespeare, Adaptation and Authorship, 1660–1769* (Oxford: Clarendon Press, 1992), 12.

67. Jane Moody, *Illegitimate Theatre in London, 1770–1840* (Cambridge: Cambridge University Press, 2000), 118–47.

68. Richard W. Schoch, *Not Shakespeare: Bardolatry and Burlesque in the Nineteenth Century* (Cambridge: Cambridge University Press, 2002).

69. Andrew Murphy, *Shakespeare for the People: Working-Class Readers, 1800–1900* (Cambridge: Cambridge University Press, 2008).

70. Caricature is discussed under the banner of "Shakespeare and popular culture" in Kathryn Prince, "Shakespeare and English Nationalism," in *Shakespeare in the Eighteenth Century,* ed. Fiona Ritchie and Peter Sabor (Cambridge: Cambridge University Press, 2012), 285.

71. See Margareta de Grazia, "Shakespeare in Quotation Marks," in *The Appropriation of Shakespeare: Post-Renaissance Reconstructions of the Works and the Myth,* ed. Jean Marsden (New York: Harvester Wheatsheaf, 1991), 57–71.

72. John Clare, "Popularity in Authorship," in *The Prose of John Clare,* ed. J. W. and A. Tibble (London: Routledge and Kegan Paul, 1951), 207.

73. See Stuart Sillars, *Painting Shakespeare: The Artist as Critic, 1720–1820* (Cambridge: Cambridge University Press, 2006), 10.

74. Rosie Dias, *Exhibiting Englishness: John Boydell's Shakespeare Gallery and the Formation of the National Aesthetic* (New Haven: Yale University Press, 2013), 52–53.

75. Christopher Rovee, *Imagining the Gallery: The Social Body of British Romanticism* (Stanford, CA: Stanford University Press, 2006), 5.

76. [Humphrey Repton], *A Catalogue of the Pictures, &c. in the Shakespeare Gallery, Pall-Mall* (London: H. Baldwin, 1790).

77. According to Dias, viewers were especially unfamiliar with *Titus Andronicus* (*Exhibiting Englishness,* 234, n. 81).

78. James Gillray to John Boydell, 30 September 1788, Folger Shakespeare Library, Washington, D.C., Shelfmark ART Flat a5 no. 4.

79. Bate, *Shakespearean Constitutions,* 51.

80. John Sneyd to James Gillray, 13 October 1800, in *George Canning and His Friends,* ed. Josceline Bagot, 2 vols. (London: John Murray, 1909), 1:171.

81. *The Exhibition of the Royal Academy, MDCCLXIX. The First* (London: T. Cadell, 1769), 2.

82. Luisa Calè, *Fuseli's Milton Gallery: "Turning Readers into Spectators"* (Oxford: Oxford University Press, 2006), 37–38.

5. Paradise Lost, *from the Sublime to the Ridiculous*

1. Lucy Newlyn, *Paradise Lost and the Romantic Reader* (Oxford: Clarendon Press, 1993), 4. For reception histories of *Paradise Lost* in the period, see Dustin Griffin, *Regaining Paradise: Milton and the Eighteenth Century* (Cambridge: Cambridge University Press, 1986); and Leslie Moore, *Beautiful Sublime: The Making of Paradise Lost, 1701–1734* (Stanford, CA: Stanford University Press, 1990).

2. See Griffin, *Regaining Paradise,* 11–21.

3. *The History of King-Killers,* quoted in Griffin, *Regaining Paradise,* 11; *The Critical Review; or, Annals of Literature,* vol. 5 (London: A. Hamilton, 1758), 321; Samuel Johnson, *Lives of the Poets,* ed. Roger Lonsdale, 4 vols. (Oxford: Oxford University Press, 2006), 1:276. On Johnson's view of Milton's politics, see Christine Rees, *Johnson's Milton* (Cambridge: Cambridge University Press, 2010), 191–210.

4. Newlyn, *Paradise Lost and the Romantic Reader,* 35; Jackie DiSalvo, *War of Titans: Blake's Critique of Milton and the Politics of Religion* (Pittsburgh: University of Pittsburgh Press, 1983), 29.

5. John Toland, *The Life of Milton,* in *The Early Lives of Milton,* ed. Helen Darbishire (London: Constable, 1932), 182.

6. See, e.g. Newlyn, *Paradise Lost and the Romantic Reader,* 19.

7. See Griffin, *Regaining Paradise,* 62–71.

8. *The State of Innocence: And Fall of Man. Described in Milton's Paradise Lost. Render'd into Prose* (London: T. Osborne and J. Hildyard, 1745); John Buchanan, *The First Six Books of Milton's Paradise Lost, Rendered into Grammatical Construction* (Edinburgh: A Kincaid, W. Creech, and J. Balfour, 1773), title page; John Wesley, *An Extract from Milton's Paradise Lost. With Notes* (London, 1791), A2.

9. Thomas Cooper, *The Life of Thomas Cooper* (London: Hodder and Stoughton, 1872), 35.

10. Lord Chesterfield, *Letters*, ed. David Roberts (Oxford: Oxford University Press, 1992), 280.

11. *True Briton*, 19 May 1800, in Luisa Calè, *Fuseli's Milton Gallery: "Turning Readers into Spectators"* (Oxford: Oxford University Press, 2006), 51.

12. James Boswell, *The Life of Samuel Johnson*, ed. David Womersley (London: Penguin, 2008), 699.

13. For surveys of this period, see L. G. Mitchell, *Charles James Fox and the Disintegration of the Whig Party, 1782–1794* (Oxford: Oxford University Press, 1971), 9–91, and *Charles James Fox* (Oxford: Oxford University Press, 1992), 46–71; John Cannon, *The Fox-North Coalition: Crisis of the Constitution, 1782–4* (Cambridge: Cambridge University Press, 1969); and Boyd Hilton, *A Mad, Bad, Dangerous People? England, 1783–1846* (Oxford: Oxford University Press, 2006), 39–57.

14. Mitchell, *Charles James Fox*, 47.

15. Ibid., 60–61; Cannon, *Fox-North Coalition*, 46–47; Hilton, *Mad, Bad, Dangerous People*, 11, 47.

16. Cannon, *Fox-North Coalition*, ix.

17. *The Parliamentary History of England*, 36 vols. (London: T. C. Hansard, 1806–20), 24:216.

18. See Hilton, *Mad, Bad, Dangerous People*, 41, 45.

19. Peter A. Schock, *Romantic Satanism: Myth and the Historical Moment in Blake, Shelley and Byron* (New York: Palgrave Macmillan, 2003); William Blake, *The Marriage of Heaven and Hell* (1790), pl. 6, in *The Complete Poetry and Prose of William Blake*, ed. David V. Erdman, rev. ed. (Berkeley: University of California Press, 1988), 35.

20. Quoting John Milton, *Paradise Lost*, 12.641–49, in *The Works of John Milton*, vol. 2 pts. 1 and 2, ed. Frank Allen Patterson (New York: Columbia University Press, 1931). Hereafter cited parenthetically. Sayers changes "all th' Eastern side beheld" to "To the eastern Side" and "hand in hand" to "Arm in Arm."

21. In fact, as Mitchell notes, Fox decided to resign at the end of June (*Charles James Fox*, 50).

22. *Carlo Khan's Triumphal Entry into Leadenhall Street* (5 December 1783; BMC 6276).

23. Notebook of Lord Eldon (c. 1829), Lewis Walpole Library, Yale University, mss vol. 202, 2.

24. See Amelia F. Rauser, "The Butcher-Kissing Duchess of Devonshire: Between Caricature and Allegory in 1784," *Eighteenth-Century Studies* 36, no. 1 (2002): 23–46.

25. *Rambler's Magazine,* July 1784, 257, and August 1784, 314.

26. Boswell, *Life of Samuel Johnson,* 113.

27. *A Political History of the Years 1756 and 1757; In a Series of Seventy-five Humorous and Entertaining Prints* (London: E. Morris, 1757), 12. Townshend's *Gloria Mundi* is pl. 55.

28. *Morning Post,* 3 August 1782.

29. For the allegiances of the *Morning Herald,* see Lucyle Werkmeister, *The London Daily Press, 1772–1792* (Lincoln: University of Nebraska Press, 1963), 128.

30. *Morning Herald,* 3 October 1782; *Public Advertiser,* 29 March 1783, 25 March 1784.

31. Cannon, *Fox-North Coalition,* 169.

32. John Dryden, *Absalom and Achitophel,* l. 205, in *The Poems of John Dryden,* ed. James Kinsley, vol. 1 (Oxford: Clarendon Press, 1958).

33. *London Chronicle,* 12–14 November 1763. I quote *The Scot's Magazine,* vol. 25 (Edinburgh: W. Sands, A. Murray, and J. Cochran, 1763), 616–17, which reprinted the essay.

34. See Francis Blackburne, *Memoirs of Thomas Hollis,* 2 vols. (London: J. Nichols, 1780), 1:226.

35. *London Chronicle,* 5–7 June 1764, 561. See also *London Chronicle,* 26–28 April 1761, 403.

36. *Parliamentary History,* 24:597.

37. Hilton, *Mad, Bad, Dangerous People,* 43.

38. George Selwyn to Lord Carlisle, 19 March 1782, in Historical Manuscripts Commission, *Fifteenth Report, Appendix, Part VI: The Manuscripts of the Earl of Carlisle* (London: Her Majesty's Stationary Office, 1897), 599.

39. Richard Fitzpatrick to Lord Ossory, 3 July 1782, in *Memorials and Correspondence of Charles James Fox,* ed. Lord John Russell, 2 vols. (London: Richard Bentley, 1853), 1:459.

40. See Cindy McCreery, "Satiric Images of Fox, Pitt, and George III: The East India Bill Crisis, 1783–84," *Word and Image* 9, no. 2 (1993): 163–85.

41. *Parliamentary History,* 23:1427, 23:1403.

42. John King, *Thoughts on the Difficulties and Distresses in which the Peace of 1783, has involved the People of England* (London: J. Fielding, T. Davies, J. Southern, and W. Deane, 1783), 10.

43. Edmund Burke, *A Philosophical Enquiry into the Origin of Our Ideas of the Sublime and Beautiful,* ed. David Womersley (London: Penguin, 1998), 105.

44. *Morning Herald,* 18 February 1782.

45. *European Magazine,* March 1782, 180.

46. See, e.g., *Morning Post,* 12 February 1784.

47. Marcia R. Pointon, *Milton and English Art* (Manchester: Manchester University Press, 1970).

48. For more on the Eidophusikon, see Iain McCalman, "Magic, Spectacle, and the Art of de Loutherbourg's Eidophusikon," in *Sensation and Sensibility: Viewing Gainsborough's "Cottage Door,"* ed. Ann Bermingham (New Haven: Yale University Press, 2005), 181–97.

49. Raymond B. Waddington, "Appearance and Reality in Satan's Disguises," *Texas Studies in Literature and Language* 4, no. 3 (1962): 398.

50. William Empson, *Milton's God,* rev. ed. (London: Chatto and Windus, 1965), 13; Stanley Eugene Fish, *Surprised by Sin: The Reader in Paradise Lost* (London: St. Martin's Press, 1967), 38.

51. "Satan Reformer," *Blackwood's Magazine* 31 (January–June 1832): 592–97.

52. John Upton, *Critical Observations on Shakespeare* (London: G. Hawkins, 1746), 162.

53. Vic Gatrell, *City of Laughter: Sex and Satire in Eighteenth-Century London* (London: Atlantic, 2006), 258–92.

54. David V. Erdman, *Blake: Prophet against the Empire,* 3rd ed. (Princeton, NJ: Princeton University Press, 1977), 217; Ian Haywood, *Romanticism and Caricature* (Cambridge: Cambridge University Press, 2013), 15.

55. Joseph Addison, *Critical Essays from the Spectator,* ed. Donald F. Bond (Oxford: Oxford University Press, 1970), 83. The eighteen essays originally appeared in the *Spectator* between January and May 1712.

56. Ibid., 110.

57. Ibid., 113.

58. See, e.g., Thomas Rowlandson's *Prospect before Us* (20 December 1788; BMC 7383).

59. See Calè, *Fuseli's Milton Gallery,* 178–80; Haywood, *Romanticism and Caricature,* 12–32.

60. *Milton; Proposal for Engraving and Publishing by Subscription Thirty Capital Plates, from Subjects in Milton* (London: J. Johnson, 1791).

61. See *Oracle,* 13 January 1792.

62. Burke, *Philosophical Enquiry,* 103, quoting *Paradise Lost,* 2.666–73.

63. W. J. T. Mitchell, *Iconology: Image, Text, Ideology* (Chicago: University of Chicago Press, 1986), 116–49; Samuel Taylor Coleridge, *Lectures 1809–1819 on Literature,* ed. R. A. Foakes, 2 vols. (Princeton, NJ: Princeton University Press, 1987), 1:311–12.

64. Calè, *Fuseli's Milton Gallery*, 151, 178–79.

65. Ronald Paulson, *Hogarth*, 3 vols. (Cambridge: Lutterworth, 1992–93), 3:243.

66. Addison, *Critical Essays*, 68.

67. Lord Kames, *Elements of Criticism*, 3rd ed., 3 vols. (Edinburgh: A. Millar and A. Kincaid and J. Bell, 1765), 1:388.

68. Johnson, *Lives of the Poets*, 1:257–58. See Rees, *Johnson's Milton*, 146–48.

69. Steven Knapp, *Personification and the Sublime: Milton to Coleridge* (Cambridge, MA: Harvard University Press, 1985), 2.

70. Samuel Johnson, *A Dictionary of the English Language*, 2 vols. (London: W. Strahan et al., 1755), s.v. "Allegory."

71. Fredric Jameson, *The Political Unconscious: Narrative as a Socially Symbolic Act* (Ithaca, NY: Cornell University Press, 1981), 106.

72. Haywood, *Romanticism and Caricature*, 12–32.

73. *Parliamentary History*, 29:418–19.

74. See, e.g., ibid., 30:1209; and *The Parliamentary Register* (London: J. Debrett, 1780–1803), 37:112, 38:143, 40:432, 43:551.

75. Newlyn, *Paradise Lost and the Romantic Reader*, 197–204.

76. John N. King, *Milton and Religious Controversy: Satire and Polemic in Paradise Lost* (Cambridge: Cambridge University Press, 2000), 80.

77. Fish, *Surprised by Sin;* Dennis H. Burden, *The Logical Epic: A Study of the Argument of Paradise Lost* (London: Routledge and Kegan Paul, 1967).

78. John Leonard, *Faithful Labourers: A Reception History of Paradise Lost, 1667–1970*, 2 vols. (Oxford: Oxford University Press, 2013), 1:266.

79. King, *Milton and Religious Controversy*, 2.

80. Ludovico Ariosto, *Orlando Furioso*, trans. Guido Waldman (Oxford: Oxford University Press, 1974), canto 34, st. 73–85. See John Wooten, "From Purgatory to the Paradise of Fools: Dante, Ariosto, and Milton," *ELH* 49, no. 4 (1982): 741–50.

81. Addison, *Critical Essays*, 107; Voltaire, "An Essay on Epick Poetry," in Florence Donnell White, *Voltaire's Essay on Epic Poetry: A Study and an Edition* (Albany, NY: Brandow, 1915), 141; James Beattie, *Essays; On Poetry and Music, as they affect the Mind; On Laughter, and Ludicrous Composition; On the Utility of Classical Learning* (Edinburgh: William Creech, 1776), 224; Johnson, *Lives of the Poets*, 1:262.

82. George Lavington, *The Enthusiasm of Methodists and Papists Compared, Part III* (London: J. and P. Knapton, 1751), 328–29; Sir Brooke Boothby, *A Letter to the Right Honourable Edmund Burke* (London: J. Debrett, 1791), 53;

Benjamin Fowler, *The French Constitution; with Remarks on some of its Principal Articles* (London: G. G. J. and J. Robinson, 1792), 293–94.

83. Balachandra Rajan, "*Paradise Lost:* The Uncertain Epic," *Milton Studies* 17 (1983): 105–19.

84. Christine Banerji and Diana Donald, eds. and trans., *Gillray Observed: The Earliest Accounts of His Caricatures in "London und Paris"* (Cambridge: Cambridge University Press, 1999), 236, 242.

85. Roland Mushat Frye, *Milton's Imagery and the Visual Arts: Iconographic Tradition in the Epic Poems* (Princeton, NJ: Princeton University Press, 1978), 213–14.

86. Banerji and Donald, *Gillray Observed*, 242.

87. Ibid., 240.

88. Alexander Pope, *The Iliad of Homer*, vol. 2 (London: W. Bowyer, for Bernard Lintot, 1716), 95–96, n. 43; Pope, *The Rape of the Lock*, 5.113–22, in *The Poems of Alexander Pope: A One-Volume Edition of the Twickenham Text*, ed. John Butt (London: Methuen, 1963).

89. For a discussion of objecthood in *Rape of the Lock*, see Jonathan Lamb, *The Things Things Says* (Princeton, NJ: Princeton University Press, 2011), 98–125.

90. *London and Westminster Review, April–July 1837* (London: Henry Cooper, 1837), 280.

91. Raimonda Modiano, "Humanism and the Comic Sublime: From Kant to Friedrich Theodor Vischer," *Studies in Romanticism* 26, no. 2 (1987): 242.

6. Gulliver Goes to War

1. Alexandra Franklin, "John Bull in a Dream: Fear and Fantasy in the Visual Satires of 1803," in *Resisting Napoleon: The British Response to the Threat of Invasion, 1797–1815*, ed. Mark Philp (Aldershot: Ashgate, 2006), 126.

2. For Gillray's ideological slipperiness, see especially Ronald Paulson, *Representations of Revolution, 1789–1820* (New Haven: Yale University Press, 1983), 183–211; and Ian Haywood, *Romanticism and Caricature* (Cambridge: Cambridge University Press, 2013), 12–32.

3. Writing to Alexander Pope on 29 September 1725 about the progress of *Gulliver's Travels*, Swift stated: "The cheif end I propose to my self in all my labors is to vex the world rather than divert it." Jonathan Swift, *Gulliver's Travels*, ed. David Womersley, The Cambridge Edition of the Works of Jonathan Swift (Cambridge: Cambridge University Press, 2010), 592. Further references to *Gulliver's Travels* are to this edition and will be made parenthetically.

4. *Morning Post*, 23, 28 June 1803.

5. Quoted in Richard Godfrey, "Introduction," in *English Caricature 1620 to the Present: Caricaturists and Satirists, Their Art, Their Purpose and Influence* (London: Victoria and Albert Museum, 1984), 15.

6. William Bates, *George Cruikshank: The Artist, the Humorist, and the Man* (London: Houlston and Sons, 1879), 83.

7. Correspondence and Letters of James Gillray, British Library Add. MS 27337, ff. 53–54, 11, 94. These letters include numerous examples of hints sent to Gillray.

8. Draper Hill, *Mr. Gillray, the Caricaturist: A Biography* (London: Phaidon, 1965), 58, 64 n.1.

9. Sir Andrew Francis Barnard to his half-sister Isabella, 25 February 1802, in Andrew Barnard, *Barnard Letters, 1778–1824*, ed. Anthony Powell (London: Duckworth, 1928), 153–54; *Monthly Mirror* 13 (1802): 219–20.

10. Quoted in *For King and Country: The Letters and Diaries of John Mills, Coldstream Guards, 1811–14*, ed. Ian Fletcher (Staplehurst: Spellmont, 1995), 88.

11. Braddyll also designed *The King of Brobdingnag and Gulliver (Plate 2d)* (10 February 1804, BMC 10227), *The Genius of France nursing her darling* (26 November 1804, BMC 10284), and *Farmer Giles & his Wife shewing off their daughter Betty to their Neighbours* (1 January 1809, BMC 11444).

12. See Joseph Farington, *The Diary of Joseph Farington*, vol. 3: *September 1796—December 1798*, ed. Kenneth Garlick and Angus Macintyre (New Haven: Yale University Press, 1979), 927–28.

13. Jeanne K. Welcher, *Gulliveriana VII: Visual Imitations of Gulliver's Travels, 1726–1830* (Delmar, NY: Scholars' Facsimiles and Reprints, 1999), lxvii.

14. Claude Rawson, *Gulliver and the Gentle Reader: Studies in Swift and Our Time* (London: Routledge and Kegan Paul, 1973), 37. John F. Sena registers many of these confluences in "*Gulliver's Travels* and the Genre of the Illustrated Book," in *The Genres of Gulliver's Travels*, ed. Frederik N. Smith (Newark: University of Delaware Press, 1990), 101.

15. Ronald Paulson, "Putting Out the Fire in Her Imperial Majesty's Apartment: Opposition Politics, Anticlericalism, and Aesthetics," *ELH* 63, no. 1 (1996): 82.

16. In the 1740s–50s, Bowles published three sets of engravings entitled *The Lilliputian Dancing School*, *The Lilliputian Riding School*, and *Lilliputian Figures*, as well as a *Lilliputian Calendar*. See Jeanne K. Welcher, *Gulliveriana*

VIII: An Annotated List of Gulliveriana, 1721–1800 (Delmar, NY: Scholars' Facsimiles and Reprints, 1988), lxxii–lxxxviii.

17. See Douglas Fordham, *British Art and the Seven Years' War: Allegiance and Autonomy* (Philadelphia: University of Pennsylvania Press, 2010), 85.

18. In *Gulliveriana VII*, Welcher catalogs a number of midcentury satirical prints that do very briefly allude to *Travels* (lxxxix–cx, 161–6).

19. See, e.g., Rawson, *Gulliver and the Gentle Reader;* Womersley in Swift, *Travels,* lxxxv–xcii; and Frederick N. Smith, "The Danger of Reading Swift: The Double Binds of *Gulliver's Travels,*" *Studies in the Literary Imagination* 17, no. 1 (1984): 35–47.

20. See Robert Halsband, "Eighteenth-Century Illustrations of *Gulliver's Travels,*" in *Proceedings of the First Münster Symposium on Jonathan Swift,* ed. Herman J. Real and Heinz J. Vienken (Munich: Wilhelm Fink, 1985), 83–112.

21. See M. Sarah Smedman, "Like Me, Like Me Not: *Gulliver's Travels* as Children's Book," in *Genres of Gulliver's Travels,* 75–100; and Welcher, *Gulliveriana VII,* 44–45.

22. *Morning Chronicle,* 10 June 1772.

23. David Vincent, *Literacy and Popular Culture: England, 1750 to 1914* (Cambridge: Cambridge University Press, 1989), 61; Sheila O'Connell, *The Popular Print in England* (London: British Museum, 1999), 32.

24. Robert Heron, *A Letter from Ralph Anderson, Esq. to Sir John Sinclair, Bart. M. P. &c. on the necessity of an instant change of ministry, and an immediate peace* (Edinburgh: G. Mudie and Son, 1797), 80.

25. Robert Orr, *An Address to the People of Ireland, against an Union* (Dublin: J. Stockdale, 1799), 26; Matthew Weld, *Constitutional Considerations, interspersed with Political Observations, on the Present State of Ireland* (Dublin: J. Moore, 1800), 37.

26. George Edward, *The Great and Important Discovery of the Eighteenth Century, and the means of setting right the national affairs* (London: J. Ridgeway, 1791), 172; William Godwin, *Enquiry Concerning Political Justice,* 2nd ed., 2 vols. (London: G. G. and J. Robinson, 1796), 2:202; Edmund Burke, *Reflections on the Revolution in France,* ed. L. G. Mitchell (Oxford: Oxford University Press, 1993), 133.

27. Henry Redhead Yorke, *Reason Urged against Precedent, in a Letter to the People of Derby* (London, 1793), 24–26; Godwin, *Enquiry Concerning Political Justice,* 1:11–12; *Thoughts on War, Political, Commercial, Religious, and Satyrical* (London: Darton and Harvey, 1793), 51–54. Claude Rawson considers *Travels* within the context of Augustan reflections upon war in *Satire and*

Sentiment, 1660–1830: Stress Points in the English Augustan Tradition, new ed. (New Haven: Yale University Press, 2000), 29–97.

28. William Dent, *I. Frith The Unfortunate Stone-Thrower* (1790, BMC 7626).

29. Welcher, *Gulliveriana VII*, 629.

30. F. P. Lock, *The Politics of Gulliver's Travels* (Oxford: Clarendon Press, 1980), 16–17, 131–32.

31. William Cobbett, *The Political Proteus: A View of the Public Character and Conduct of R. B. Sheridan, Esq.* (London: Cox, Son, and Baylis, 1804), 188.

32. Stuart Semmel, *Napoleon and the British* (New Haven: Yale University Press, 2004), 6.

33. See, e.g., *The Corsican Crocodile dissolving the Council of Frogs!!!* (November 1799; BMC 9427).

34. James Baker, "Locating Gulliver: Unstable Loyalism in James Gillray's *The King of Brobdingnag and Gulliver*," *Image and Narrative* 14, no. 1 (2013): 142. Baker entirely disregards Thomas Braddyll's involvement.

35. See, e.g., *Farmer G——e, Studying the Wind & Weather* (1 October 1771; BMC 4883), and Isaac Cruikshank, *A Visit to the Irish Pig!!* (7 January 1799; BMC 9339).

36. Welcher, *Gulliveriana VII*, 633.

37. Vincent Carretta, *George III and the Satirists from Hogarth to Byron* (Athens: University of Georgia Press, 1990), 317.

38. Pat Rogers, "Gulliver's Glasses," in *The Art of Jonathan Swift,* ed. Clive T. Probyn (London: Vision Press, 1978), 185.

39. On Swift's attitude toward standing armies, see David Womersley's long note in Swift, *Travels,* 487–96.

40. *The Caricatures of James Gillray; with Historical and Political Illustrations, and Compendius Biographical Anecdotes and Notices* (London: John Miller, Rodwell and Martin, [1818]), 13.

41. Thomas Holcroft, *Memoirs of Late Thomas Holcroft,* 3 vols. (London: Longman et al., 1816), 1:132–33.

42. E. H. Gombrich, *Meditations on a Hobby Horse and Other Essays on the Theory of Art* (London: Phaidon, 1963), 142.

43. James Boswell, *The Life of Samuel Johnson,* ed. David Womersley (London: Penguin, 2008), 434.

44. John Ashton, *English Caricature and Satire on Napoleon I,* 2 vols. (London: Chatto and Windus, 1884), 2:3. A copy of the Spanish version is in the Curzon Collection at the Bodleian Library, shelfmark Curzon b.08(150).

45. *Annual Register . . . of the Year 1827* (London: Baldwin and Cradock et al., 1828), 242.

7. Harlequin Napoleon; or, What Literature Isn't

1. See A. M. Broadley, *Napoleon in Caricature, 1795–1821*, 2 vols. (London: John Lane, Bodley Head, 1911); and Tim Clayton and Sheila O'Connell, *Bonaparte and the British: Prints and Propaganda in the Age of Napoleon* (London: British Museum, 2015).

2. James Gillray, *News from Calabria!—Capture of Buenos Ayres!—i.e. the Comforts of an Imperial Déjeuné at St Cloud's, 13 Sept. 1806* (BMC 10974); *Patriotic Visions Appearing to N. Buonaparte* (c. 1808).

3. Samuel Taylor Coleridge, *Shakespearean Criticism*, ed. Thomas Middleton Raysor, 2 vols., 2nd ed. (London: J. M. Dent and Sons, 1960), 2:225; Simon Bainbridge, *Napoleon and English Romanticism* (Cambridge: Cambridge University Press, 1995), 13, 108–19, 130–33, 147, 163–65, 183–87, 201–5.

4. *Morning Post*, 10 January 1800.

5. Paul Keen, *The Crisis of Literature in the 1790s: Print Culture and the Public Sphere* (Cambridge: Cambridge University Press, 1999), 2.

6. "Harlequin's Invasion," *Morning Post*, 9 August 1803. The poem is collected in James Smith, *Memoirs, Letters and Comic Miscellanies in Prose and Verse of the Late James Smith*, ed. Horace Smith, 2 vols. (London: Henry Colburn, 1840), 1:282–87.

7. David Mayer, *Harlequin in His Element: The English Pantomime, 1806–1836* (Cambridge, MA: Harvard University Press, 1969), 23–31.

8. Ibid., 23.

9. Melynda Nuss, *Distance, Theatre, and the Public Voice, 1750–1850* (New York: Palgrave Macmillan, 2012), 16. See also Jane Moody, *Illegitimate Theatre in London, 1770–1840* (Cambridge: Cambridge University Press, 2000), 210.

10. *Gentleman's Magazine* 73 (November 1803): 1056–57; *The Spirit of the Public Journals for 1803* (London: James Ridgway, 1804), 291–93; *The Anti-Gallican; or Standard of British Loyalty, Religion and Liberty* (London: Vernor and Hood; J. Asperne, 1804), 69–70.

11. On radical mock playbills of the 1790s, see *Exhibition Extraordinary!!: Radical Broadsides of the Mid-1790s*, ed. John Barrell (Nottingham: Trent Editions, 2001).

12. Gillian Russell, " 'Announcing Each Day the Performances': Playbills, Ephemerality, and Romantic Period Media/Theater History," *Studies in Romanticism* 54, no. 2 (2015): 244.

13. Richard Schechner, *Between Theater and Anthropology* (Philadelphia: University of Pennsylvania Press, 1985), 36.

14. Stuart Semmel, *Napoleon and the British* (New Haven: Yale University Press, 2004), 6, 19–37.

15. Charles Maclean, *An Excursion in France, and Other Parts of the Continent of Europe* (London: T. N. Longman and O. Rees, 1804), 51.

16. Semmel, *Napoleon and the British*, 33.

17. David Garrick, *Harlequin's Invasion; or, A Christmas Gambol,* 1.2.4, in *The Plays of David Garrick*, vol. 1: *Garrick's Own Plays, 1746–1766,* ed. Harry William Pedicord and Fredrick Louis Bergman (Carbondale: Southern Illinois University Press, 1980). References to the play will hereafter be made parenthetically and by the act, scene, and line number given in this edition.

18. Judy A. Hayden, "Harlequin, the Whigs, and William Mountfort's *Doctor Faustus,*" *SEL* 49, no. 3 (2009): 573–93, and "Of Windmills and Bubbles: Harlequin Faustus on the Eighteenth-Century Stage," *Huntington Library Quarterly* 77, no. 1 (2014): 1–16.

19. John O'Brien, *Harlequin Britain: Pantomime and Entertainment, 1690–1760* (Baltimore: John Hopkins University Press, 2004), 181–208. Robert Walpole is cast as Harlequin in *Robin's Reign or Seven's the Main* (1731; BMC 1822) and *Magna Farta or the Raree Show at St. J——'s* (1742; BMC 2575).

20. For George Whitefield as Harlequin, see *Harlequin Methodist* (c. 1763; BMC 4092). Pitt the Elder is Harlequin in an untitled print published in the *Political Register* of January 1768 (BMC 4180); his son takes the role in *The Covent Garden Pantomime or the Westminster Candidates* (22 April 1784; BMC 6545); and Charles James Fox is Harlequin in *A New Pantomime. Harlequine* (25 February 1784; BMC 6424). Thomas Paine appears as Harlequin in *French Liberty* (July 1793; BMC 8334).

21. John Thelwall, *The Rights of Nature, against the Usurpations of Establishments* (London: H. D. Symonds, 1796), 56.

22. Henry Redhead Yorke, *On the Means of Saving our Country* (Dorchester: T. Lockett, 1797), 103; Charles Pigott, *The Jockey Club; or, A Sketch of the Manners of the Age, Part the First,* 6th ed. (London: H. D. Symonds, 1792), 121; *A Rod in Brine; or, A Trickler for Tom Paine* (Canterbury: printed for the author, 1792), 83.

23. David Francis Taylor, *Theatres of Opposition: Empire, Revolution, and Richard Brinsley Sheridan* (Oxford: Oxford University Press), 238–47.

24. On Sheridan's class status, see Christopher Clayton, "The Political Career of Sheridan," in *Sheridan Studies,* ed. James Morwood and David Crane (Cambridge: Cambridge University Press, 1995), 146.

25. O'Brien, *Harlequin Britain*, 117–37; David Worrall, *The Politics of Romantic Theatricality, 1787–1832: The Road to the Stage* (Basingstoke: Palgrave, 2007), 94–95, and *Harlequin Empire: Race, Ethnicity and the Drama of the Popular Enlightenment* (London: Pickering and Chatto, 2007), 24–26.

26. *Harlequin Student; or, The Fall of Pantomime* (London: Thomas Harris, 1741), staged at Goodman's Field Theatre in 1741. The young Garrick likely appeared in this pantomime. See Denise S. Sechelski, "Garrick's Body and the Labor of Art in Eighteenth-Century Theater," *Eighteenth-Century Studies* 29, no. 4 (1996): 369–89.

27. O'Brien, *Harlequin Britain*, xxiv.

28. Alexander Pope, *The Dunciad in Four Books* (1743), ed. Valerie Rumbold (London: Longman, 1999), 3.238–40.

29. Henry Fielding, *The Champion*, 3 May 1740, in *Contributions to the Champion and Related Writings*, ed. W. B. Coley (Oxford: Clarendon Press, 2003), 302, and *The History of Tom Jones*, ed. Thomas Keymer (London: Penguin, 2005), 190.

30. See *Satirist*, January 1808, 337–41.

31. *The Age of Folly: A Poem* (London: printed for the author, [1797]), 31.

32. Marmaduke Myrtle [Thomas Dermody], *The Histrionade; or, Theatric Tribunal* (London: R. S. Kirby, 1802), 10.

33. *The Druriad; or, Strictures on the Principal Performers of Drury-Lane Theatre: A Satirical Poem* (London: W. J. and J. Richardson, 1798), 27–28.

34. Jacky Bratton, *New Readings in Theatre History* (Cambridge: Cambridge University Press, 2003), 8.

35. O'Brien, *Harlequin Britain*, xvii.

36. Raymond Williams, *Keywords: A Vocabulary of Culture and Society*, rev. ed. (New York: Oxford University Press, 1983), 183–88; Roger Chartier, *The Order of Books: Readership, Authors, and Libraries in Europe between the Fourteenth and Eighteenth Centuries*, trans. Lydia G. Cochrane (Cambridge: Polity, 1994), 37–38; Trevor Ross, *The Making of the English Literary Canon: From the Middle Ages to the Late Eighteenth Century* (Montreal: McGill-Queen's University Press, 1998).

37. William Wordsworth, preface to *Lyrical Ballads* (1800), in *Lyrical Ballads, and Other Poems, 1797–1800*, ed. James Butler and Karen Green (Ithaca, NY: Cornell University Press, 1992), 747.

38. Michel Foucault, "What Is an Author?," trans. Donald F. Bouchard and Sherry Simon, in *Language, Counter-Memory, Practice: Selected Essays and Interviews*, ed. Donald F. Bouchard (Ithaca, NY: Cornell University Press, 1977), 126.

39. Edmond Malone, *An Inquiry into the Authenticity of Certain Miscellaneous Papers and Legal Instruments* (London: H. Baldwin, 1796), 2. For the politics of this editorial project, see Margreta de Grazia, *Shakespeare Verbatim: The Reproduction of Authenticity and the 1790s Apparatus* (Oxford: Clarendon Press, 1991); and Bratton, *New Readings*, 87–88.

40. Edmund Burke, *The Writings and Speeches of Edmund Burke*, vol. 9, ed. R. B. McDowell and William B. Todd (Oxford: Oxford University Press, 1991), 73.

41. Edmund Burke, *The Correspondence of Edmund Burke*, gen. ed. Thomas W. Copeland, 10 vols. (Cambridge: Cambridge University Press, 1958–78), 8:456.

42. O'Brien, *Harlequin Britain*, 210.

43. Lance Bertelsen, "Popular Entertainment and Instruction, Literary and Dramatic: Chapbooks, Advice Books, Almanacs, Ballads, Farces, Pantomimes, Prints and Shows," in *The Cambridge History of English Literature, 1660–1780*, ed. John Richetti (Cambridge: Cambridge University Press, 2005), 82; Jackson I. Cope, *Dramaturgy of the Daemonic: Studies in Antigeneric Theater from Ruzante to Grimaldi* (Baltimore: Johns Hopkins University Press, 1984), 111–13.

44. O'Brien, *Harlequin Britain*, xxiv.

45. Peter Stallybrass and Allon White, *The Politics and Poetics of Transgression* (Ithaca, NY: Cornell University Press, 1986), 5–6.

46. Smith, *Memoirs, Letters and Comic Miscellanies*, 1:29.

47. See Oskar Cox Jensen, *Napoleon and British Song, 1797–1822* (Basingstoke: Palgrave Macmillan, 2015), 48.

48. Smith, *Memoirs, Letters and Comic Miscellanies*, 1:34, 278–80.

49. William Wordsworth, *The Prelude: The Four Texts (1798, 1799, 1805, 1850)*, ed. Jonathan Wordsworth (London: Penguin, 1995), 7.296–97.

50. Stallybrass and White, *Poetics and Politics of Transgression*, 108. The authors are writing about Pope and Augustan poetry.

51. For an elaboration of this bi-polar model of culture, see Peter Burke, *Popular Culture in Early Modern Europe*, rev. ed. (Aldershot: Scholar Press, 1994), and for a critique of it, see Philip Connell and Nigel Leask, "What Is the People?," in *Romanticism and Popular Culture in Britain and Ireland*, ed. Connell and Leask (Cambridge: Cambridge University Press, 2009), 3–48.

52. Morag Shiach, *Discourse on Popular Culture: Class, Gender and History in Cultural Analysis, 1730 to the Present* (Cambridge: Polity, 1989).

53. Deidre Shauna Lynch, *Loving Literature: A Cultural History* (Chicago: University of Chicago Press, 2014), 28.

54. Semmel, *Napoleon and the British*, 4.

55. Linda Colley, *Britons: Forging the Nation, 1707–1837*, new ed. (London: Pimlico, 2003), 17–18.

56. Jonathan Brody Kramnick, *Making the English Canon: Print-Capitalism and the Cultural Past, 1700–1770* (Cambridge: Cambridge University Press, 1998), 45. Kramnick is quoting Joseph Warton in *The Adventurer; Volume the Fourth* (London: H. Goldney, 1783), 291.

57. The checkered sign that can be seen on the corner of the inn in Cruikshank's print was a common means by which an establishment indicated that it sold beer and wine. Here, it also alludes to the harlequinade.

58. Leigh Hunt, "On Pantomime," in *Examiner*, 5, 26 January 1817, in *The Selected Writings of Leigh Hunt*, ed. Greg Kucich and Jeffrey N. Cox, 6 vols. (London: Pickering and Chatto, 2003), 2:81–86, 94–95 (quotation at 85).

59. Walter Scott, *The Life of Napoleon Buonaparte*, 9 vols. (Edinburgh: Ballantyne and Co., 1827), 8:395.

60. Semmel, *Napoleon and the British*, 147–74.

61. Northrop Frye, *Anatomy of Criticism: Four Essays* (Princeton, NJ: Princeton University Press, 1957), 164.

62. Mayer, *Harlequin in His Element*, 2–3.

63. Moody, *Illegitimate Theatre*, 209–18 (215).

64. On pantomime's topicality, see Mayer, *Harlequin in His Element*, 2, 6, 52–56; and Jeffrey N. Cox, " 'Illegitimate' Pantomime in the 'Legitimate' Theater: Context as Text," *Studies in Romanticism* 54, no. 2 (2015): 159–86.

65. Richard Findlater, *Joe Grimaldi: His Life and Theatre*, 2nd ed. (London: Cambridge University Press, 1978), 99–100.

66. Haywood, *Romanticism and Caricature*, 80.

67. Steven E. Jones, *Satire and Romanticism* (Basingstoke: Macmillan, 2000), 176; Nuss, *Distance, Theatre, and the Public Voice*, 22.

68. Harlequin jumps through a clockface in *Harlequin and Mother Goose* (Covent Garden, 1808).

69. Marshall McLuhan, *Understanding Media: The Extensions of Man* (London: Routledge and Kegan Paul, 1964).

70. See Vic Gatrell, *City of Laughter: Sex and Satire in Eighteenth-Century London* (London: Atlantic, 2006), 388–405.

71. See Mikhail Bakhtin, *Rabelais and His World*, trans. Hélène Iswolsky (Bloomington: Indiana University Press, 1984); and Marilyn Gaull, "Pantomime as Satire: Mocking a Broken Charm," in *The Satiric Eye: Forms of Satire in the Romantic Period*, ed. Steven E. Jones (New York: Palgrave, 2003), 207–24.

72. Moody, *Illegitimate Theatre*, 12.

73. Sechelski, "Garrick's Body and the Labor of Art," 376.

74. Hunt, "On Pantomime," 2:94.

75. *Times*, 27 December 1825. Quoted in Mayer, *Harlequin in His Element*, 51.

76. Hunt, "On Pantomime," 2:84.

77. Gatrell, *City of Laughter*, 396. See also Ronald Paulson, *Representations of Revolution, 1789–1820* (New Haven: Yale University Press, 1983), 178.

78. John O'Brien, "Pantomime," in *The Cambridge Companion to British Theatre, 1730–1830*, ed. Jane Moody and Daniel O'Quinn (Cambridge: Cambridge University Press, 2007), 103–14 (quotation at 113).

79. *Songs, Chorusses, &c. in the New Comic Pantomime, called Harlequin & Fancy; or, the Poet's Last Shilling* (London: C. Lowndes, [1815]), 6–7.

80. Ibid., 18–19. On the generic anxiety of pantomime, see Nuss, *Distance, Theatre, and the Public Voice*, 14.

81. *Songs, Chorusses*, 17.

82. *Times*, 27 December 1815.

Acknowledgments

The development of this book has been profoundly shaped by the institutions I've been lucky enough to work at and the colleagues I've been lucky enough to work alongside. At the Jackman Humanities Institute, University of Toronto, the way I think about images was enriched by the many conversations I had with Tania Ahmed, Stefan Dolgert, Nicole Blackwood, Brad Rogers, and Julie Boivin. The Department of English at Toronto was a thrilling environment for a young scholar of eighteenth-century literature, and Tom Keymer, Deidre Lynch, and Terry Robinson have all at some point shown themselves to be acute readers of my work. Since moving to the University of Warwick I've been the willing beneficiary of the insights of Kate Astbury, Tess Grant, Mark Knights, Mark Philp, Paul Prescott, and, most especially, the wonderful Tina Lupton.

This book is better thanks to the advice and suggestions of Kristina Straub, Ashley Cohen, Rebecca Tierney-Hynes, Ros Ballaster, Danny O'Quinn, and Oskar Cox Jensen. I owe special thanks to Thomas Pfau and David Womersley, who invited me to participate in their SIAS summer institute "Scenes from the History of the Image." The warmth and unassuming brilliance of this group modeled a genuinely efficacious interdisciplinarity, and I'm especially grateful to Antoinina Bevan Zlatar, who was among this number, for reading a draft of my Milton chapter.

A preliminary version of Chapter 3 appeared as "The Disenchanted Island: A Political History of *The Tempest*, 1760–1830," *Shakespeare Quarterly* 63, no. 4 (2012): 487–517, while an early version of Chapter 6 was published as "Gillray's Gulliver and the 1803 Invasion Scare," in *The Afterlives of Eighteenth-Century Fiction*, ed. Daniel Cook and Nicholas Seager (Cambridge: Cambridge University Press, 2015), 212–32. I'm grateful to Johns Hopkins University Press and Cambridge University Press for granting me permission to reuse this material here.

The Paul Mellon Centre for Studies in British Art awarded me a grant to cover the costs of obtaining illustration rights, and research for this book has also been supported by the University of Toronto's Connaught Fund and the University of Warwick's Humanities Research Fund. I'm greatly indebted to the staff at the British Museum, the British Library, the Huntington Library, and the Lewis Walpole Library for their help and patience, and to the last of these I'm especially grateful for making so many images of satirical prints freely available to me. At Yale University Press, I owe huge thanks to Laura Jones Dooley, Ash Lago, and Margaret Otzel—who guided this book through production—and in particular to my editor, Sarah Miller, for having faith in this unusual project. I'm also tremendously grateful to my anonymous readers, for advice and suggestions that were helpful and encouraging in equal measure.

It's impossible here to give an accurate sense of how much I've depended—and continue to depend—on the love, intelligence, and encouragement of Jennifer Gold. This book is dedicated both to her and to our little daughter, Mathilda, whose exemplary sleeping habits have meant that its completion has been far less painful than I'd dared imagine.

Index

Page numbers in *italic* type indicate images.

Abbott, Charles, 108
Abingdon, Earl of, 44, 45
Ackermann, Rudolph, 41
Act of Union (1800), 190, 192
Adam and Eve, 147–48, 149, 153, 168
Addington, Henry, 1st Viscount Sidmouth, 120–21, *120*, 249
Addison, Joseph: *Cato*, 28, 29, 141; on *Paradise Lost*, 140, 166, 167, 168, 172, 175, 176–77
aesthetics, 131, 140, 227
allegory, 15–16, 18, 27, 77, 127, 248; national, 98–99, 208; *Paradise Lost and*, 141, 142, 158, 165, 171–77; *Tempest* as, 81, 90–91, 93, 99, 100
allusion, 4, 10, 16, 17, 27, 30, 72, 77; literary parody vs., 32, 132–33
Altick, Richard, 31
amateurs, 184–86, 208–9
American colonies, 73, 74, 128
American War of Independence, 28, 78, 80, 81, 109, 143; peace treaty, 144, 161
Amiens, Peace of (1802–3), 120–21, 122–23, 124; collapse of, 181–82, 199
androgyny, 126
Anne, Lady (*Richard III*), 6–7, 10, 27
Anti-Gallican, The (anthology), 214
Anti-Jacobin, The (periodical), 28, 30, 62
Ariel (*Tempest*), 77, 87, 93, 94, 192
Ariosto, *Orlando Furioso*, 176, 177, 179
Ashton, John, 201
Asperne, James: *Cruce Dignus*, 237, 238–39; *Harlequin's Invasion*, 216–17, *218*, 219, 223, 224, 231, 232, 234; *Shakespeare's Ghost*, 233, 234, *234*

Bainbridge, Simon, 211
Baker, James, 196
Bakhtin, Mikhail, 36, 116, 243–44
Banks, Sarah Sophia, 35
bardolatry, 71, 72
Barré, Isaac, 147
Barrell, John, 55, 56
Barry, James, 34, 134
Barthes, Roland, 8
Bate, Jonathan, 16, 26, 72, 94, 101–2, 112, 115, 125, 137
Baxandall, Michael, 5
Beattie, James, 177
Bell, John, 84–85, *85*, 129
Berkeley, Grantley, 41
Bertelsen, Lance, 228
Bible, 35, 142
Bindman, David, 8, 24
blackness, 222, 223
Blair, Cherie, 131
Blake, William, 14, 138, 141, 146; reading of *Paradise Lost*, 158, 165
Blessings of Peace, The (anon. print), 109, *110*, 118
Bogel, Frederic, 54
Bonaparte. *See* Napoleon
book prices, 31
Boswell, James, 143, 149
Bourbon monarchy, 74, 236, 242, 244
Bourdieu, Pierre, 31, 35, 55, 138
bourgeoisie, 34, 38, 42, 54, 134
Bowles, Carington, 58
Bowles, John, 50, 188
Boydell, John, 170; Shakespeare Gallery, 23, 134–39, 169, 179